THE ELEPHANT IN THE WOMB

THE ELEPHANT IN THE WOMB

Written by
KALKI KOECHLIN

Illustrated by
VALERIYA POLYANYCHKO

PENGUIN BOOKS

An imprint of Penguin Random House

PENGUIN BOOKS

USA | Canada | UK | Ireland | Australia
New Zealand | India | South Africa | China

Penguin Books is part of the Penguin Random House group of companies
whose addresses can be found at global.penguinrandomhouse.com

Published by Penguin Random House India Pvt. Ltd
4th Floor, Capital Tower 1, MG Road,
Gurugram 122 002, Haryana, India

First published in Penguin Books by Penguin Random House India 2021

10 9 8 7 6 5 4 3 2 1

The views and opinions expressed in this book are the author's own and the facts are as reported by him which have been verified to the extent possible, and the publishers are not in any way liable for the same.

ISBN 9780143454052

Typeset in
Book design and layout by Valeriya Polyanychko
Printed at Replika Press Pvt. Ltd, India

The views and opinions are solely based on the author's knowledge and understanding of her strategies and do not reflect the publisher's intentions, beliefs and/or opinions. The examples used in the book are for illustrative purposes only and sourced from research findings, resources and references available in the public domain and from sources for which the requisite permissions were available with the author at the relevant time. The author has strived to ensure the book's contents are correct at the time of publication; however, no part of the book shall mean to be representations or warranties, express or implied, concerning accuracy, reliability, suitability or otherwise. The book is strictly for educational purposes—the author or the publisher shall not be responsible for any action taken by any person by relying upon this book. The author shall not be liable/responsible absolutely, strictly, vicariously and/or otherwise for any remote or direct loss, damage or disruption suffered on account of the actions taken by relying upon this book. This book is for persons who are at least twenty-one years of age. Sale of this book to persons below twenty-one years of age is illegal and prohibited. The seller/reseller shall be liable for such illegal/prohibited sale.

www.penguin.co.in

MIX
Paper from responsible sources
FSC® C016779

This book is dedicated to

_____

Dear Reader,

Hello.

I'm an actor and a celebrity, writing a book for the first time (and thankfully, I am being supported by the very talented artist, Val, to really hammer my points in.) I know that my position in society is one of privilege and not everyone will be able to relate to everything I share in this book. But I hope some of you will relate to some of the things I confess to, complain about or care for.

In any case, keep calm and consume this book with a sense of irony. It is a personal recipe and will require your own adjustments to it as you go along. The empty pages after each chapter are for you to create, vent and scribble on.

Also, guys, both figuratively and literally, this book isn't just for women or mothers. This is for anyone who wants to veer away from some of the clichés attached to birth and babies, and discover messy and marvellous secrets to parenting.

Please, I beg of you, do not use this book for medical guidance, it is not a prescription given to you by a medical authority. And finally, be careful, contents may be HOT, if you know what I mean... If you don't, I mean keep it the fuck away from children's reach!

Yours till the last page,
Kalki

CONTENTS

Sept 2017

I'm tired of ambition

And sick of responsibility

I want to hear myself think

And find myself involved in others and [redacted] ready to learn

Not guarded or uninterested or motivated by opportunity

I would like to breathe and not feel my lungs pressed against my

chest from guilt or fear or anger

I want peace and a child growing in my belly

I want to transform.

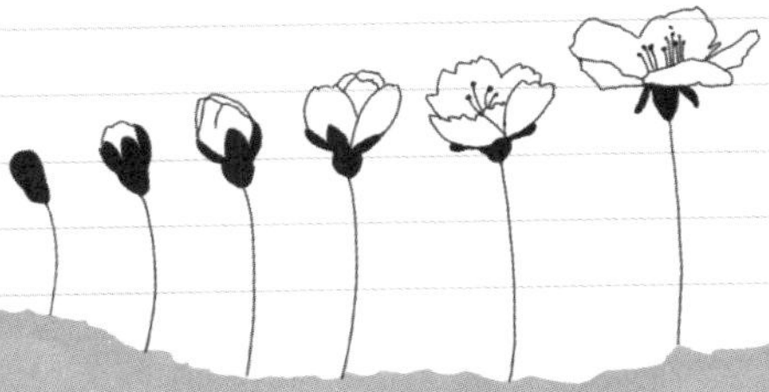

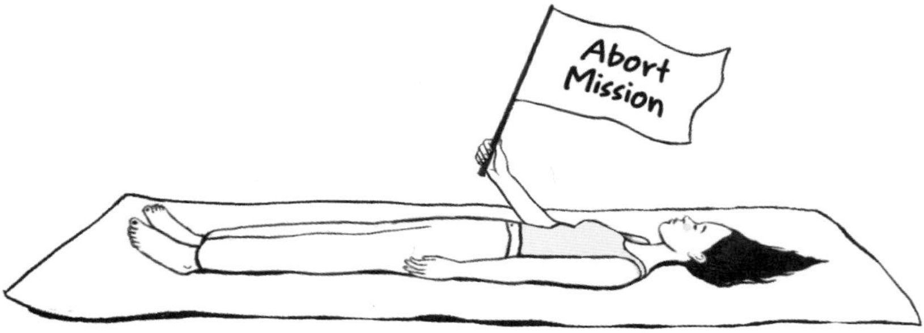
Abort
Mission

Before we celebrate the gift of life, I'd like to start with celebrating the gift of science. I have had two abortions in my life. The first was in my twenties when not only was I unprepared to have a child but I was passionately against having children, and even wrote an article questioning why women are always expected to have children, especially after marriage.

When I went to see a nearby gynaecologist, one of the first questions she asked me was, 'Are you married?' (I wasn't at the time). I felt myself shrinking under the guilt of I don't even know what —societal expectations? God? Judgemental (and unprofessional) doctors and nurses who measured the length of my shorts with their eyes as I entered a 'family' clinic?

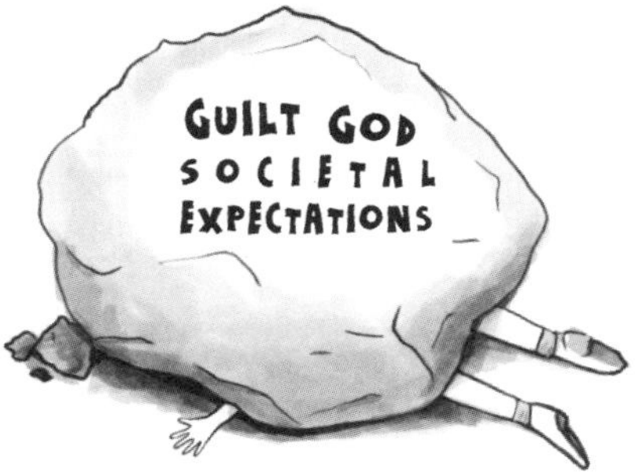
GUILT GOD
SOCIETAL
EXPECTATIONS

Anyway uncomfortable with the attitude of this clinic, I asked my partner for help and he took me to his GP, who passed me the pills surreptitiously as though we were executing a drug deal, scolded us like two naughty kids on the playground, and then asked me and my partner at the time to 'be more careful'.

Cut to 2016 where my life was significantly more independent and I had my basic health backed up with a regular gynaecologist, homeopath and GP who all interacted with each other and cooperated when it came to my choices about allopathy, like professional adults. I told my gynaecologist that I had decided on an abortion, and we opened up the calender together and agreed on a date for the operation (for reasons related to work I couldn't take the pill this time around). Obviously, the second experience was far less traumatic than the first.

Abortion A

After 'sorting it out' with the pills, my partner left town for work, leaving me alone to deal with the profuse bleeding and intense cramps.

I hadn't told anyone about my abortion except my partner so I found myself completely alone.

I didn't know the doctor and so didn't feel comfortable to call him and ask about what I was going through.

I started having a r e c u r r i n g nightmare about my foetus coming back to life that haunted me.

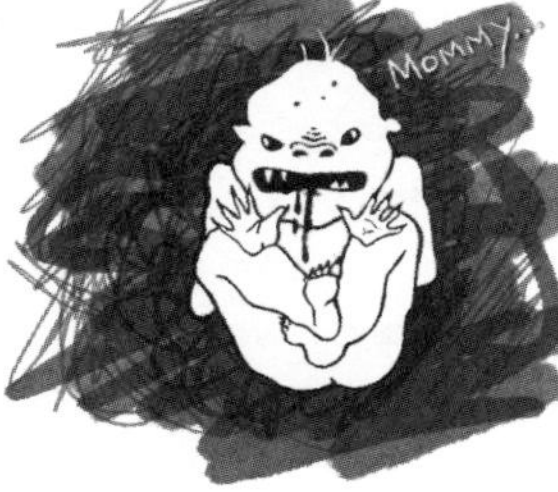
MOMMY...

Abortion B

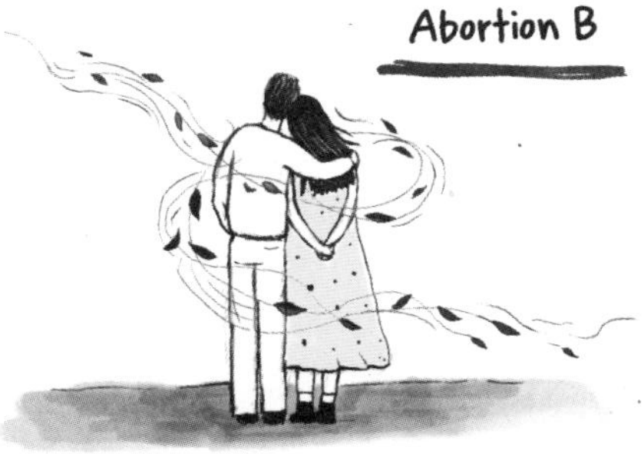

My partner came to the clinic for the procedure and took me home.

My brother and his girlfriend were staying with me, and my friends were available on the phone so I wasn't alone.

My gynaecologist regularly texted me to check how I was doing.

I was sad about the situation but not traumatized by it.

Let's just drill this in for the sake of social prejudices that jar with the law and scientific reasoning. Taking the abortion pill is physiologically indistinguishable from a miscarriage that occurs on its own. So if you criminalize medical abortions, you are basically criminalizing miscarriages! And of course, there are many reasons to not have a child:

SOCIAL PREJUDICE

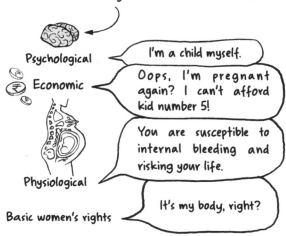

Psychological

Economic

> I'm a child myself.

> Oops, I'm pregnant again? I can't afford kid number 5!

> You are susceptible to internal bleeding and risking your life.

Physiological

Basic women's rights

> It's my body, right?

Abortions, like miscarriages, occur way more often than we are aware, or are willing to accept as a society. And this is because we're so silent about them.

ALL MY PROBLEMS

ALL THE WORLD'S PROBLEMS

I know, I know, it's a bit *GASP* to begin a book on motherhood with a cold plunge into abortion rights, but I feel the decision to have a child is so colossal, and no one really asks us to prepare psychologically or spiritually for a child. Instead, the preparation is usually something like:

Do I have money to raise a child?

Is it a good time in my career for this?

Do we have access to good schools?

Do I submit to family pressure?

Isn't having a child what everyone expects after marriage?

When really, it should be more like:

How good am I at handling stressful situations?

How willing am I to change my routine, let go of control and rework my entire life around a new person?

Do I have a reliable support system? Friends, family and help, including but not exclusively or necessarily a partner?

Do I want to make the world a safer, cleaner and more compassionate place? (Where are our taxes going? Why are people still starving when we have the technology to make more food than we need? Why do I feel the need to protest? Is global warming going to destroy the human species?)

In 2016, I got pregnant. I really wanted a child but the pregnancy was unplanned and I didn't feel ready.

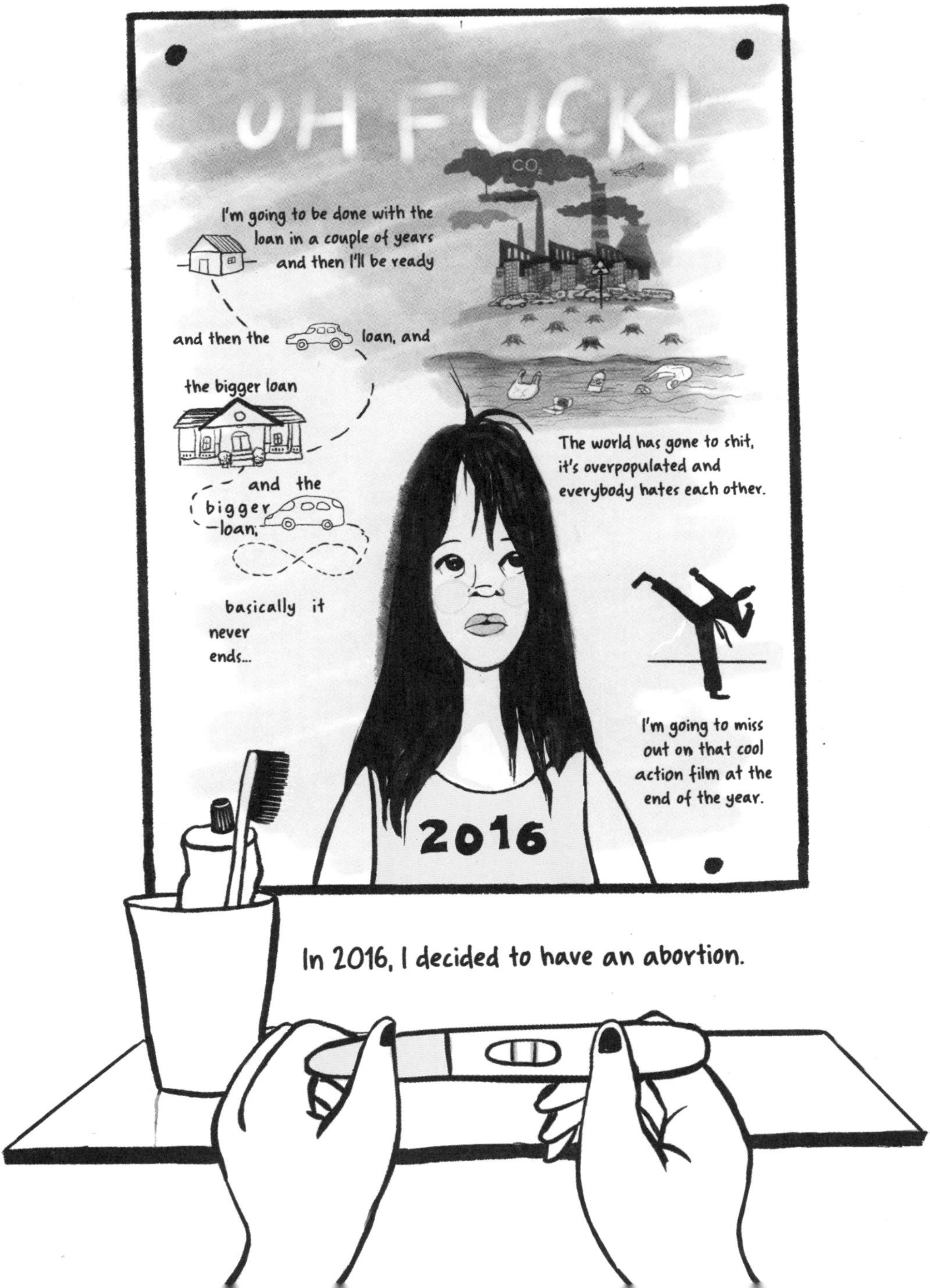
OH FUCK!
CO_2
I'm going to be done with the loan in a couple of years and then I'll be ready
and then the loan, and
the bigger loan
and the bigger loan,
basically it never ends...
The world has gone to shit, it's overpopulated and everybody hates each other.
I'm going to miss out on that cool action film at the end of the year.
2016
In 2016, I decided to have an abortion.

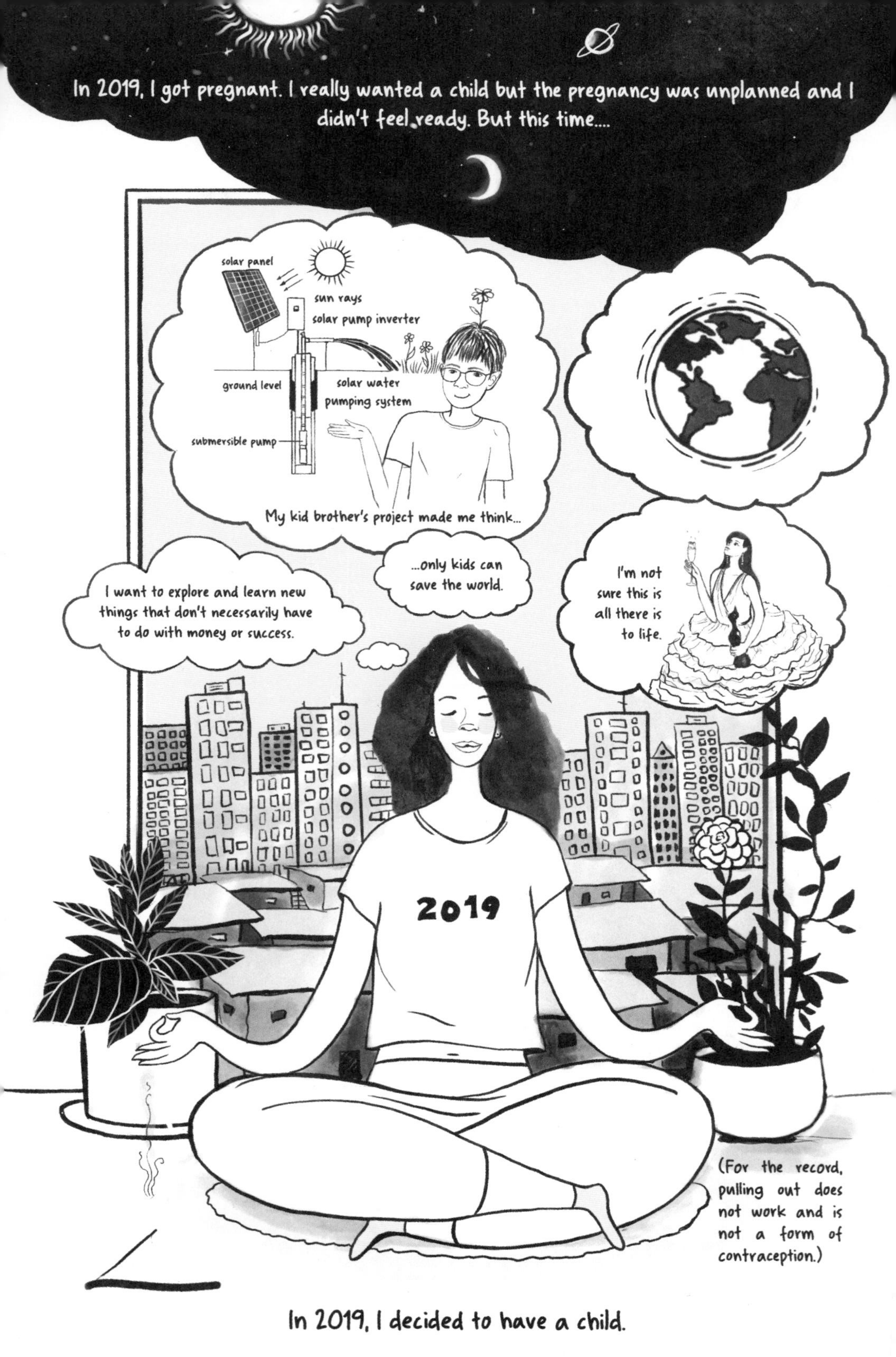
In 2019, I got pregnant. I really wanted a child but the pregnancy was unplanned and I didn't feel ready. But this time....
solar panel
sun rays
solar pump inverter
ground level
solar water pumping system
submersible pump
My kid brother's project made me think...
...only kids can save the world.
I want to explore and learn new things that don't necessarily have to do with money or success.
I'm not sure this is all there is to life.
2019
(For the record, pulling out does not work and is not a form of contraception.)
In 2019, I decided to have a child.

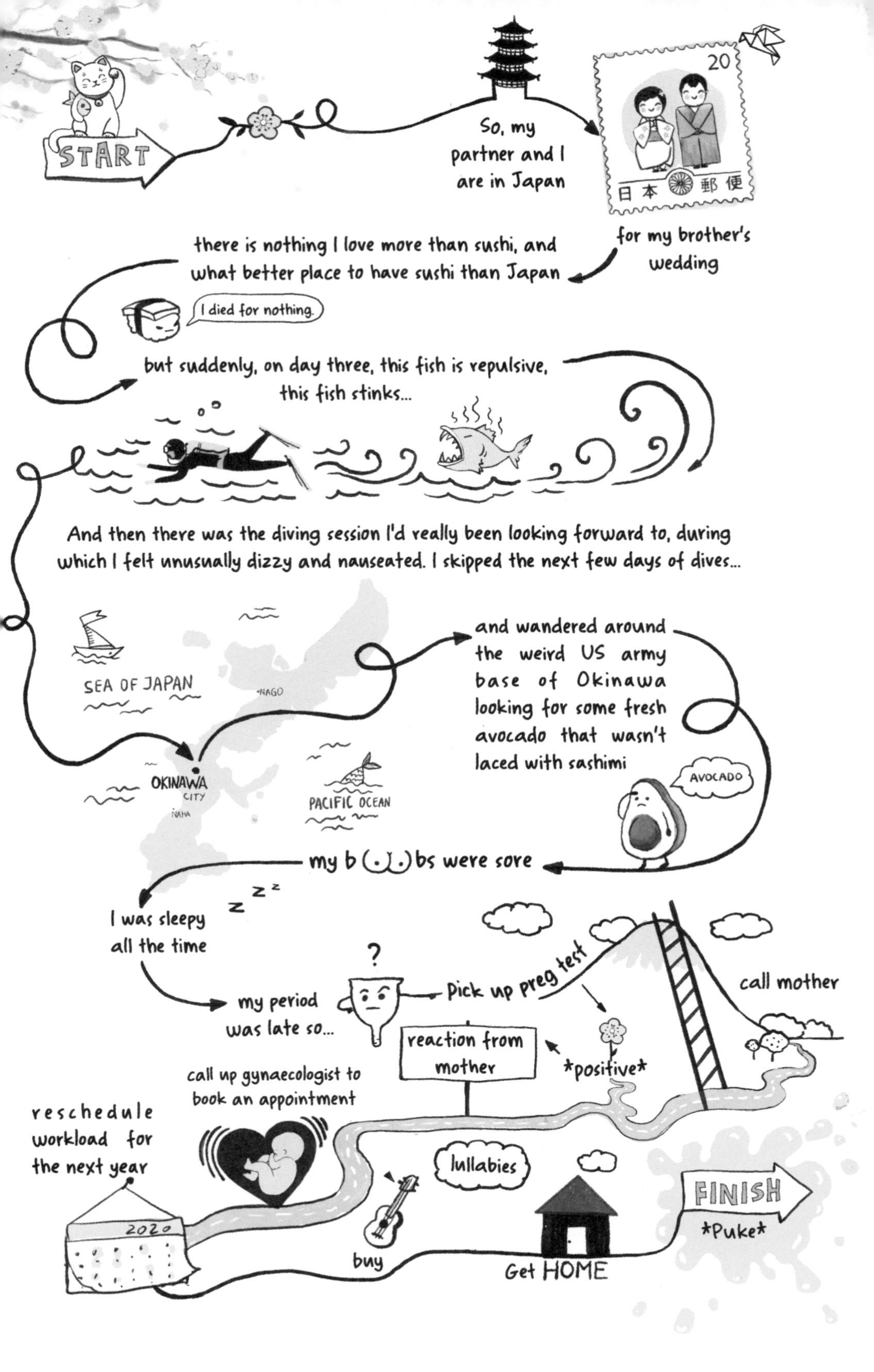

START
So, my partner and I are in Japan
20
日本郵便
for my brother's wedding
there is nothing I love more than sushi, and what better place to have sushi than Japan
I died for nothing.
but suddenly, on day three, this fish is repulsive, this fish stinks...
And then there was the diving session I'd really been looking forward to, during which I felt unusually dizzy and nauseated. I skipped the next few days of dives...
SEA OF JAPAN
NAGO
OKINAWA CITY
NAHA
PACIFIC OCEAN
and wandered around the weird US army base of Okinawa looking for some fresh avocado that wasn't laced with sashimi
AVOCADO
my b(.)(.)bs were sore
I was sleepy all the time
z z z
my period was late so...
?
Pick up preg test
positive
reaction from mother
call mother
call up gynaecologist to book an appointment
reschedule workload for the next year
2020
lullabies
buy
Get HOME
FINISH
Puke

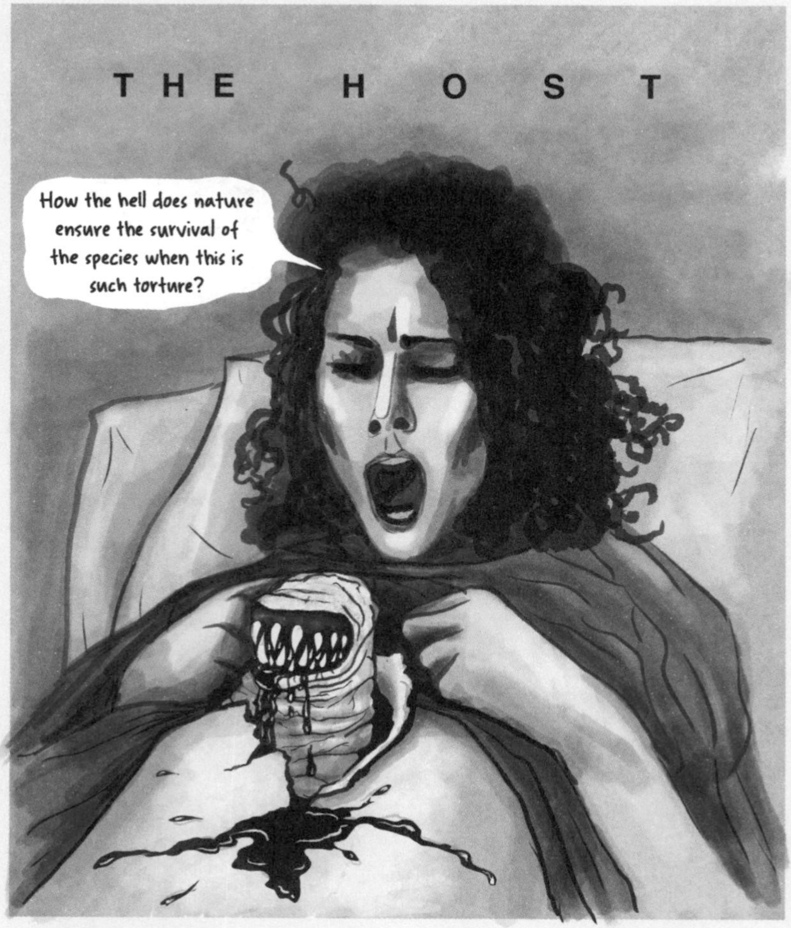
THE HOST
How the hell does nature ensure the survival of the species when this is such torture?

THE HOST

Before I got pregnant, I had a vague idea that one has to 'rest' in the first trimester and that it is a 'sensitive' time, but nobody told me to prepare for an alien invasion that would turn my insides out and transform me into a human incubating system of toxic gases and chemical imbalances.

Imagine you've just reached work and your face turns a shade of pale yellow...
and you rush to the bathroom and vomit.
WC
...this isn't a baby, this is a virus, this thing is eating me from the inside.
And you come out and someone says:
moody, probably has her period.
All-night party, huh?
A few hours later, you smell something funny, you go to the loo and your underwear is wet through with mucus-like discharge.
...ugh
And it happens again, the next day.
you OK?
Do I look OK?
Don't fucking tell me to calm down.
OK, calm down.
Nothing.
sorry... What's the matter ?
And you're trying to concentrate on your work.
Has the AC stopped working?
nd the next day...
Why does she dress like a chudail these days?
burp
SCRIPT
Do you think she is an alcoholic?
...ookaaay divaaaaa...
Your director comes in smoking a cigarette, you walk out of the room.
OUCH! Don't fucking touch me!
sore boobs
And then you go home and your boyfriend tries to hug you.
?
You decide to get some air and so you take your dog out for a walk.
?
nd he has made dinner but the smell makes you auseated.
Crossing the road because of garbage dump smell.
rossing the road again because of chaatwallah smell.
गौरव चाट भण्डार
गौरव पानीपतासे भण्डार
This exhausts you so much you want to cry.

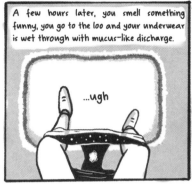

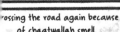

And crying has become so routine that your BF cuddles you while he is watching something on his phone.

wow babe, you've p r o b a b l y contributed to a hole in the ozone layer.

And then in the middle of the night

And in the morning you ask your doctor what's wrong and they say:

Hormonal imbalance

And scribble some illegible pill names at you.

Every single one of you fuckers tortured your mothers at one point in your ungrateful lives and you don't even know it.

And at the supermarket you hate on the check-out guy for taking his own sweet time.

That was my first few months—every day a struggle, every smell a possible trigger, every effort disorienting, and no one around me seemed to understand.

To be honest, the only time I felt any sense of relief in these months was when I drove off to a remote cottage in Kamshet for a week. God bless the few parts of the world left with no network. Thanks to a phone mostly switched off, I could really slow down. There was no pressure to post something motivational online and seek validation from strangers, nor the anxiety of a work call that might or might not happen, nor sensational news that made me worry about what kind of world I was choosing to bring this child into.

I spoke only at mealtimes to the staff there and spent the rest of the time reading, learning to play the ukulele and napping a lot.

I would wake up wanting to nap, I would eat breakfast and nap, or do some sluggish yoga which was more an excuse to get to nap again. I would nap between every little effort I made in the day.

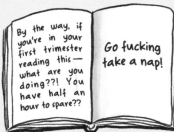

By the way, if you're in your first trimester reading this— what are you doing??! You have half an hour to spare??

Go fucking take a nap!

Shhh...it's a secret

Does it really have to be? I understand that because of high miscarriage rates and out of a general fear of something going wrong, we are advised to keep quiet in the first trimester. But isn't this the time we need the most support and understanding? Just imagine how different things could be if people knew...

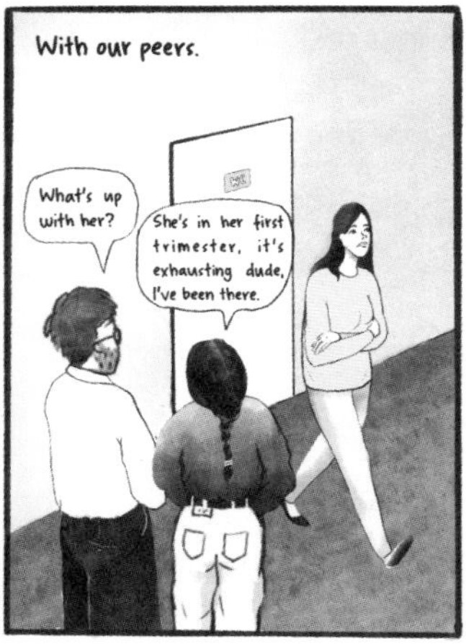
With our peers.
What's up with her?
She's in her first trimester, it's exhausting dude, I've been there.

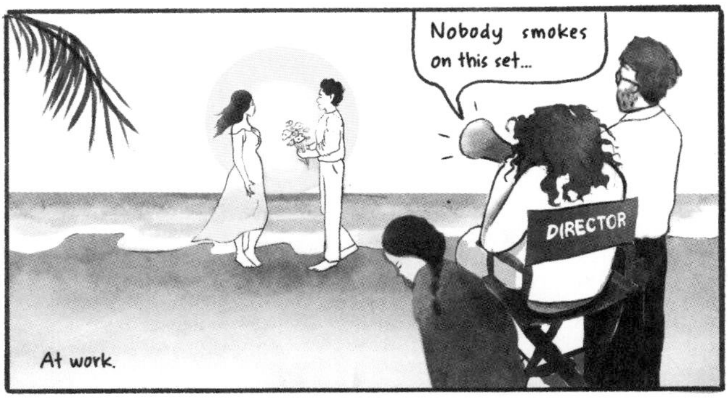
Nobody smokes on this set...
DIRECTOR
At work.

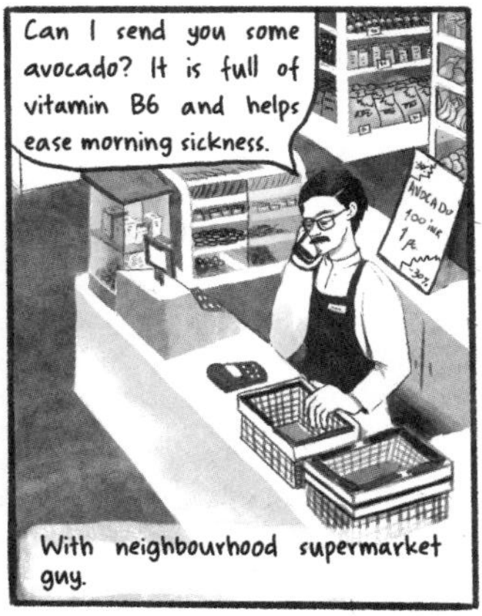
Can I send you some avocado? It is full of vitamin B6 and helps ease morning sickness.
With neighbourhood supermarket guy.

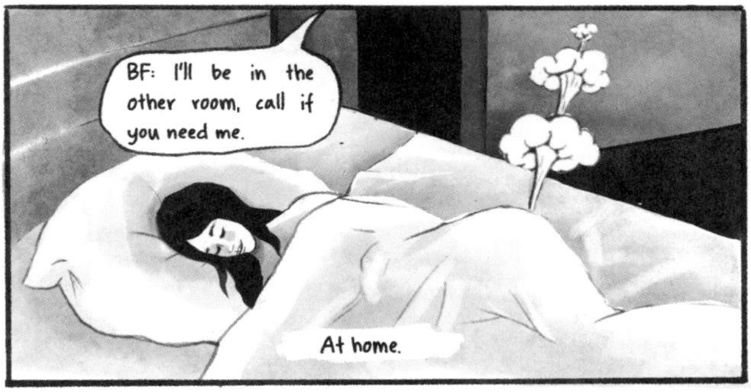
BF: I'll be in the other room, call if you need me.
At home.

And when it comes to miscarriages, the word itself gives away its societal prejudice.

Mis-carriage. You mis-carried. Like you carried this wrong. You, as a woman, failed to let this tiny little baby live.

When in reality, 85 per cent of miscarriages happen in the first trimester.

And one in four pregnancies experience miscarriages.

It happens a lot. And if we understand that as a fact of life instead of...

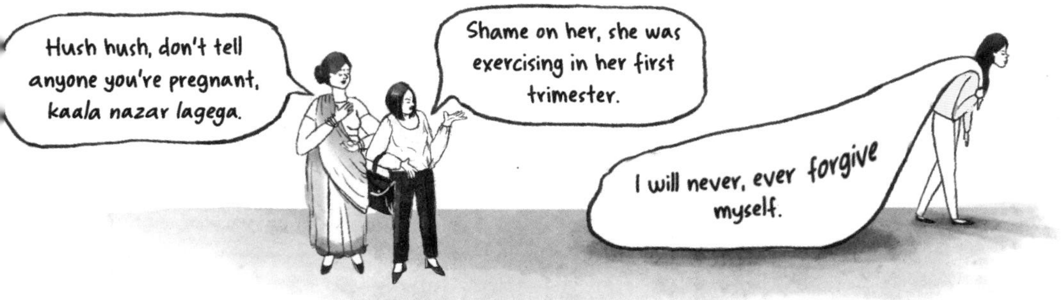
Hush hush, don't tell anyone you're pregnant, kaala nazar lagega.
Shame on her, she was exercising in her first trimester.
I will never, ever forgive myself.

If we learnt early in school how to deal with failures and disappointments, as much as we learn about success...
If we explored how being aware of our vulnerabilities instead of ignoring them can be a strength, that finding our pain points can help us develop self-worth and trust others around us, and can help us overcome negative emotions quicker over time...

Then maybe, just maybe, we could relax even in this stressful time and let our body do the work it has to do.

Certificate Of Failure

Presented to:

Name Kalki

Date 20/03/1993

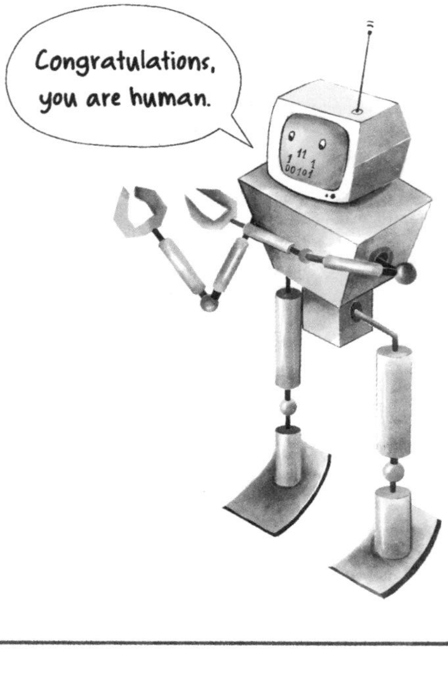
Congratulations,
you are human.

I don't know anything again, my thoughts are abstract and short-lived like textures in the sand before a wave sweeps it away. And what a comfort that is, not knowing. When something is beyond your control, it goes on, even when you don't pay attention to it. It's automatic, like breathing. And I go on being busy with things that now seem like all the wrong things, getting myself to zip up too tight, high-waisted jeans along with an equally taut smile for some crowd that knows nothing about me nor I about them. And I wonder how much we have in common, how many untold truths we bear, and how much more real this performance could get if we knew each other's secrets. The thought is swept away as I try to make the next appointment, lugging along the distractions of my little rectangular gadget for company, while all along I'm thinking, nothing really matters, not really, not the big CEO's fancy event, not the new lines I've been given to regurgitate, not the dreams of winning an award, nor any of our attempts to defy death, to outlive our past, or take hold of our future, because life is a quiet little thing that grows in the dark and that's all the glory in the world.

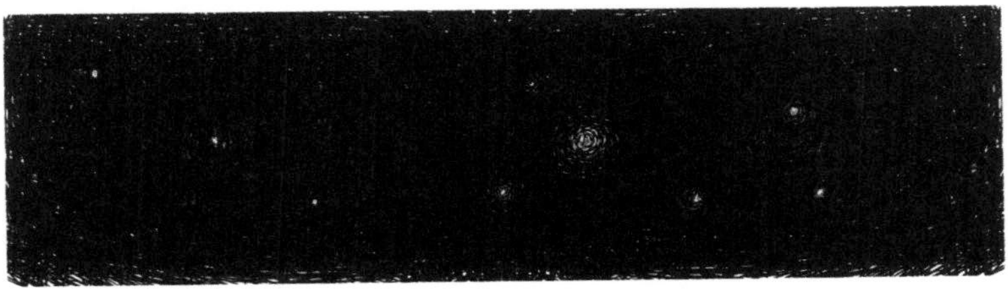

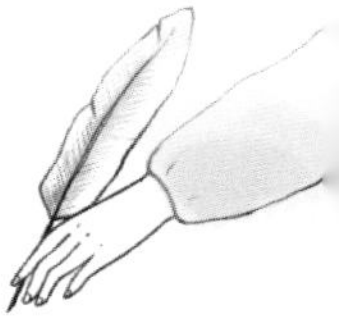

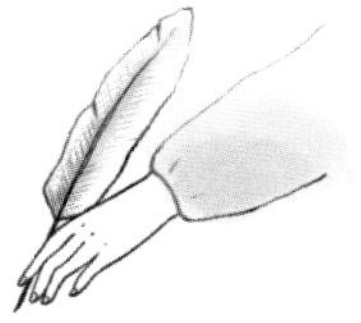

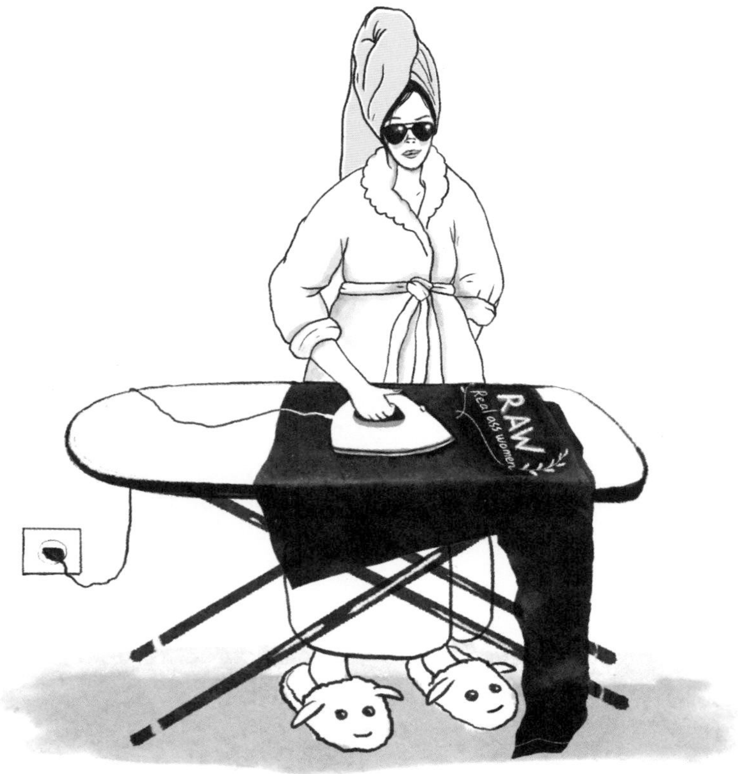
RAW
Real ass women

If you're lucky like me, you'll get your appetite and libido back after about four months. Still, 15–20 per cent of women experience the nasty symptoms of the first trimester throughout the pregnancy, and some suffer from hyperemesis gravidarum, a case of morning sickness so severe, the mother needs clinical intervention to prevent dehydration. Like its name suggests, it is a grave condition that requires the attention of your doctor. Nobody really knows why HG happens to some women, which makes me wonder why no one has researched it properly. Is suffering once again something a woman must bear? Is the health and comfort of a mother being sidelined?

The short answer is, yes. There is far less research on women's health than there is on men's health. One *Forbes* article points out, 'It's really only since the early '90s that the research community has begun to recognize the importance of including women and paying attention to the possibility that there may be sex/gender differences.' This implies, on the one hand, that most of the medicines we use today have been tested on only half the population, the male half, and we have a lot of catching up to do on how this affects women. While on the other hand, a woman's symptoms can be dismissed by doctors as 'emotional' and 'not real' because of the lack of research on how her body functions. All this leaves women to deal with a bunch of untreated symptoms and unaddressed suffering.

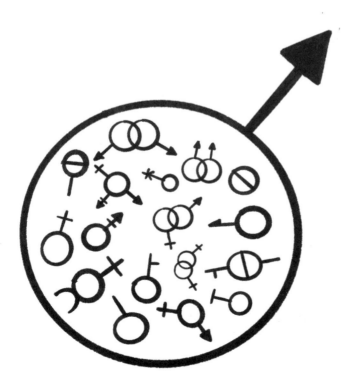

♂ Male
♀ Female
⚣ Gay
⚢ Lesbian
⚲ Neutrois
⚲ Nonbinary
⚲ Genderless
⚲ Demigender
⚤ Homosexual
♂ Travesti
⊖ Agender
⚥ Hermaphroditus
⚥ Bisexual
⚤ Heterosexual
♀ Demigirl
♂ Demiboy
⚧ Transgender
⚨ Genderqueer

And well, that just allows me to take off on a feminist tangent here. While research in women's health is lacking, the market for women's contraceptive methods seems to be thriving. There are exactly three forms of contraception for men. Abstinence, unrealistic. Vasectomy, extreme. OK, let me start again. There's only one practical form of contraception for men. The condom. And men often don't want to use condoms saying they're a moodkill, and they can say this casually because they know they are not going to have to pay the price. It's women who pay the price for an unplanned pregnancy. And so the onus on contraception is on women. Women have the IUD, the implant, the diaphragm, the ring. Women have pills, more pills and the morning-after pill. While we all know how slow the progress on the male contraception pill has been, we women have a bewildering assortment of hormonal pills we can choose from and pop every day of the month, along with varying degrees of side effects.

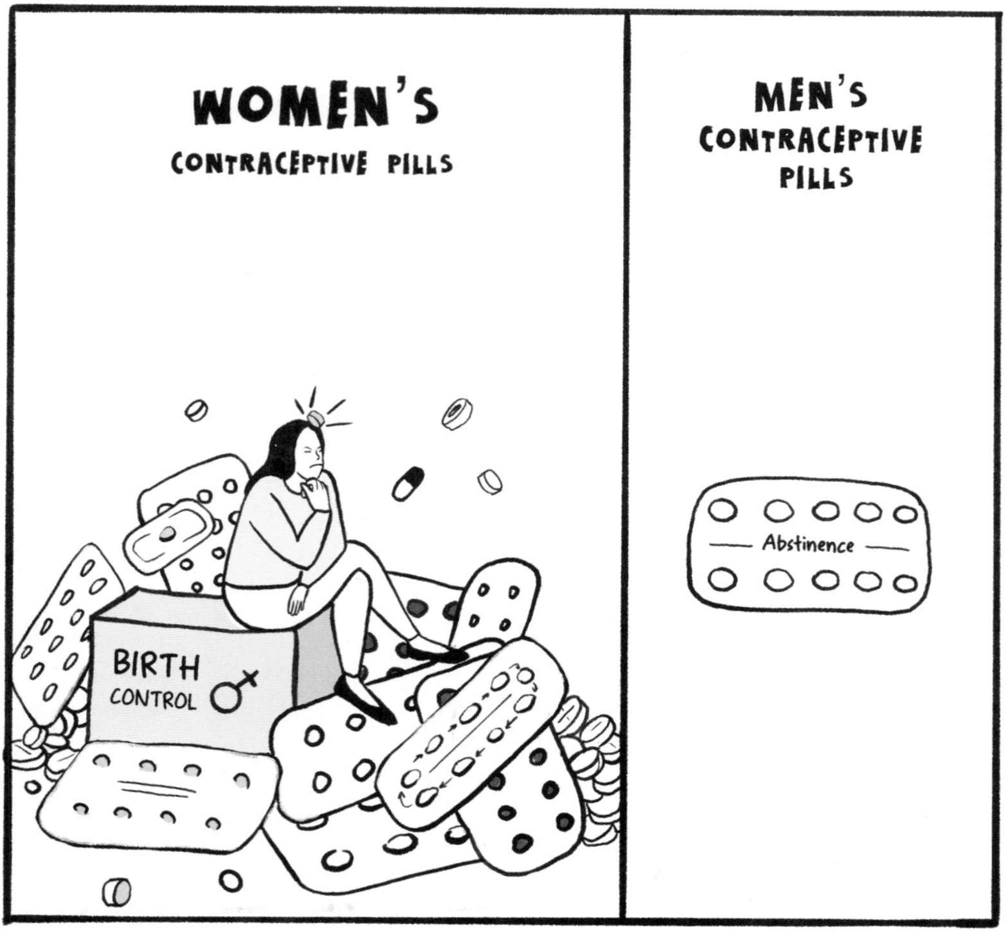
WOMEN'S
CONTRACEPTIVE PILLS
BIRTH
CONTROL
MEN'S
CONTRACEPTIVE
PILLS
Abstinence

MOM-TO-BE

Generally, popular culture doesn't talk about pregnancy, except in stereotypes. She's either the crazy hormonal bitch who needs to park herself on the sofa for nine months and eat a lot of junk, or the magical, maternal and filtered Instagram mum, who seems perpetually caught photographed in soft sunlight falling on her newly found curves. It's only when you get pregnant that you delve into a mountain of books and online forums acknowledging the reality, and in your search for corroboration and comfort, you're relieved to find out you're not alone in whatever horror you might be dealing with.

Yet, somehow this is kept in a tight little circle of mummyhood, and the outward projection to the rest of society tends to be one of maternal beauty, grace, meditation and fulfilling a woman's life purpose. I am wary of this way of making women a separate species, by putting them on a pedestal or isolating them. While I have immense respect for the sisterhood and draw much strength in our solidarity, I know I have also fallen into the trap of creating unreal expectations by only showing the celebratory side of my pregnancy or my sex, and not acknowledging the hardships, and I realize that that's how we keep myths alive and give birth to witches and princesses instead of regular human beings. The truth is, pregnancy is a raw and overwhelming journey at best, and the more we talk about our real experience of it, the more the world around will accommodate our real needs.

In my case, months five and six were good months, I was told to look forward to these months. I got gifts and hugs, and people knowing I was pregnant meant they offered me a seat or water which was nice. But let's just say it wasn't all cupcakes and baby showers. I had burps that burnt my entire chest, perhaps because I'd want to eat Cadbury Nutties, whole packs at a time in a monstrous and desperate attempt to ease my literally growing discomfort. My back would ache so much that I found myself sitting on the pavement one day, just plonked there for everyone to stare at while I gathered each vertebra from the swamp of exhaustion they'd sunk into and pulled myself back up, turning on all fours first, into a deep squat, keeping my knees bent, and lifting with that little bounce at the end like a heavyweight champion at the critical moment when pulling up their dumb-bells.

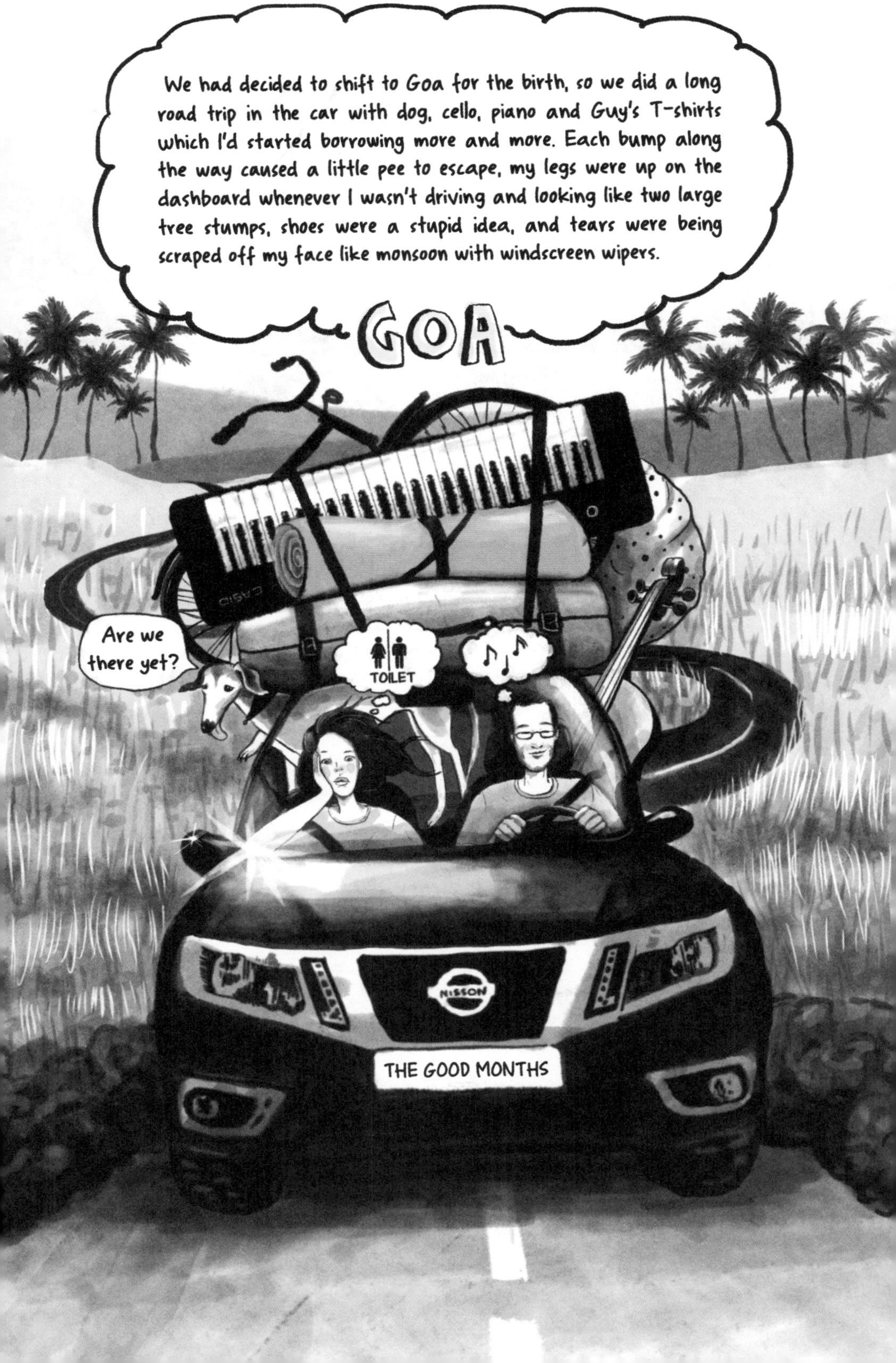
We had decided to shift to Goa for the birth, so we did a long road trip in the car with dog, cello, piano and Guy's T-shirts which I'd started borrowing more and more. Each bump along the way caused a little pee to escape, my legs were up on the dashboard whenever I wasn't driving and looking like two large tree stumps, shoes were a stupid idea, and tears were being scraped off my face like monsoon with windscreen wipers.
GOA
Are we there yet?
TOILET
CASIO
NISSON
THE GOOD MONTHS

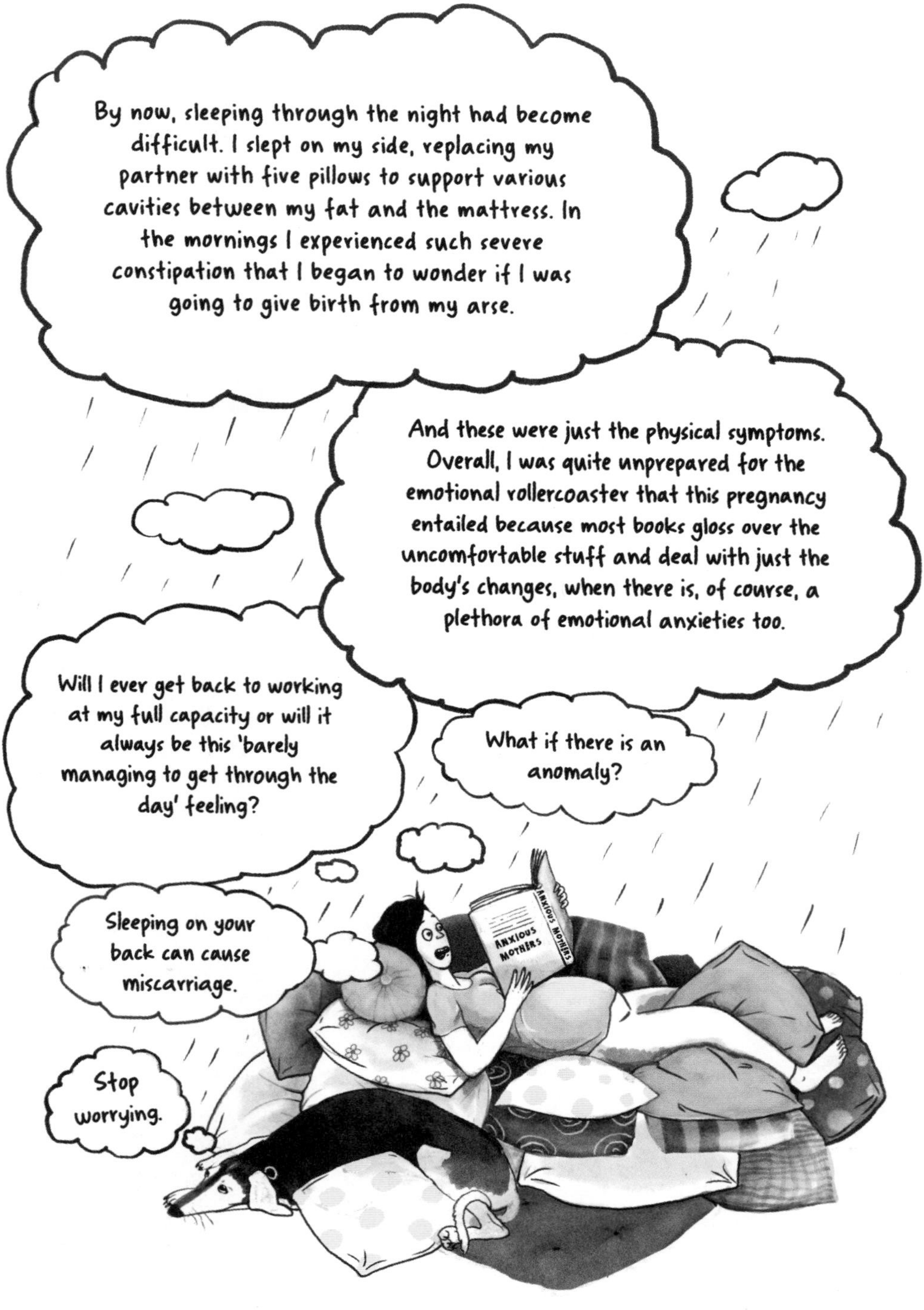
By now, sleeping through the night had become difficult. I slept on my side, replacing my partner with five pillows to support various cavities between my fat and the mattress. In the mornings I experienced such severe constipation that I began to wonder if I was going to give birth from my arse.
And these were just the physical symptoms. Overall, I was quite unprepared for the emotional rollercoaster that this pregnancy entailed because most books gloss over the uncomfortable stuff and deal with just the body's changes, when there is, of course, a plethora of emotional anxieties too.
Will I ever get back to working at my full capacity or will it always be this 'barely managing to get through the day' feeling?
What if there is an anomaly?
ANXIOUS MOTHERS
Sleeping on your back can cause miscarriage.
Stop worrying.

Perhaps the peak of my pregnancy anxiety came when I had to go for the second anomaly scan. This is a scan that is 'offered' to you at about eighteen weeks, 'offered' being the caustic word here, because I later learnt that you don't have to get this scan done, that it's your choice. But no one tells you that.

Anyway, the scan is a useful one—it's to check your baby's growth and development, check for abnormalities and principally to rule out the possibility of your child having Down's syndrome. The thing is, by this point, you're likely to feel like this is your child, your kicking, breathing force of life and no longer a far removed and invisible foetus. And therefore, this scan triggers a series of 'what ifs'.

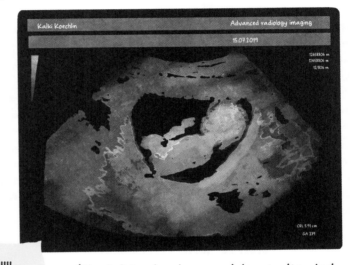

What if my child has Down's syndrome? What if there is something majorly wrong which will make her suffer all her life? What if the scan got it wrong? I mean the scan is not perfect, right?

Kalki Koechlin
Advanced radiology imaging
15.07.2019

I was told casually that abortions are legal till twenty weeks but...

...I've heard her heartbeat!!!!
Due Date
26/01/20

(No, I did not get a sex determination test, not even when I went abroad at eight months, not for any other reason than that I didn't want to spend my holiday time in a clinic, but I had this intuition I was going to have a girl, and referred to 'it' as 'she' quite often.)

The anomaly scan was a nerve-racking test. I remember holding Guy's hand so tight in the radiologist's waiting room, he had my fingernail marks to complain about later. Again I was lucky to not have to deal with bad news, but I wonder if, given a choice, I would have wanted to know—wanted to put myself in a position to make that impossible decision. My best friend from school was also pregnant two months after me and I asked her how she felt about it. She said it's better to know, to be prepared, even if abortion is not an option, but her mother, who was from a generation where they didn't have 'all these fancy machines', thought it would lead to unnecessary worry. I spoke to another friend, who doesn't have children, and she said that for someone from a poorer family this choice to abort so late is very important, because they would not be able to look after a child with such a severe disability. I agree with all of them.

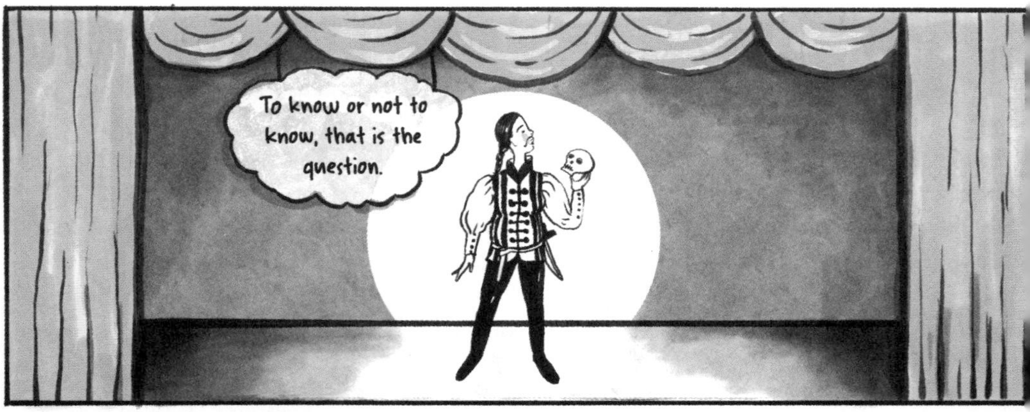
To know or not to know, that is the question.

There's gritty realities to pregnancy, and the constant fear that at any point you could lose th growing life. I think the least we can do for pregnant women is present their choices to them a inform them of their rights openly. In this case, the choice is to know and take a decisive course action or to not know and live with life-altering possibilities.

Halfway through my anomaly scan I had to go out and drink something sweet as the doctor w unable to see my baby properly and needed her to move positions. I sipped a mango milkshake loud through my straw in the quiet sanitized clinic, feeling much like Sappho does today when she do something audacious but cute in front of strangers. Then I went back to lying down and watchi that grey blob on a screen with a heart rate of 120 kicking and turning in my stomach. The ba is healthy, said the doctor. My jaw released, the grip of my fingers against my palms loosened an went to work that day, with a skip to my step and grinning at everyone I met. That's what it fe like to be alive, I thought to myself.

STEP 1

While I was juggling these existential questions with my therapist, friends and family, I was nevertheless determined to enjoy some part of this pregnancy, and remembering the words of my gynaecologist: 'People can't expect a natural birth if they sit around and eat sugar for nine months, it's called labour for a reason, it requires

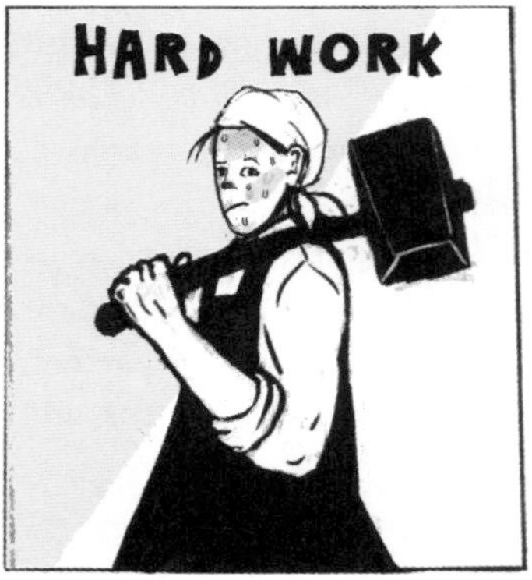
HARD WORK

STEP 2

I started to pay attention to the difference between a **HEALTHY CRAVING**, like waking up at 4 A.M., my mouth watering at the thought of grapefruit, maybe a signal for vitamin C, versus a false one. Like eating mutton biryani with a sprinkle of chips and then chocolate cake with a glass of milk which was perhaps, just perhaps, a big fat excuse to pig out and wallow in my acid reflux.

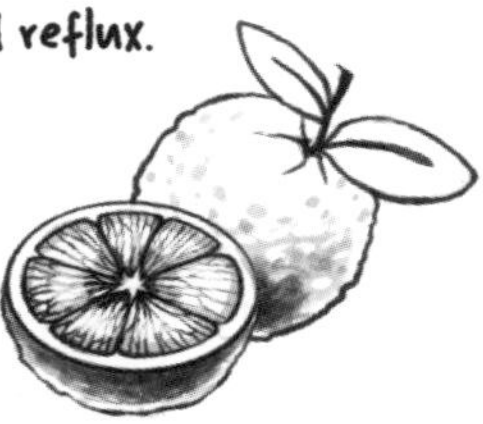

STEP 3

And hanging on to the adv of one down-to-ear mother: 'You won't feel like but use these ever-so-sligh better months (the seco trimester) to get yours strong for what you're abo to go through.'

I went back to **EXERCISING** seriously...

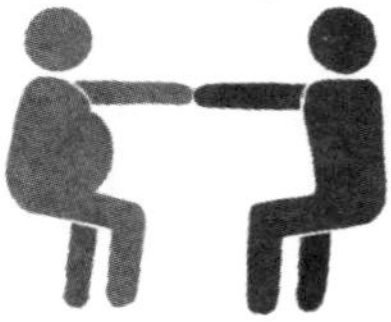

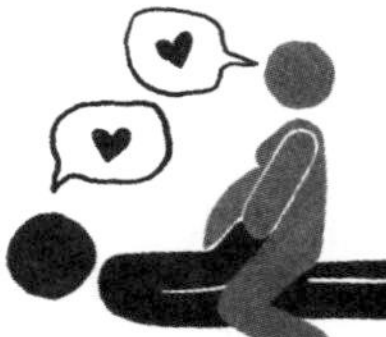

and sometimes creatively.

Apart from the things I could do for myself, here are some things I wished would have happened in the social sphere when I was pregnant.

Do not stare

Unlike how leering at a woman's body is generally frowned upon, leering at a pregnant woman's belly seems to be just fine.

Do not touch

Forget leering, touching the belly seems to be acceptable for certain middle-aged aunties, kids and elders. No, it is not okay to stare, touch or put your unfamiliar hand on her belly without her consent.

Do I look OK?

DON'T MESS WITH PREGGOES

Don't, DO NOT tell her how to dress!

Do find out her dietary requirements.
I don't need cake. I need iron, B6, protein and folic acid ie. spinach, fish, eggs, broccoli.

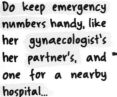

Do keep emergency numbers handy, like her gynaecologist's her partner's, and one for a nearby hospital...

PREGNANCY ETIQUETTE

Do invite her to PARTIES.

Do offer water, a chair and something to put her feet up, if you're having her over, but don't treat her like she's breakable, let her struggle if she wants to.

Even when there's dancing, alcohol and smoking, you can ask smokers to use the balcony or have a designated smoking room. It is very isolating when people treat their pregnant friend like a fragile egg that must hibernate and not have a social life.

I confess I didn't read much about my pregnancy during my pregnancy. I would read the weekly reports on my BabyCentre app, and when I had some doubts about what was happening in my body, I would look up the classic *What To Expect When You're Expecting*. Mostly I was reading 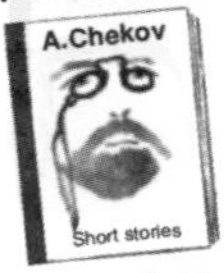
A.Chekov
Short stories
and learning lines. What I did do is speak to mother friends who had experienced many of the symptoms I'd had, some far worse than mine. In traffic, or on set, I listened to podcasts 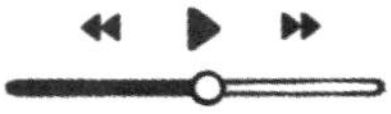 like The Birth Hour and Parentland, and heard the audiobook 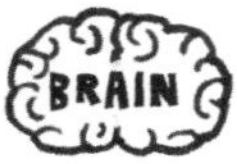
BRAIN
RULES FOR BABY. Somehow grounding myself in scientific facts about the baby's development, or a real mother's experience, helped me stay focused. I was in touch with two doulas who would answer my questions on mucus plugs, water bursting, interventions, labour stages and other things that I simply wanted to understand from a technical perspective. I watched birth stories and birth recordings on **YOUTUBE**, mostly for how women moved during labour, the active positions they took, the sounds they made. Sometimes I would close the door and practise those movements and sounds along with my yoga routine. I saw pregnancy as a sort of intense form of exercise, or as a mother friend of mine called it, 'an extreme sport', where being informed about correct posture and which muscles needed to work was important, but being in the body, physically doing it, was the only way to actually prepare for it. This, however, didn't stop many people from lending their theories, books and secrets on pregnancy to me, even though I had never asked them for their advice...

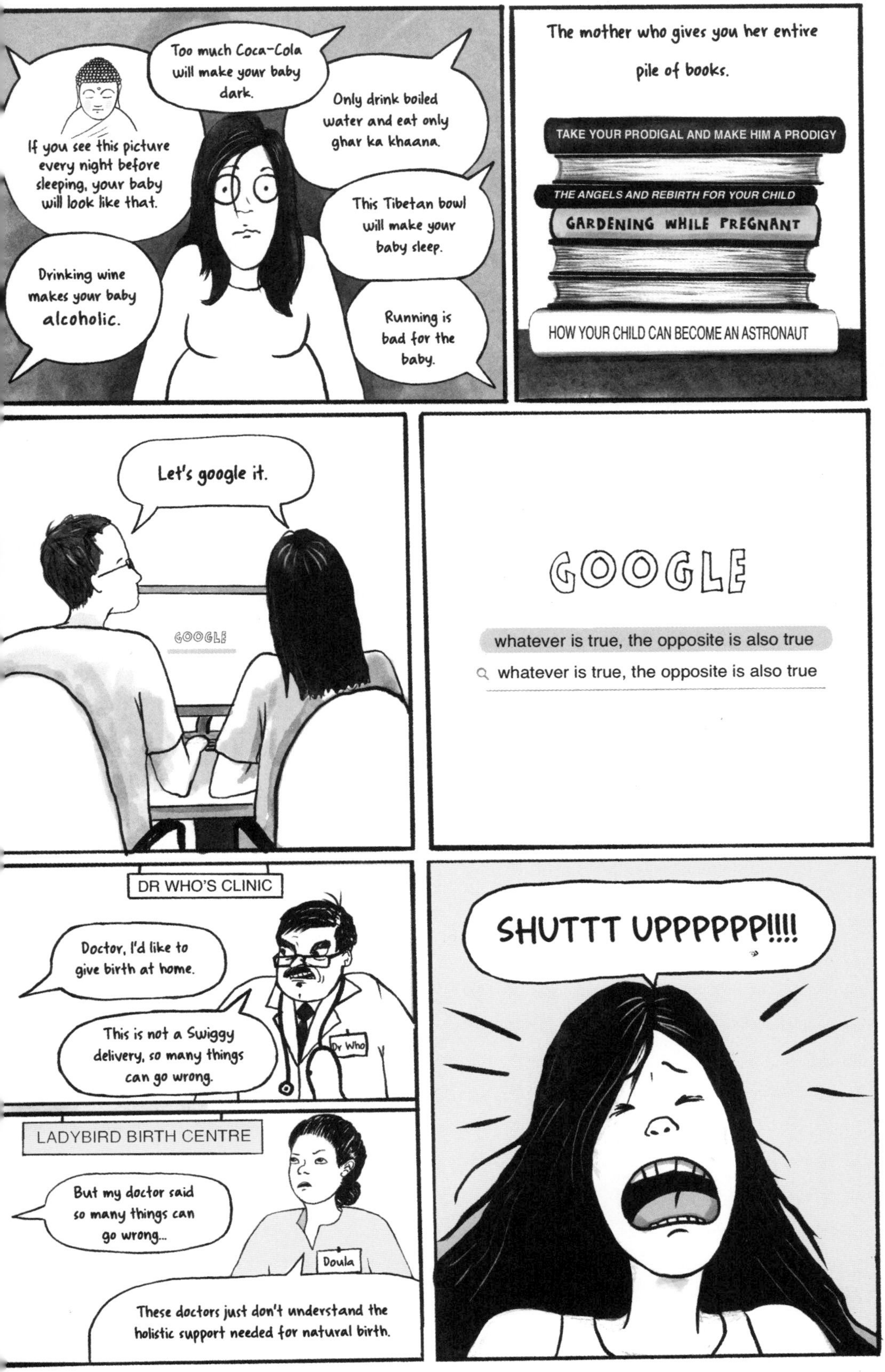

Too much Coca-Cola will make your baby dark.
If you see this picture every night before sleeping, your baby will look like that.
Only drink boiled water and eat only ghar ka khaana.
This Tibetan bowl will make your baby sleep.
Drinking wine makes your baby alcoholic.
Running is bad for the baby.
The mother who gives you her entire pile of books.
TAKE YOUR PRODIGAL AND MAKE HIM A PRODIGY
THE ANGELS AND REBIRTH FOR YOUR CHILD
GARDENING WHILE PREGNANT
HOW YOUR CHILD CAN BECOME AN ASTRONAUT
Let's google it.
GOOGLE
GOOGLE
whatever is true, the opposite is also true
whatever is true, the opposite is also true
DR WHO'S CLINIC
Doctor, I'd like to give birth at home.
This is not a Swiggy delivery, so many things can go wrong.
Dr Who
LADYBIRD BIRTH CENTRE
But my doctor said so many things can go wrong...
Doula
These doctors just don't understand the holistic support needed for natural birth.
SHUTTT UPPPPPP!!!!

It's hard not to get angry or completely confused with all this information coming at you. I found the best way to deal with it was with a smile, a 'thank you' and a

mental note:

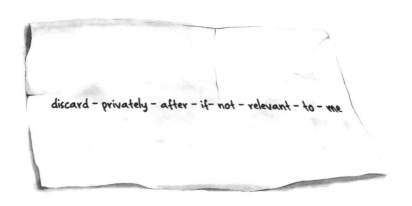

discard – privately – after – if– not – relevant – to – me

After all, this age is just full of fragmented short rants for an invisible public from an anonymous mass of well-intentioned but under-informed self-proclaimers. Social media has become a cute way to drop a bomb of your opinion on a big debate and leave whenever the debris and human annihilation gets too much to handle. Sometimes I do wish people would keep their opinions to themselves so that we can get on with world peace.

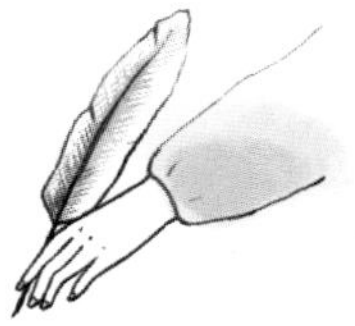

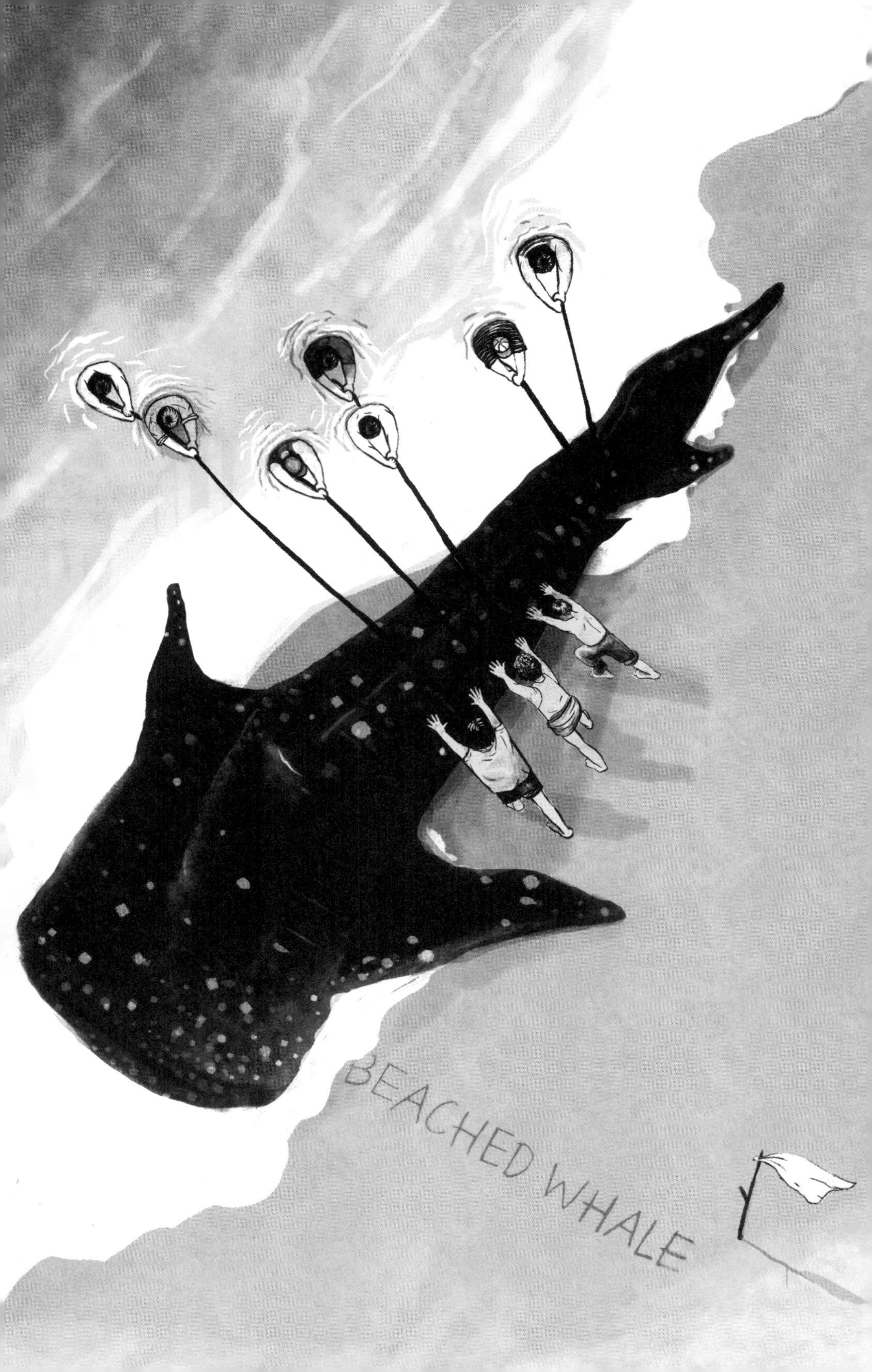
BEACHED WHALE

When whales are stranded on a beach, they're in danger of dying of dehydration or collapsing under their own weight.
The whale is used to pressure from all sides being equal as a result of living in water, and so the downward pull of gravity exhausts her completely. Towards the end of my pregnancy, I really began to feel like a fish out of water, or more specifically, a whale out of water. This last trimester is just like the first; the nausea is back, and although the vomiting is less frequent, it's compensated by its projectile nature, and of course, I'm 15 kilos heavier, making me want to quit, retire

or

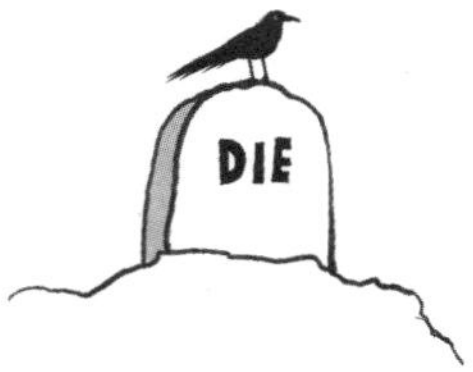
DIE

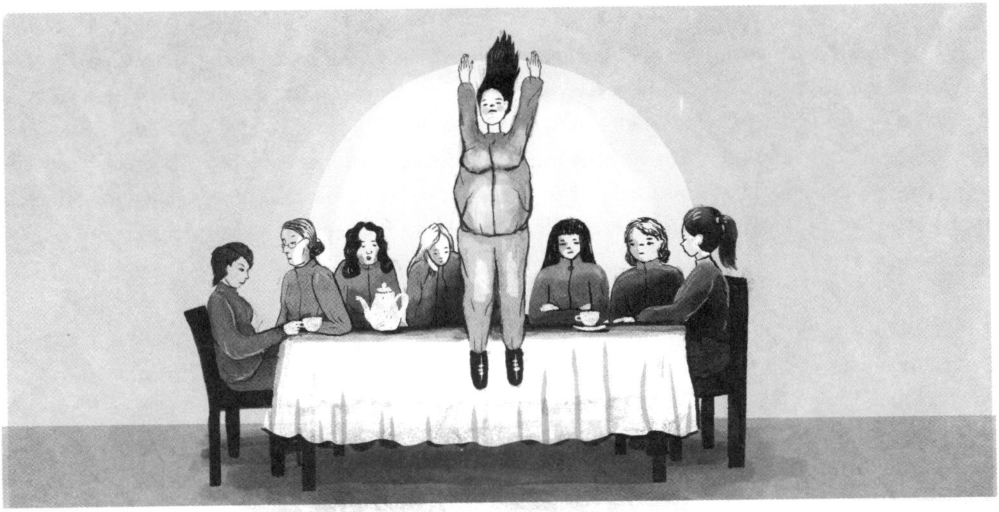

I'm doing this play with eight girls working on a version of *Uncle Vanya*, a two-hour-forty-five-minute play where none of the actors ever leave the stage during the performance. Six hours of rehearsals a day for a month and a couple of weeks performing and travelling, sometimes two shows a day, meant six hours on stage, not including warm-ups, travel and getting ready. I've always felt great on stage; once the lights are up I have no time to judge myself, I'm immersed in the role and the hours just fly by. This wasn't the case when I was eight months pregnant. I felt highly inadequate on stage and unable to reach my goals on a daily basis during rehearsals. And yet my body seemed to accommodate my efforts better than my mind. There was this one jump I would do in a scene, from the table to the floor, landing with a little bounce in the knees to accommodate my big belly, and after it, we would always hear a collective gasp from the audience – it must have looked shocking from the outside. One woman came to me after the show and said, 'You mustn't do that; your baby might slip out.'

Needless to say, it was intense. But I believe working throughout this last trimester really helped me keep a routine and not spend too much time on Google researching

all the things that can go wrong before a birth	Search

or reading about all the things you're expected to get right before becoming a parent.

The truth is, there is a certain amount of letting go one has to do after a point, because this is bigger than anyone and has a working of its own.

I was excited, after all, the biggest premiere of my life was coming up in 2020. We had a cosy holiday home in Goa, a midwife we barely knew but whom many had recommended for a water birth, and as soon as the last show was over, I was getting on a flight—with the intention of wearing my most anti-fit black dress, hoping they wouldn't notice I was beyond the flyable weeks, and where I could finally spend my last month yoga-ing, feeling my way through hypnobirthing and (responsibly) sunbathing.

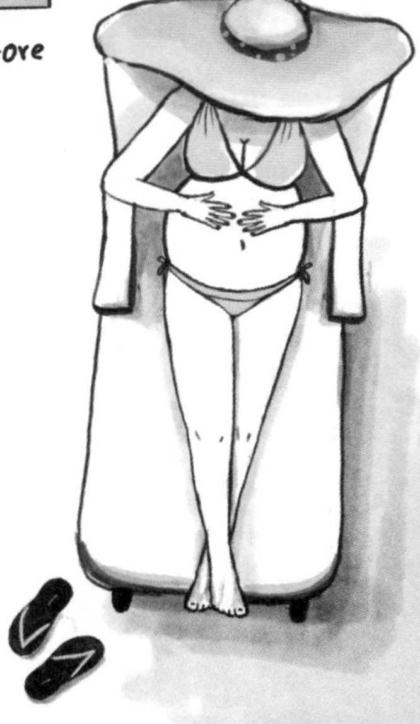

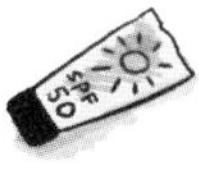
SPF 50

It's the last night of shows in a Mumbai performance space called G5A, about forty-five minutes till doors open to the audience, and I get a call from an acquaintance. She speaks to me for forty-six minutes about her really, really difficult birthing experience with the same midwife we were going with. She needed medical intervention, she had to rush somewhere else at the last minute, her baby needed tubes, it was traumatic. She wishes nothing like that to happen to me or other mothers, she feels it's her duty to tell me since she knew I am planning the same.

I'm just sitting there, in this exhibition room showcasing images from the Bhopal gas tragedy— I'd gone there to get away from the chatter of eight girls pre-show—and I am looking at a poster of a dilapidated building and a stranded child, with stunned tears rolling down my cheeks silently. I ask if she and her baby are OK now—yes—she says. I say a quick bye and hang up. I go into the green room and my face must reflect what I am feeling, like my whole world has just shattered, because my director notices first, then my partner walks into the room which makes me cry, and then there is a collective hug from eight girls and two of my favourite men before we all shuffle on stage and I shove away this feeling of the universe collapsing for the next three hours.

After a long night of discussion with my partner, we decide to change all our plans. So instead of chilling on a beach in Goa, the last three weeks of my pregnancy were spent shifting everything back from Goa, shifting into a new flat close to my clinic, finding a new doula so we could take a crash course in birthing, breastfeeding and not dropping the baby, drawing up a new birth plan, and generally being utterly exhausted.

I tell you all this in detail because things will change. At some point, in the labour room or before, because no amount of science, knowledge or preparation can make you ready for what is, in my opinion, the greatest act of surrender.

This act of birthing, of parenting, in fact of life-ing, requires at all times a certain flexibility from us, and like an actor who learns their lines over and over a hundred times before finally performing on a stage, we must know that even if these lines don't change, their rhythm and intonation changes every night, depending on what your co-actor does, or depending on whether or not you get a laugh at a certain line from your audience. And sometimes even the lines change. Sometimes you have to improvise on the spot. No day is the same for an actor performing the same play again and again. And no birth is the same for you or me even though birthing is an age-old story.

So when that unexpected change comes—and it will never be when you're sitting comfortably waiting for it—when your idealism is smashed into a million broken pieces at an inconvenient moment and everything you worked for in the past nine months seems to dissolve into the unknown waters of

what the fuck am I supposed to do now

REMEMBER

That you've got more stamina inside you than you ever dreamed of

That we have a structure around us, doctors, family, friends, therapists, who can guide us, remember to trust them even though you're scared to death

That your body has a memory of its own, separate from the mind, which is subject to panic

Remember to take a walk, or a jog, or a swim or a jump on stage, to shift your thoughts and let this body do what it has been engineered to do for millions of years

And remember to breathe for four counts in and eight counts out!

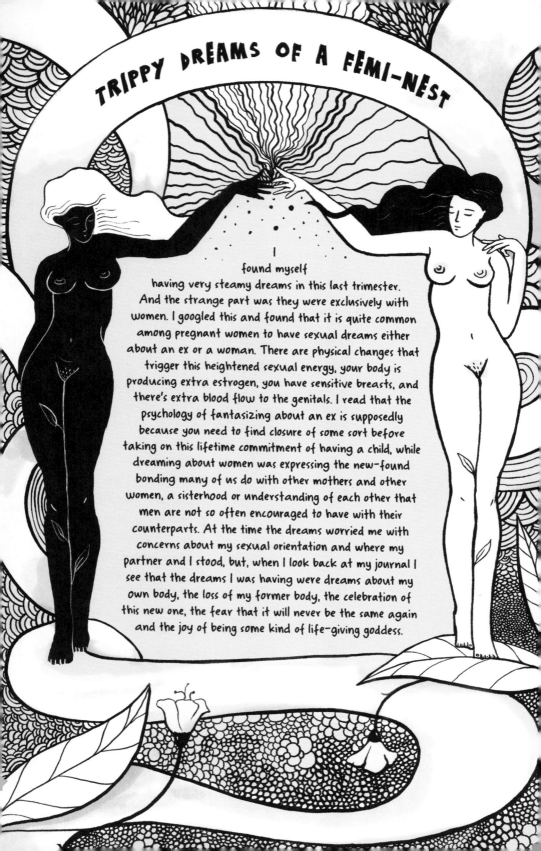

TRIPPY DREAMS OF A FEMI-NEST

I found myself having very steamy dreams in this last trimester. And the strange part was they were exclusively with women. I googled this and found that it is quite common among pregnant women to have sexual dreams either about an ex or a woman. There are physical changes that trigger this heightened sexual energy, your body is producing extra estrogen, you have sensitive breasts, and there's extra blood flow to the genitals. I read that the psychology of fantasizing about an ex is supposedly because you need to find closure of some sort before taking on this lifetime commitment of having a child, while dreaming about women was expressing the new-found bonding many of us do with other mothers and other women, a sisterhood or understanding of each other that men are not so often encouraged to have with their counterparts. At the time the dreams worried me with concerns about my sexual orientation and where my partner and I stood, but, when I look back at my journal I see that the dreams I was having were dreams about my own body, the loss of my former body, the celebration of this new one, the fear that it will never be the same again and the joy of being some kind of life-giving goddess.

There is something to be said about the pregnant woman's body here. The sheer physical transformation is so rapid and so unlike any other natural cycle that its easy to just skip past it. It's like, oh that was a weird year, but now I have the perfect family and I can forget all about that lonely, sexually repressed, far from perfect state of mind.

As an actor, I'm of a rare privileged class that gets someone else to dress me up for red carpets and glamorous events. During this time, my stylists searched high and low for maternity glamour, but fashion didn't seem to see the pregnant body as a thing worth investing in, at least here in India. We were forced to take large-size dresses, tailor them, put on a belt, add an elastic band to the trouser button and other such resourceful but worrying adjustments. And when I went to the maternity section of the limited stores that had them, I found the dresses I so distinctly remember seeing throughout my life on neighbouring 'aunties', you know the kaftan-cum-nightie-cum-tent dress that strips you of all your sexuality and makes you look like a nice bundle of shapeless comfort and soft opinions?

Yup

That

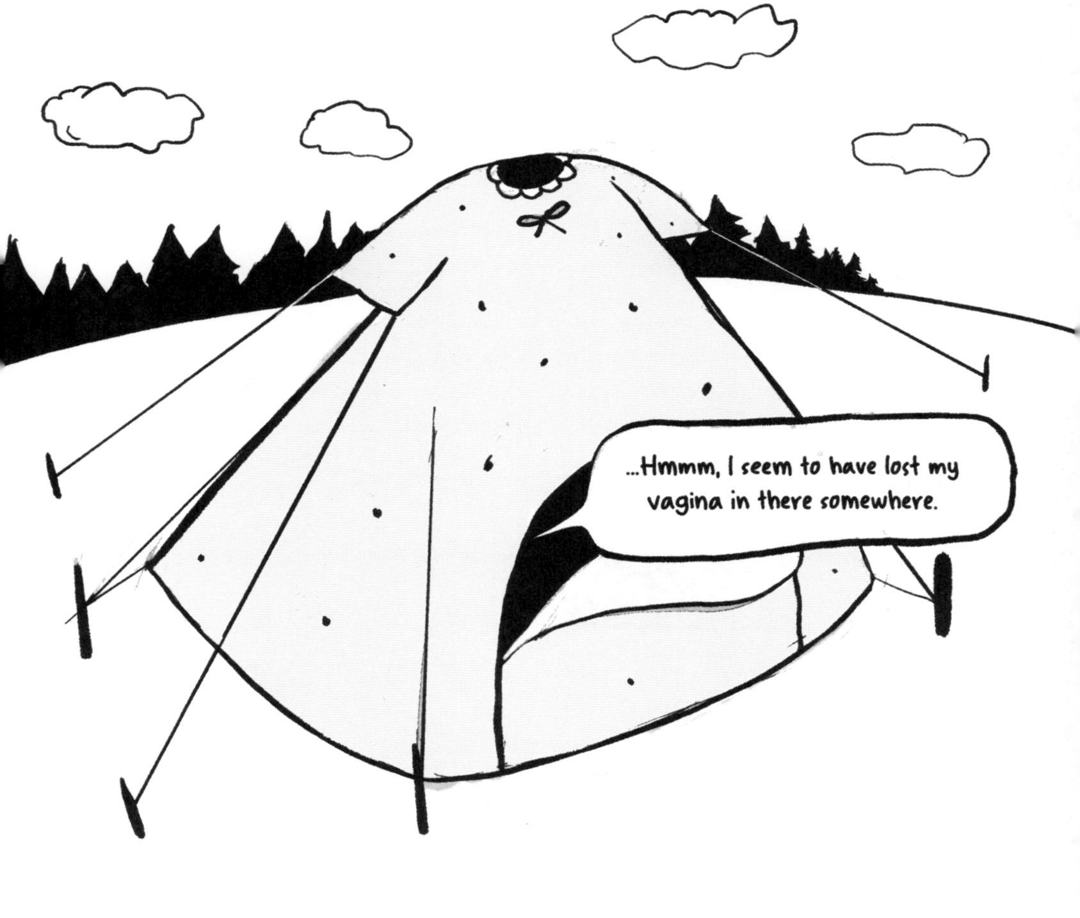

...Hmmm, I seem to have lost my vagina in there somewhere.

Is desexualizing the pregnant woman's body convenient because the stages of growth are too fast and people don't want to spend money on clothes they'll only wear for a few months? I don't know. We seem to have no problem investing in expensive baby clothes that your baby will wear only for a month or so—there are clothes my baby wore once, before she outgrew them. No, I believe if there was profit to be made, the seven-to-nine-month pregnancy catsuit would be available at our nearest mall. I wonder if this is again to be blamed on patriarchal systems at play. If it is because we, as a society, need this woman to be available for all the invisible, unpaid work that exists in the domestic realm, and if she gets all uppity, fashionable and non-maternal during her pregnancy, then who will bring up our children?

I've noticed this in my line of work, when a woman gets married or decides to have children, the questions journalists ask are:

> Will you still be working after marriage?

> As though maybe I lost a limb in the dowry deal or something.

> How will you manage the work-life balance?

> The answer is holding my baby in one hand, the phone between my shoulder and neck and grabbing the diaper bag with the other hand, while my partner wipes her bum and gets rid of the nuclear waste.

Whereas the questions posed to men in the same league tend to be more like:

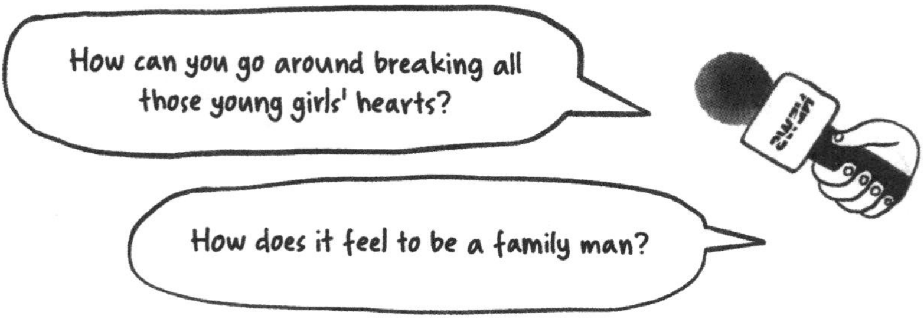

> How can you go around breaking all those young girls' hearts?

> How does it feel to be a family man?

The body
machine
flexibility, but it is
is fragile and subject
how we view each other.
not wearing a bra, but I
made sexy pink bikini and
large hat that received
being a mother, an actor, a sexually
a committed relationship. What I
don't nurture the capacity for
everyone in neat little boxes,
irregular, we change from
and it is relentless. I think one
because it keeps changing, while,
like to pretend it's steady and
first thirty years of my life to
speaking to a fairly big cosmetic
they told her that I was too volatile,
were unpredictable and changing
they needed someone who could look
lot of our advertising and commercial
sameness. In stark contrast to this, life
when we get comfortable with one
plummets us in a different direction.

In today's world we're told to 'hold on', to
'move on', instead of being taught to let go,
reflect...

is an extraordinary
capable of unimaginable
controlled by a mind, which
to changes from society and
I liked being in a kaftan and
also loved lounging in a custom-
sunbathing. With a ridiculously
attention and admiration. I like
active and desirable woman in
mean to say is, as a society we
change very well. We like to keep
when in fact we are messy and
the moment we are born till we die
of the reasons life can be hard is
at the same time, as a society we
predictable. I think it took me the
realize this. I remember my manager
brand about endorsing them, and
that my 'look'and my choice of roles
too often for their brand vision,that
the same for years to come. And a
content is based on this idea of
tends to fluctuate relentlessly, just
way of being, something unexpected

'stick to what you believe in' or to
change our habits or look back and

During my pregnancy, I loved that I was encouraged to write things down and keep a pregnancy journal by a number of my mother friends, so that I could look back at it to get perspective (and write this book). I love that I had doctors and doulas I could express my insecurities to so they could encourage me or gently nudge me to work on them. I loved having a partner that I could exchange articles with, and share my worries with, so we could find a happy compromise between our different views and experiences. In retrospect, I loved that I had to slow down, play the ukulele and listen to my body, because it helped me clear the clutter in my mind and think about what actually makes me happy. All these little support systems helped me love my body and help me still, when it fluctuates in size and capability as it inevitably will through childbearing or ageing. And more importantly, I can allow myself to change my mind about the way I look at life and relearn how to interact with the world, in a more conscious and gentle manner.

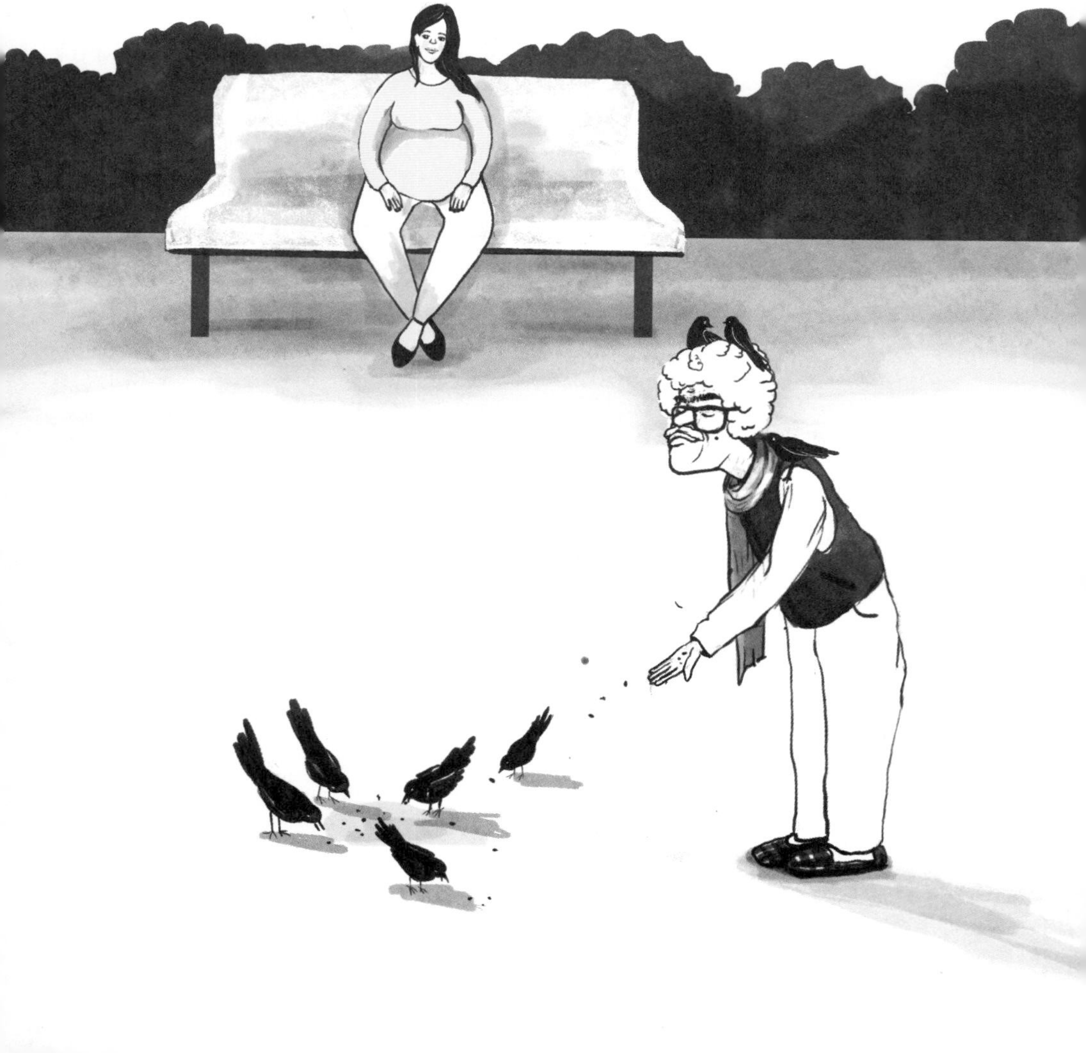

Philosophies

LOVE and HATE. Seems to be everywhere these days. A worldwide debate. But I don't need to look far to find it. I see this cycle of love and hate in my own family. We curse each other and scream and shout and break things, until we ourselves break. Then we cry, feel the guilt and look down at our feet. We hug gingerly, love reluctantly and forget quickly until it is repeated again. Love and hate. A habit.

Like two magnets, 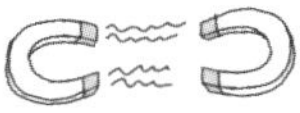 in constant repulsion.

Perhaps the opposite of hate is not love, but understanding. And the opposite of love is not hate, but neglect. There are so many uncomfortable extremes that make us feel we must react at once and put a stop to it – slam the door, walk away, shout your way to the other person's silence, unleash unthinkable acts of violence.

But living with discomfort all the time, as I do now, because it is inside me and I cannot escape it, I have no choice but to be PATIENT. My body demands it, my mind shuts down, my heart can only beat. If I erupt, it is inward and I alone feel the heat. I feel small, very small, from the sheer mystery and unfamiliarity of the grand workings inside me. And so, eventually, I'm reduced to baby steps, forced to listen and respond, to note down and break years of habit in this moment. Today the cycle will not repeat.

Today I will plant a seed, 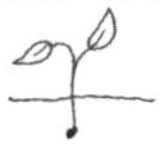 allowing my intentions to grow into another being – another me, but more conscious, more careful. I feel as if this creature, which began as a virus of discomfort inside me, slowly threatening my independence, stalling my capacity to create or think for myself, and eating into my daily routine, is now firmly a mirror of my own insecurities, a counter to my fear, a soul that can evolve and grow more rapidly than I have in all my years.

So perhaps the opposite of destruction is not creation, but simply balance. And the opposite of creation is not destruction, but constant distraction.

So I sit and wait.

Write and read.

Try to keep my balance.

And BREATHE.

Because that's all I can get right sometimes.

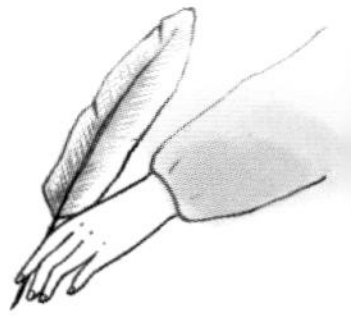

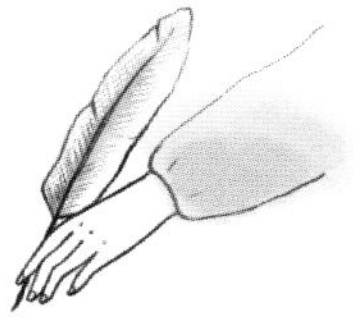

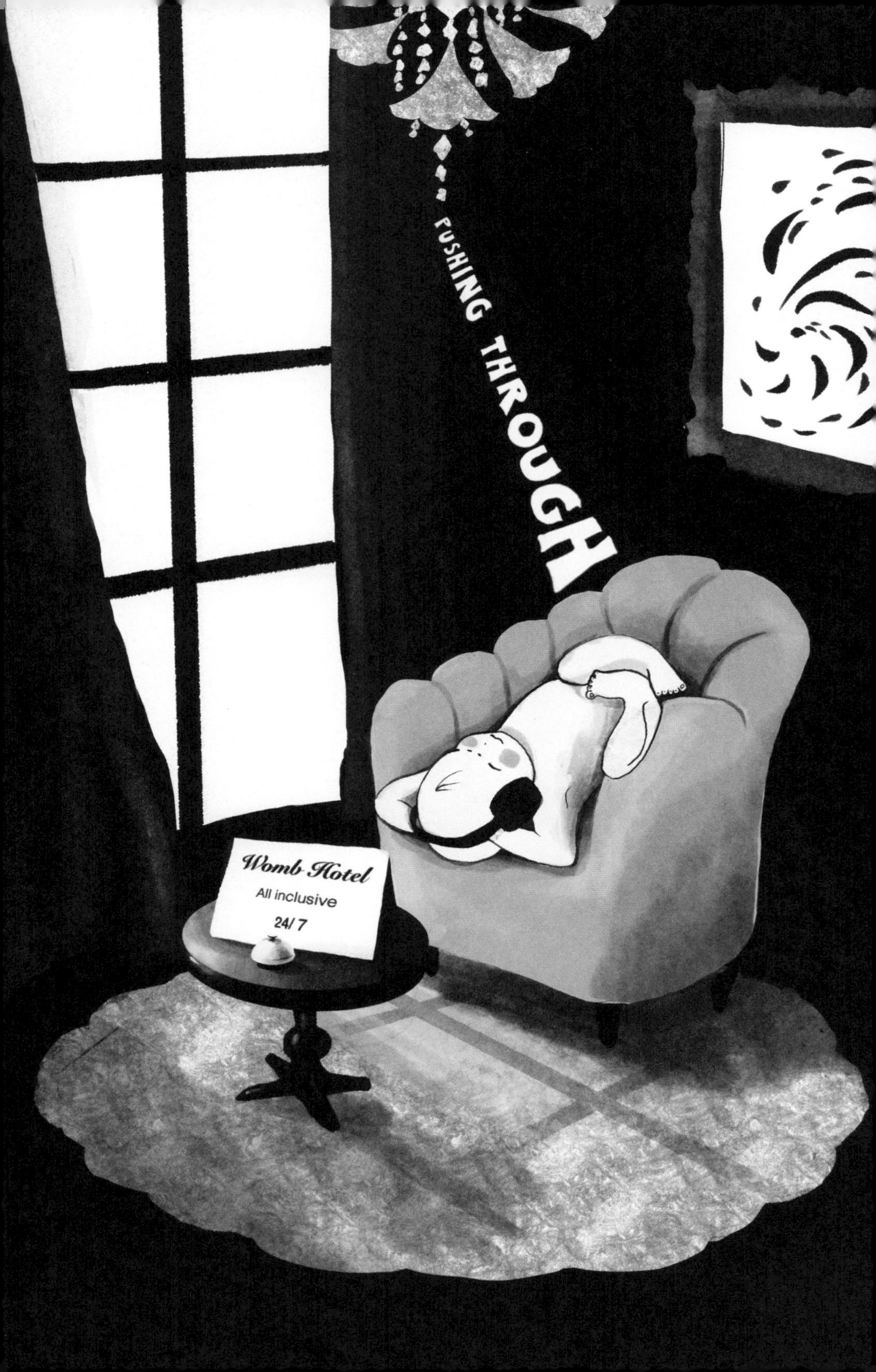

PUSHING THROUGH
Womb Hotel
All inclusive
24/ 7

How will I know I'm going into labour?

It was impossible not to lose sleep in the last few weeks before giving birth.

Will my dog Kiara try to attack the baby?

And, in my case, will this baby ever decide to come out?

Is the cord around the neck going to tighten?

My due date was Republic Day, and my baby was born on 7 February; for anyone who's had a late birth, you will appreciate how exasperating this wait is. I was going for weekly ultrasounds at this point, and a doctor I had never met before was taking my scan. He said, 'Your amniotic fluid is very low, you really can't wait more than two days, you should induce immediately', in a way that made me also panic even though what he said was inaccurate and it really wasn't his business to tell me what to do. I was getting daily messages on my WhatsApp from friends, colleagues and family asking if the baby's arrived, followed by exclamation marks, question marks and unicorn emojis. My partner looked at me with fear, as we both got into bed to have 'labour -inducing' sex again. By this point I was speaking to all the mothers I knew, even neighbours whom I hardly knew, for any recommendations to make this happen now. I was drinking castor oil, taking homeopathy, doing various types of squats and giving myself perineal massages with aromatherapy on a daily basis.

And still...

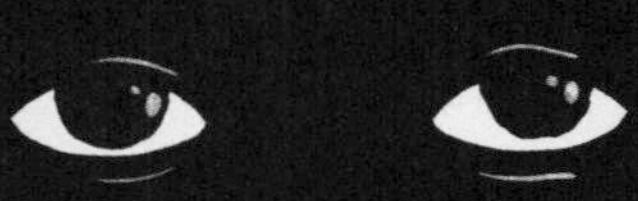

...nothing.

On 6 February, out of frustration from this wait, my partner and I went to the cinema hall to watch the newest festival film that everybody was praising called Parasite. The film, for those who haven't seen it, turns abruptly and stunningly violent towards the end, and at this point I start feeling a vague pain in my back. I dismiss it, thinking it's because I have been sitting for too long. But later that night, the pain in my lower back is back.

Midnight
I can't sleep.

I open the contractions app on my phone, the pain repeats itself every fifteen minutes.

I wake Guy up.

I think it's happening.

I call my gynaecologist, almost apologetically, I mean what if I'm wrong and I'm waking her up for nothing?

She answers sleepily but with clarity.

OK keep an eye on it, in a few hours when you're at ten minutes, head to the clinic.

01:30

02:00

We pack
✓ the dog
✓ the baby bag
✓ the exercise ball
✓ the ukulele
✓ water bottles
✓ the grown-up bag
and shove our panic below the list of all the things that need to be done.

02:15   I'm somehow down to seven minutes between contractions.

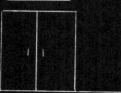

✦ CLINIC ✦

We reach the clinic.
Contractions are coming in every five minutes now.

02:30

03:00

My doula reaches the clinic, helps me count my breaths during contractions.

06:00

The contractions are every three minutes.
I'm already so tired, I'm passing out in between them.

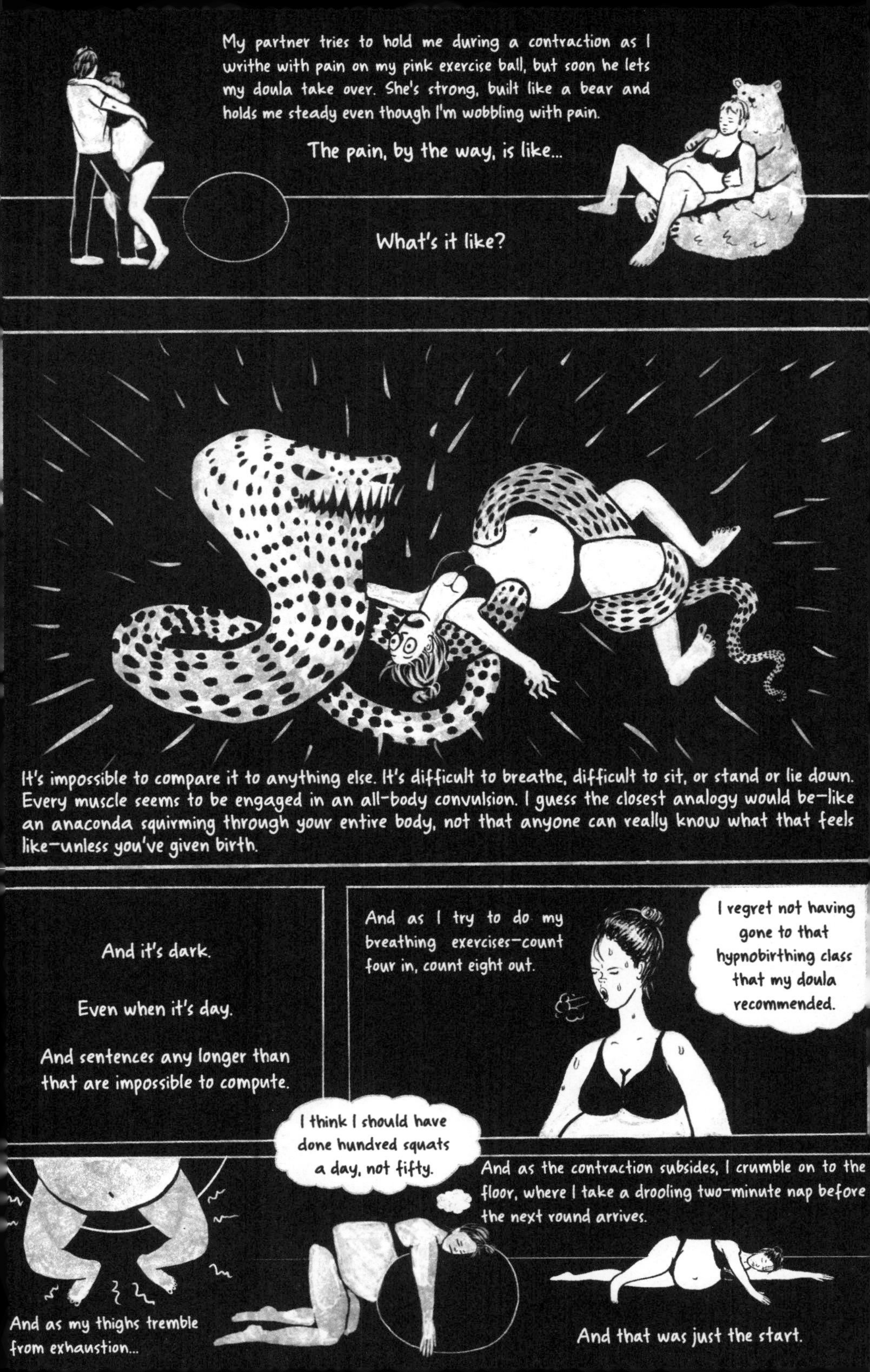

My partner tries to hold me during a contraction as I writhe with pain on my pink exercise ball, but soon he lets my doula take over. She's strong, built like a bear and holds me steady even though I'm wobbling with pain.
The pain, by the way, is like...
What's it like?
It's impossible to compare it to anything else. It's difficult to breathe, difficult to sit, or stand or lie down. Every muscle seems to be engaged in an all-body convulsion. I guess the closest analogy would be—like an anaconda squirming through your entire body, not that anyone can really know what that feels like—unless you've given birth.
And it's dark.
Even when it's day.
And sentences any longer than that are impossible to compute.
And as I try to do my breathing exercises—count four in, count eight out.
I regret not having gone to that hypnobirthing class that my doula recommended.
I think I should have done hundred squats a day, not fifty.
And as my thighs tremble from exhaustion...
And as the contraction subsides, I crumble on to the floor, where I take a drooling two-minute nap before the next round arrives.
And that was just the start.

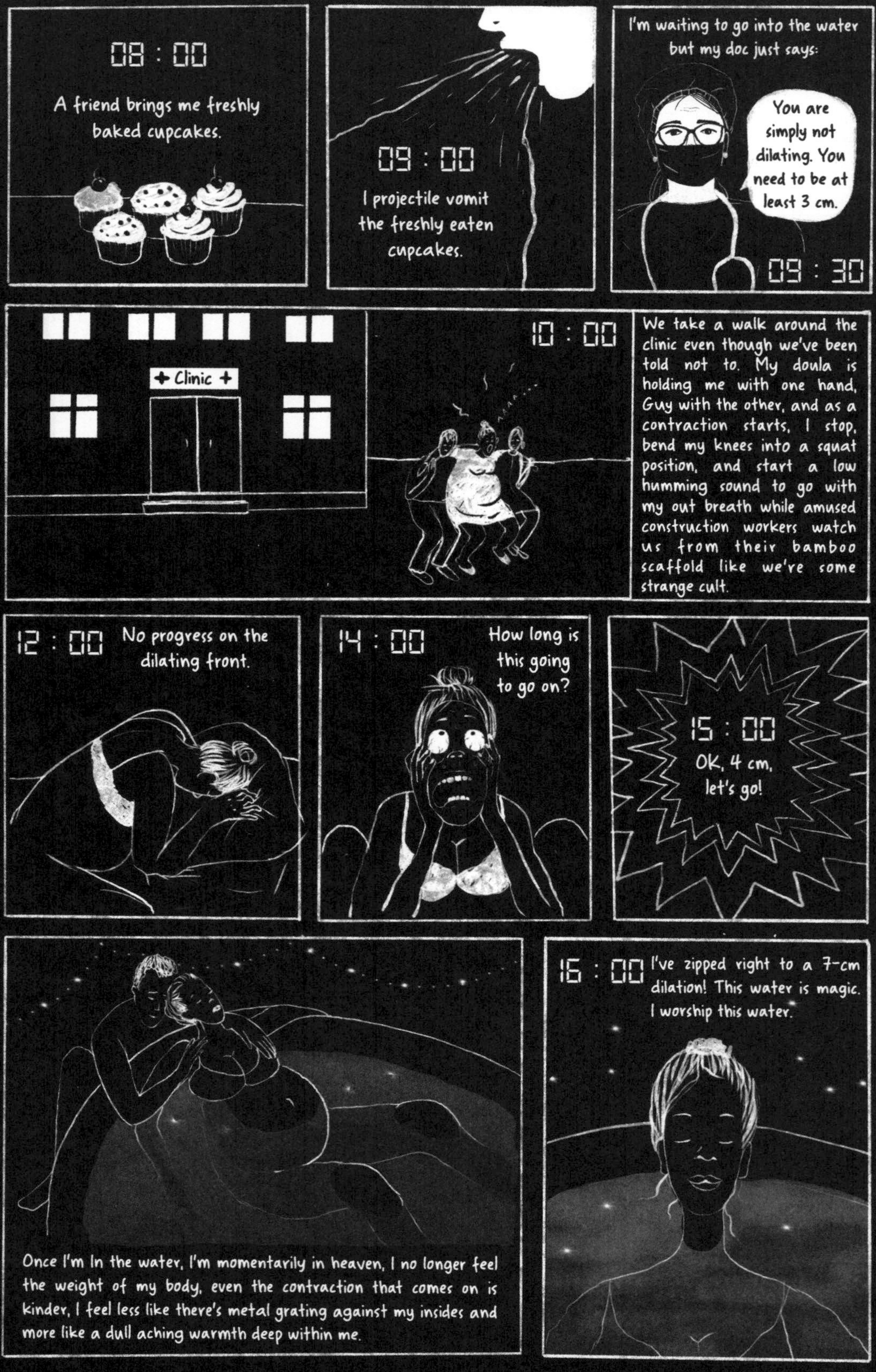
08 : 00
A friend brings me freshly baked cupcakes.
09 : 00
I projectile vomit the freshly eaten cupcakes.
I'm waiting to go into the water but my doc just says:
You are simply not dilating. You need to be at least 3 cm.
09 : 30
+ Clinic +
10 : 00
We take a walk around the clinic even though we've been told not to. My doula is holding me with one hand, Guy with the other, and as a contraction starts, I stop, bend my knees into a squat position, and start a low humming sound to go with my out breath while amused construction workers watch us from their bamboo scaffold like we're some strange cult.
12 : 00
No progress on the dilating front.
14 : 00
How long is this going to go on?
15 : 00
OK, 4 cm, let's go!
Once I'm In the water, I'm momentarily in heaven, I no longer feel the weight of my body, even the contraction that comes on is kinder, I feel less like there's metal grating against my insides and more like a dull aching warmth deep within me.
16 : 00
I've zipped right to a 7-cm dilation! This water is magic. I worship this water.

And then it starts. … the every minute contraction.

I'm so tired, I collapse after each contraction, the contractions themselves are tired, I can feel the energy draining out of my body every minute and my consciousness is slipping away with it. The next few hours are a blur.

There are regular internal checks, baby's heartbeat checks, and repositioning of my body from sitting on my haunches to leaning back into Guy's arms, I can barely breathe. People's voices are far away and muffled, even though I find out later that my doula was speaking firmly and loudly and Guy was constantly murmuring encouragement while holding me up from under my arms.

I am only concentrating on breathing. I can hear my breath louder than anybody in the room, and it's dark and I'm vaguely aware that my voice is growling lower and lower as though trying to reach deep down inside me, and the pain is actually no longer pain, it's more like my body has become a strange place that's expanding and I'm shrinking, like going into a deep meditation that you're not sure you can return from, you simply try to live through every breath, and I can barely breathe...

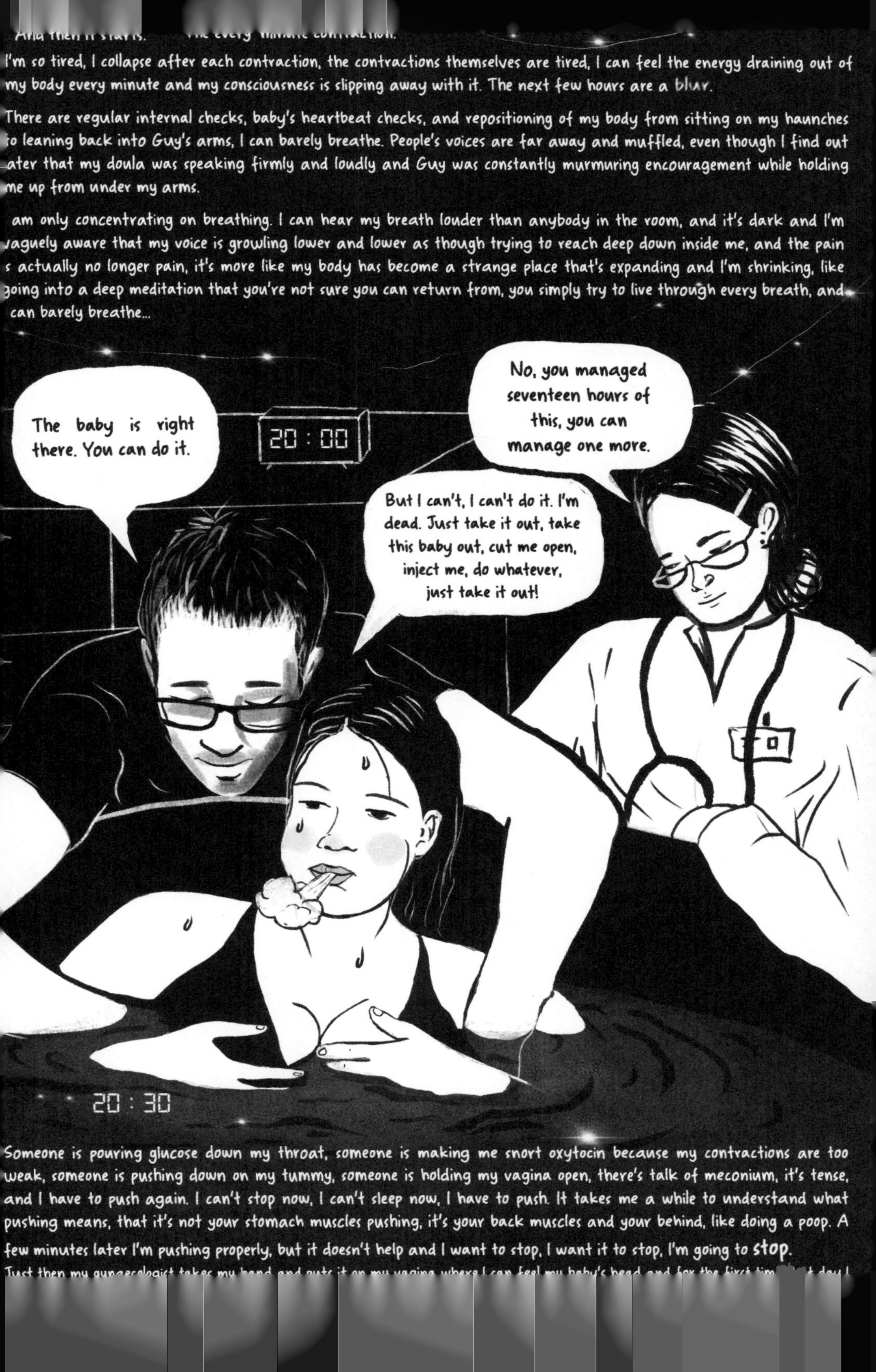

The baby is right there. You can do it.
20:00
No, you managed seventeen hours of this, you can manage one more.
But I can't, I can't do it. I'm dead. Just take it out, take this baby out, cut me open, inject me, do whatever, just take it out!
20:30

Someone is pouring glucose down my throat, someone is making me snort oxytocin because my contractions are too weak, someone is pushing down on my tummy, someone is holding my vagina open, there's talk of meconium, it's tense, and I have to push again. I can't stop now, I can't sleep now, I have to push. It takes me a while to understand what pushing means, that it's not your stomach muscles pushing, it's your back muscles and your behind, like doing a poop. A few minutes later I'm pushing properly, but it doesn't help and I want to stop, I want it to stop, I'm going to **stop**.

Just then my gynaecologist takes my hand and puts it on my vagina where I can feel my baby's head and for the first time … day I

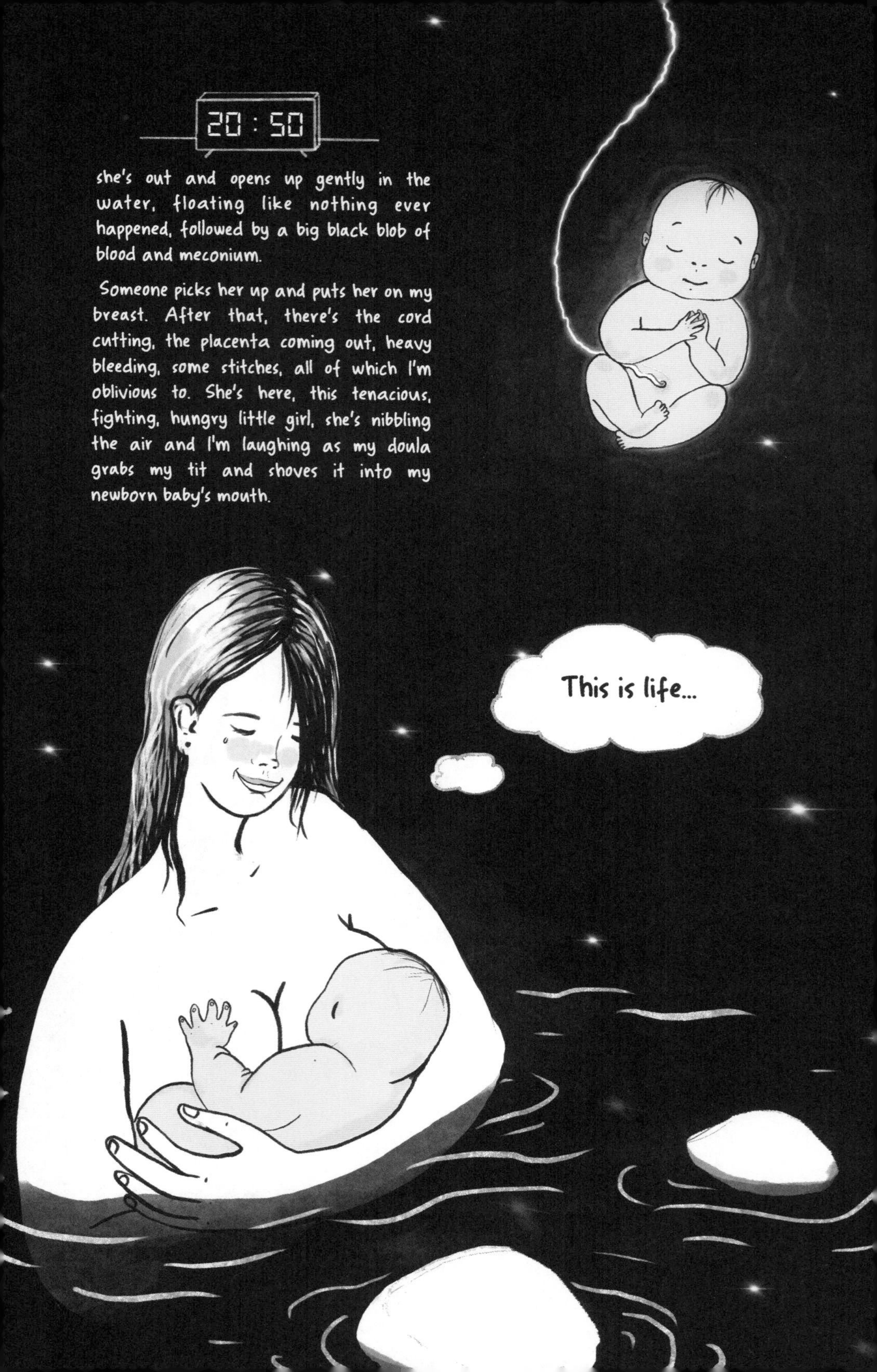
20:50
she's out and opens up gently in the water, floating like nothing ever happened, followed by a big black blob of blood and meconium.
Someone picks her up and puts her on my breast. After that, there's the cord cutting, the placenta coming out, heavy bleeding, some stitches, all of which I'm oblivious to. She's here, this tenacious, fighting, hungry little girl, she's nibbling the air and I'm laughing as my doula grabs my tit and shoves it into my newborn baby's mouth.
This is life...

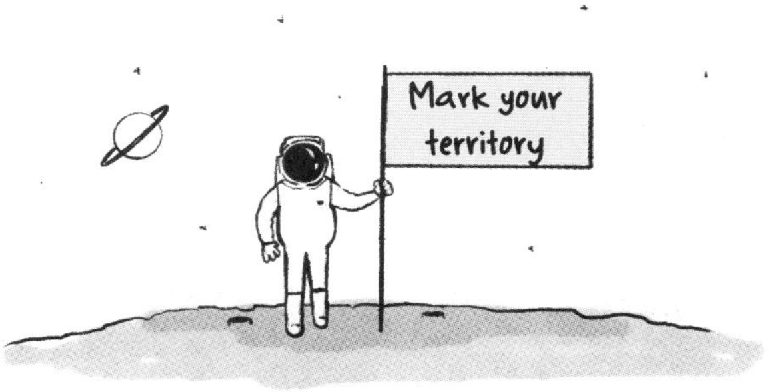
Mark your territory

I recently spoke to a woman whose birth experience reminded me how important a birth plan is. She had had a particularly gruelling twenty hours of labour, and as she reached the finish line, she was supported by a whole crowd of people, from the doctors, nurses, her husband, to people she didn't even seem to know, they were all encouraging her, holding her hand and cheering her on while she pushed. But the moment she gave birth to a baby boy, she remembers how the room emptied out as they took her baby across a glass partition to where all the family members were, and she has this image of them rejoicing and celebrating, along with the medical aids, while she was left alone on a cold slab with one nurse to birth her placenta and be stitched up. That is when I realized how important it is to demand what you want as a mother giving birth, that this is your show and remind yourself that the glory belongs to you, until the system and culture catch up.

It's tricky getting the birth you want. First, the whole thing is so unpredictable. Despite having advanced immensely in medical technology, I'm always surprised at the mystery that remains with ultrasound pregnancy scans looking more like intergalactic territory...

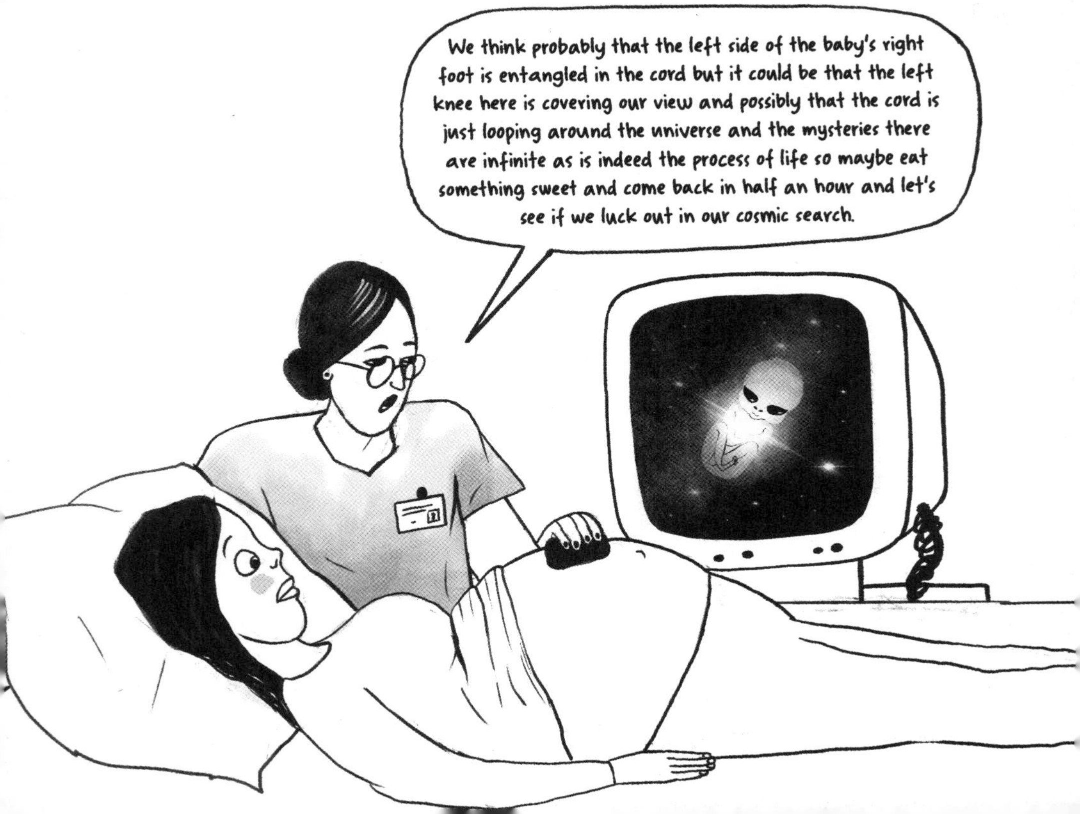
We think probably that the left side of the baby's right foot is entangled in the cord but it could be that the left knee here is covering our view and possibly that the cord is just looping around the universe and the mysteries there are infinite as is indeed the process of life so maybe eat something sweet and come back in half an hour and let's see if we luck out in our cosmic search.

And then for the natural birth that I was hoping for, there are just so many things that have to go right that you really wonder how this doesn't go wrong more often. For an ideal birth the baby's head needs to be down, facing your back and the back of her head engaged with your pelvis. You have to watch that umbilical cord closely. Mine was loosely around her neck a month before I delivered, and you have to hope your baby doesn't poop before she's out as ingesting the meconium can give her a serious infection. During the usually long hours of labour, the only way you can 'guess' if your baby is doing all right is by listening to her heartbeat at regular intervals. And these are just some from a long list of hopes and fingers crossed.

I was lucky to have a gynaecologist who fully supported my wish for a natural water birth, and not only encouraged me throughout the process but even went against 'standard procedure' in order to accommodate some of my wants.

A small deviation here:

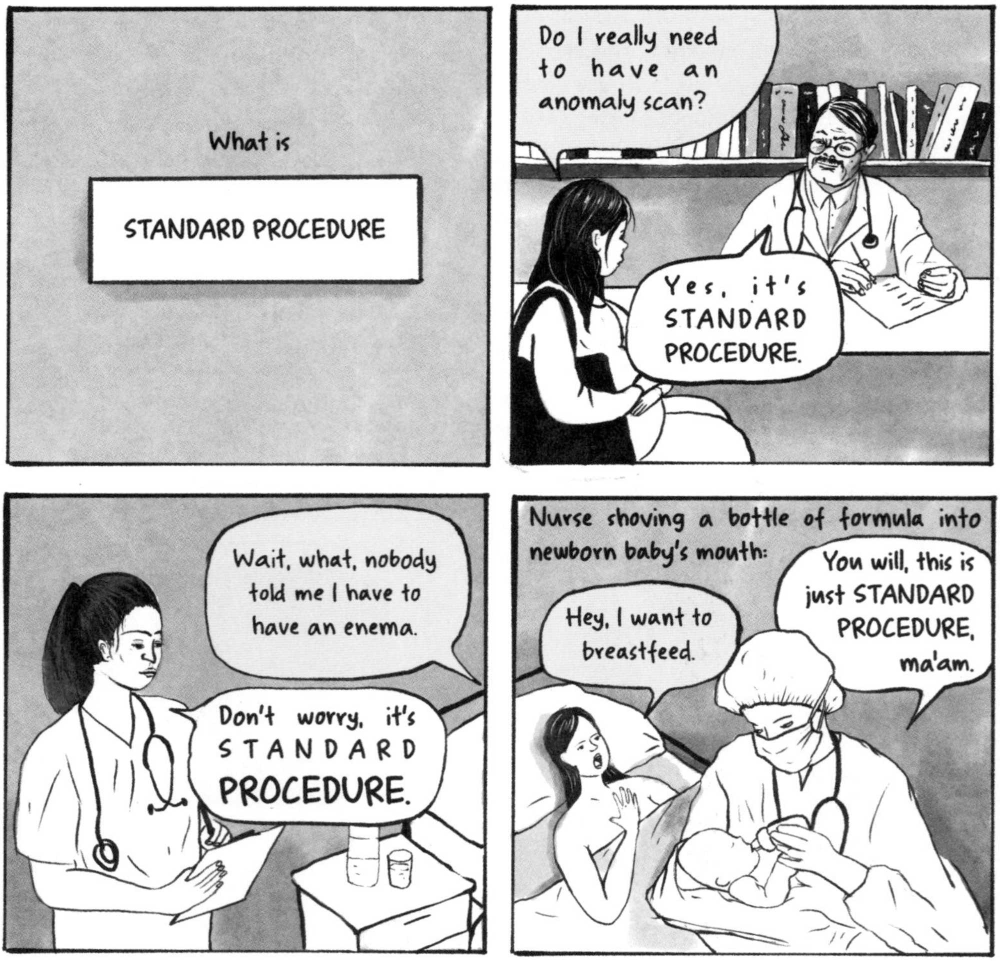
What is
STANDARD PROCEDURE
Do I really need to have an anomaly scan?
Yes, it's STANDARD PROCEDURE.
Wait, what, nobody told me I have to have an enema.
Don't worry, it's STANDARD PROCEDURE.
Nurse shoving a bottle of formula into newborn baby's mouth:
Hey, I want to breastfeed.
You will, this is just STANDARD PROCEDURE, ma'am.

The term 'standard procedure' seems to be a casual medical term for 'we know better'. And generally, yes, doctors do know better and have years of experience backing them, whereas you might be having your first baby and have a very ideal picture of how it should look. And it's important, as the pressures rise in labour, to remember that thing about flexibility and things going wrong that I wrote about in the last chapter.

However, the more I spoke to women around me who had planned natural births but were discouraged from it by medical advisers, usually at the last hour, the more I realized that there's an intricate system in place to avoid failure, save time and make money. It is not easy to understand when a medical emergency is required and when the doctor or hospital is doing something out of convenience or habit. And fear plays a big part in all of this. Fear for your baby's life, for yourself, especially in the intensity of labour, is very real and you do not want to be making a decision out of fear. That's why it's so important to be frank and open with your doctor about what you want and come to a structured agreement for your birth plan, so that you don't find yourself in the labour room having a panic attack or lifelong resentments.

It's important here to note that I have immense respect for doctors who deal with life and death on a daily basis. It requires high precision and clarity of mind, and the life of a baby is a huge pressure for any one person to have on their shoulder; believe me, we mothers know only too well. The need for medical interventions and C-sections in order to deliver safely, is no doubt one of the greatest achievements of modern medical science. But societal pressures and economic ambitions sometimes misuse medical progress for the sake of convenience and profit.

Here's some research that is cause for alarm:

17.2 per cent of births in India are C-sections which surpasses the WHO recommendations, which says that anything beyond 15 per cent can lead to maternal and perinatal morbidity—basically adds more risks to the mother's health and leads to more premature births.

The fact that the conversation on doulas is still lagging behind in India. When I was looking for a doula in Mumbai, I found only one certified doula.

There's been a decrease in home births without medical intervention, and the general perception is that home births are for the poor who can't afford medical help.

A water birth is still seen as a rare and rather mysterious method; its benefits are not widely advertised, so it remains expensive and uncommon.

Episiotomies, which is cutting the vagina at the time of birth to help the baby come out, leave both mental and physical scars on the mother which take a long time to heal. In Europe, episiotomies are practically eradicated, whereas in India, 70 per cent of natural births occur with an episiotomy, making it almost a norm and dismissing the long-term side effects it can have on mothers.

Now, I don't think there's some evil lobby of doctors who plan to cut you open every chance they get. I just think that it's very human to want to control the environment around us and the outcome we desire, without thinking of the long-term consequences. We just have to look at climate change to see that.

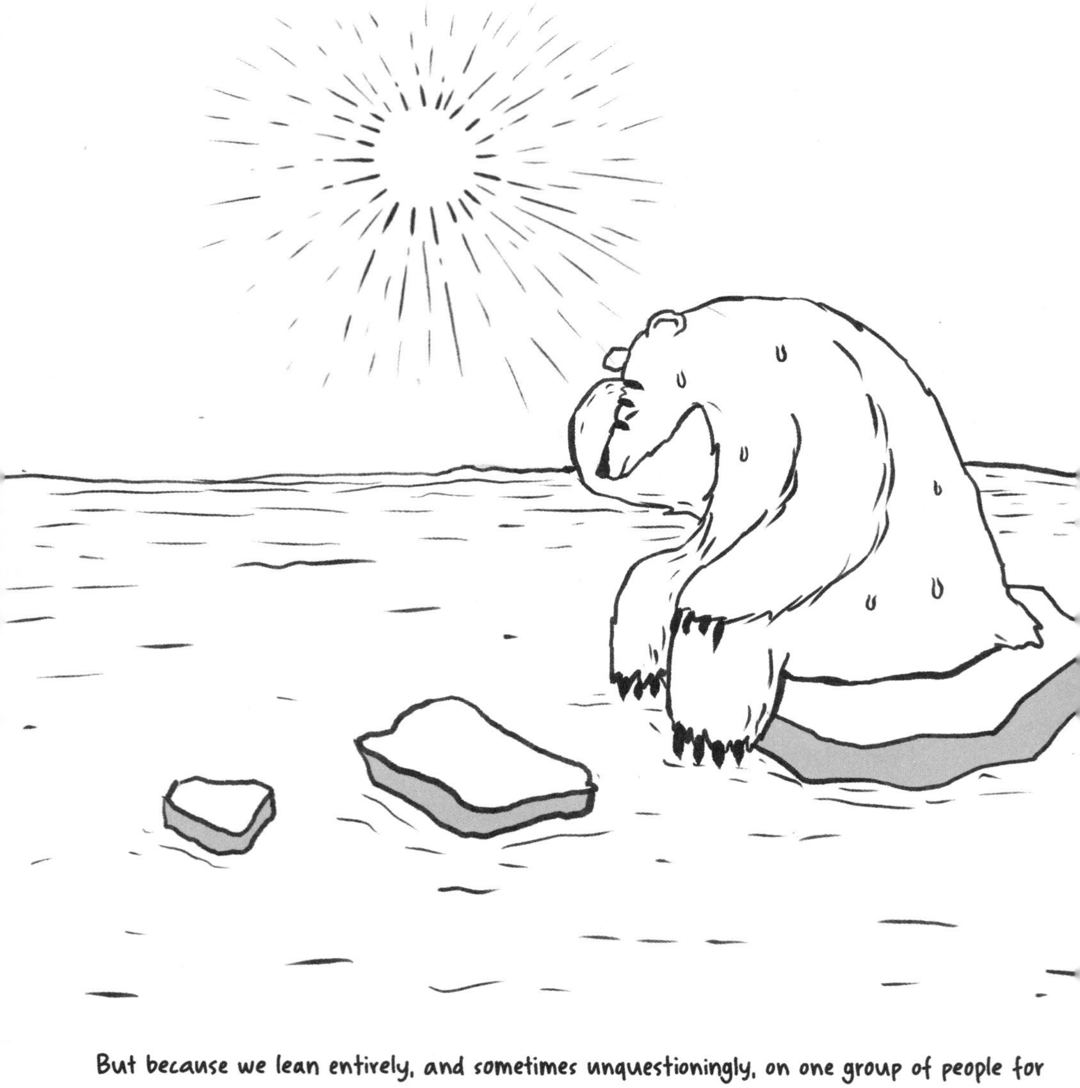

But because we lean entirely, and sometimes unquestioningly, on one group of people for all our ailments, there's enormous pressure on that section. Doctors are overworked, hospitals are understaffed and medical costs are skyrocketing. Nothing has brought this out quite as clearly as the recent global pandemic, Covid-19, where people who would normally treat themselves for a fever by just talking to their GP, are instead coming to hospitals in fear of the virus. While, on the other hand, someone with a serious chronic liver problem who clearly needs medical attention might avoid hospitals out of the same fear.

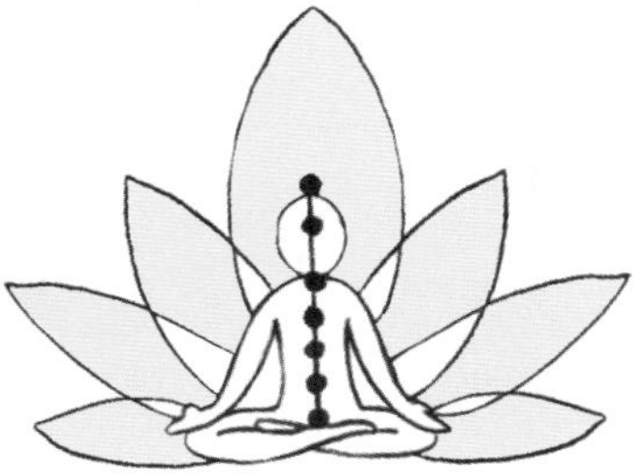

If we as a society invested more in fields that deepen the knowledge on our bodies, by promoting subjects like sex education, physical fitness, midwifery and alternative forms of physiotherapy...

If we acknowledge the tangible effects that mental health can have on physical health and popularize the benefits of therapists and psychiatrists...

If we can study our biological make-up and change our diet and habits as is the practice with nutritionists or holistic medicines...

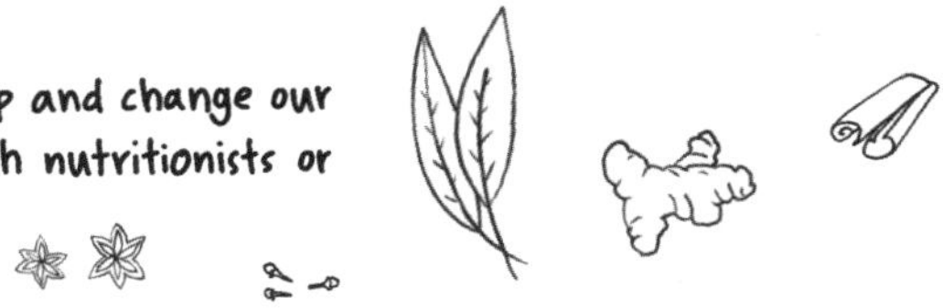

Then maybe, just maybe, we will not be entirely dependent on a few super-powered organizations to dictate our living standards.

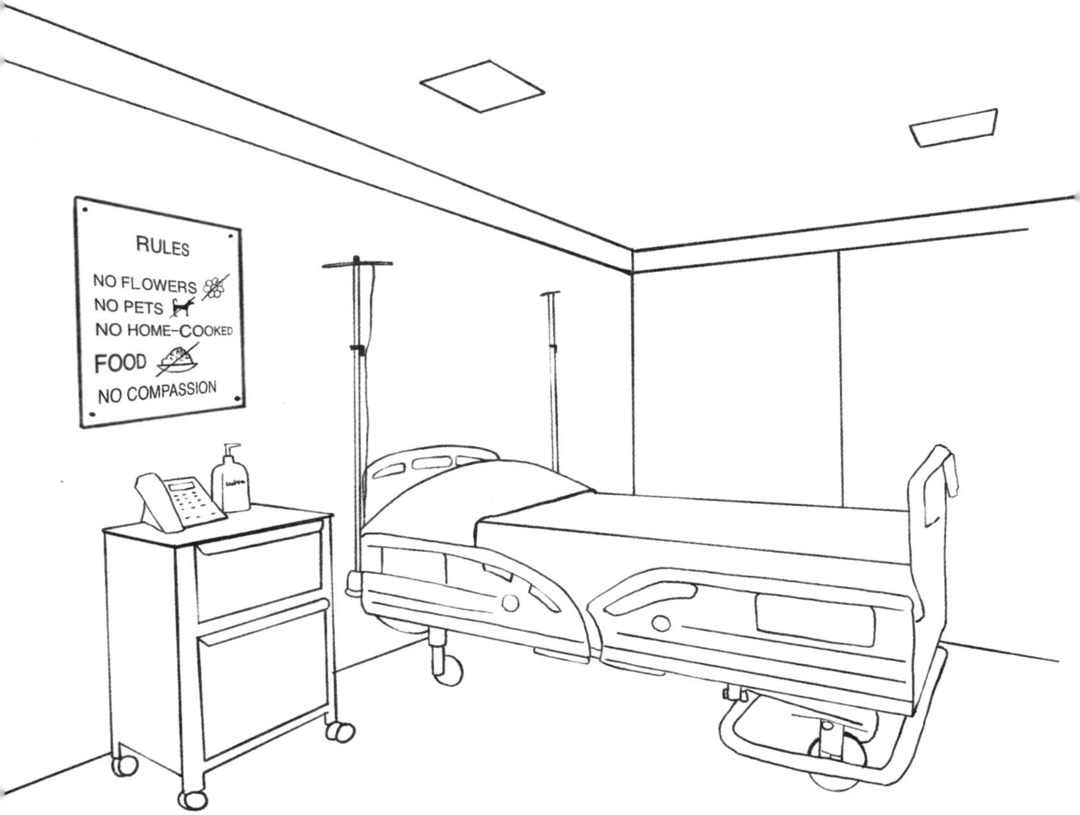
RULES
NO FLOWERS
NO PETS
NO HOME-COOKED FOOD
NO COMPASSION

MY BIRTH PLAN

Allow labour to start on its own as much as possible

Come to the clinic only after contractions are five minutes apart

Wear my own clothes, not the clinic gown

Allowed to personalize the room with lighting, music, aromatherapy, etc.

Allowed to move during labour, go for walks, get in and out of the water, etc.

Allowed to have light snacks and drink plenty during labour

Minimum interruptions, to be left alone with Guy and
my doula, as much as possible

Do not hurry the process of labour artificially if possible

No vaginal examinations without my consent

No episiotomy without my consent

No medical intervention without my consent

During the final stage, I want to know who is in the room. Limited to my partner,
my doctor, doula, pediatrician and one nurse

Delayed cord clamping

'Golden hour' with my baby, i.e. no washing and weighing the baby right away, checks
to be done while baby is on me

Immediate breastfeeding

Roomshare with my baby, either Guy or me present for any check-ups on the baby

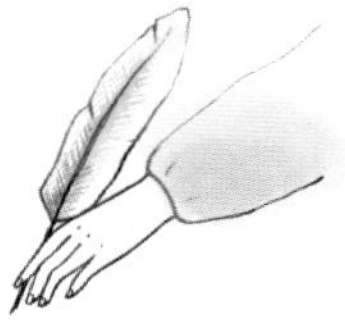

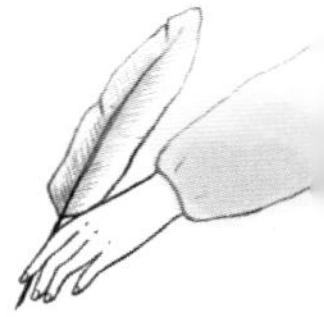

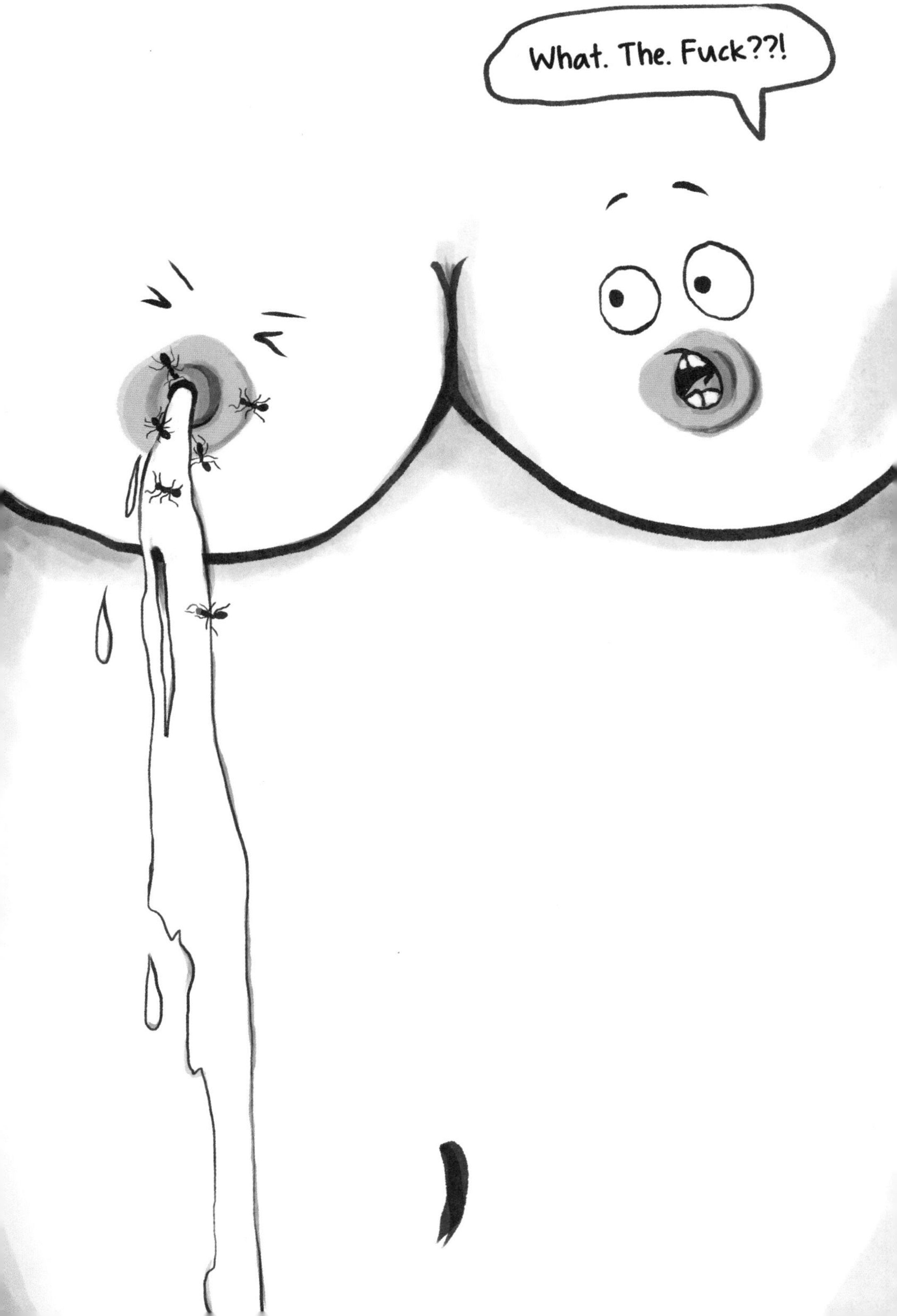
What. The. Fuck??!

These were the exact words used by my best friend when I called her a few weeks after her birth to check how her breastfeeding was going. What the fuck is this? Why does no one tell you how hard it is? Why aren't more people talking about this? She had me nodding like a dog on a dashboard. Really. This shit is hard. I wanted to breastfeed and I could do so for a long time because of a complete lockdown due to Covid and I am glad I breastfed for as long as I did, but I can completely understand why one might opt out of it and choose to remain sane instead.

I like my boobs, they're not huge, not small, not too saggy, and generally their change in size and sensitivity during pregnancy was quite welcome. However, when my breast milk came in, I quickly fell out of love with my boobs. Three days after the birth, just as the colostrum started changing into breast milk, my left boob got engorged. I remember panicking at the sight of a football on my chest.

I called up a mama friend and asked what I should do.

She said, 'Express that shit out'.

I tried until I cried. The pores from which milk usually comes out seemed to be completely blocked from some sort of swelling in the area and nothing was being expressed but my horror.

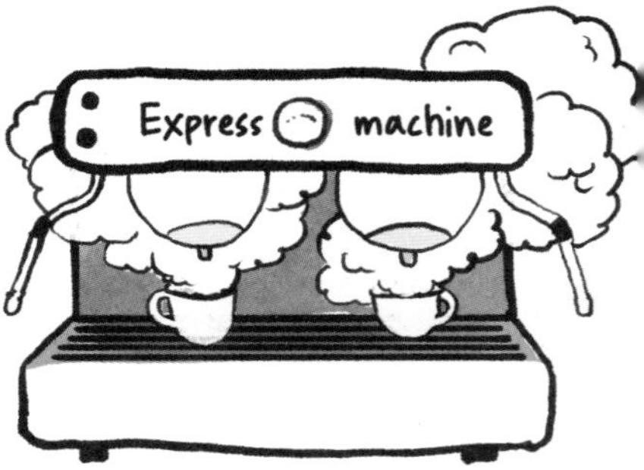
Express machine

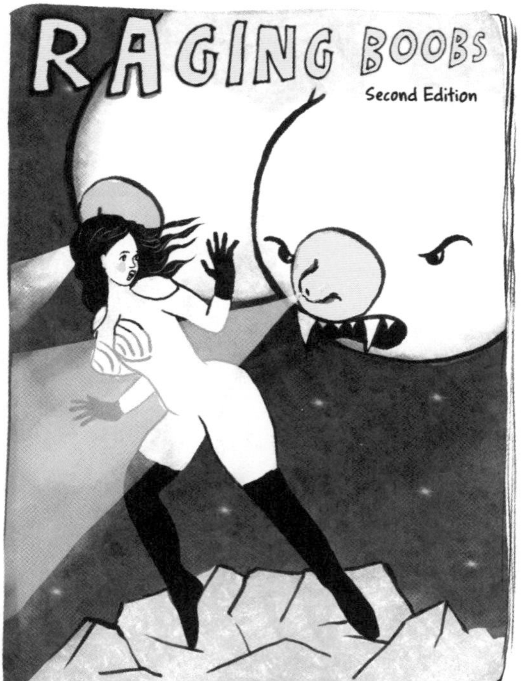
RAGING BOOBS
Second Edition

I ran to my clinic to get help from the nurses. There was the hot water bottle treatment, the ice treatment and the scream-and-bear-it treatment as they kneaded my breast like a piece of dough until some milk was released, just enough for my baby to be tempted to drink from it again.

For the next couple of weeks my milk production was all over the place. Leaky boobs at night meant I woke up with ants in bed and patchy sheets. Soreness in the day and the constant unclipping of maternity bras made me irritable and tired. And with feeds every two hours, what was once an erogenous zone was now replaced with a dull rawness that made me stiffen up at the slightest touch.

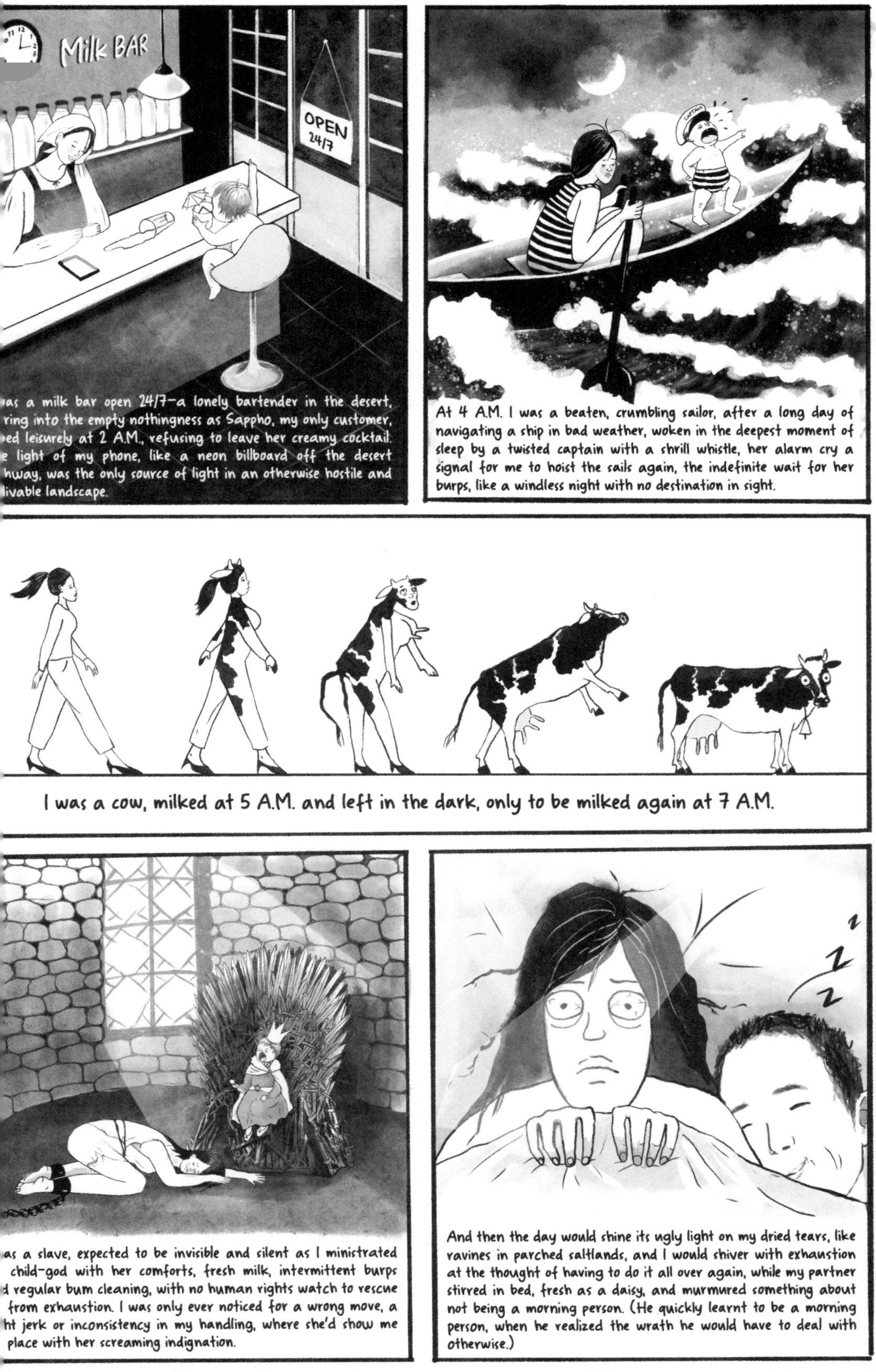
Milk BAR
OPEN 24/7
as a milk bar open 24/7—a lonely bartender in the desert, ring into the empty nothingness as Sappho, my only customer, ed leisurely at 2 A.M., refusing to leave her creamy cocktail. e light of my phone, like a neon billboard off the desert hway, was the only source of light in an otherwise hostile and livable landscape.
CAPTAIN
At 4 A.M. I was a beaten, crumbling sailor, after a long day of navigating a ship in bad weather, woken in the deepest moment of sleep by a twisted captain with a shrill whistle, her alarm cry a signal for me to hoist the sails again, the indefinite wait for her burps, like a windless night with no destination in sight.
I was a cow, milked at 5 A.M. and left in the dark, only to be milked again at 7 A.M.
as a slave, expected to be invisible and silent as I ministrated child-god with her comforts, fresh milk, intermittent burps d regular bum cleaning, with no human rights watch to rescue from exhaustion. I was only ever noticed for a wrong move, a ht jerk or inconsistency in my handling, where she'd show me place with her screaming indignation.
Z Z Z
And then the day would shine its ugly light on my dried tears, like ravines in parched saltlands, and I would shiver with exhaustion at the thought of having to do it all over again, while my partner stirred in bed, fresh as a daisy, and murmured something about not being a morning person. (He quickly learnt to be a morning person, when he realized the wrath he would have to deal with otherwise.)

In the first few months, I felt a mixture of rage and helplessness, that this was what was expected of me, that I was left to just figure this out and keep it together, or be labelled depressed and incapable. That no one was holding my hand while I sat there frozen in the dark, afraid to move lest my baby's tiny lips lost their latch on my tit. A latch that takes so much patience and practice as a flimsy posture and bulbous boobs smother your baby's face, and you try again and again to get it right and shift positions and realign and try once more, so that when she finally does latch, you usually find yourself in a very inconvenient position, one leg bent at an awkward angle holding your baby's body, one arm suspended in the air holding her head, and you stay there like a puppet on a string, for sometimes half an hour at a time, your muscles spasming, and wonder why the whole world around you isn't celebrating this incredible feat of endurance. I remember feeling anxious when I went to sleep at 11 P.M. and really having to gear myself up mentally to take on the night shift as I'd hardly slept in the day.

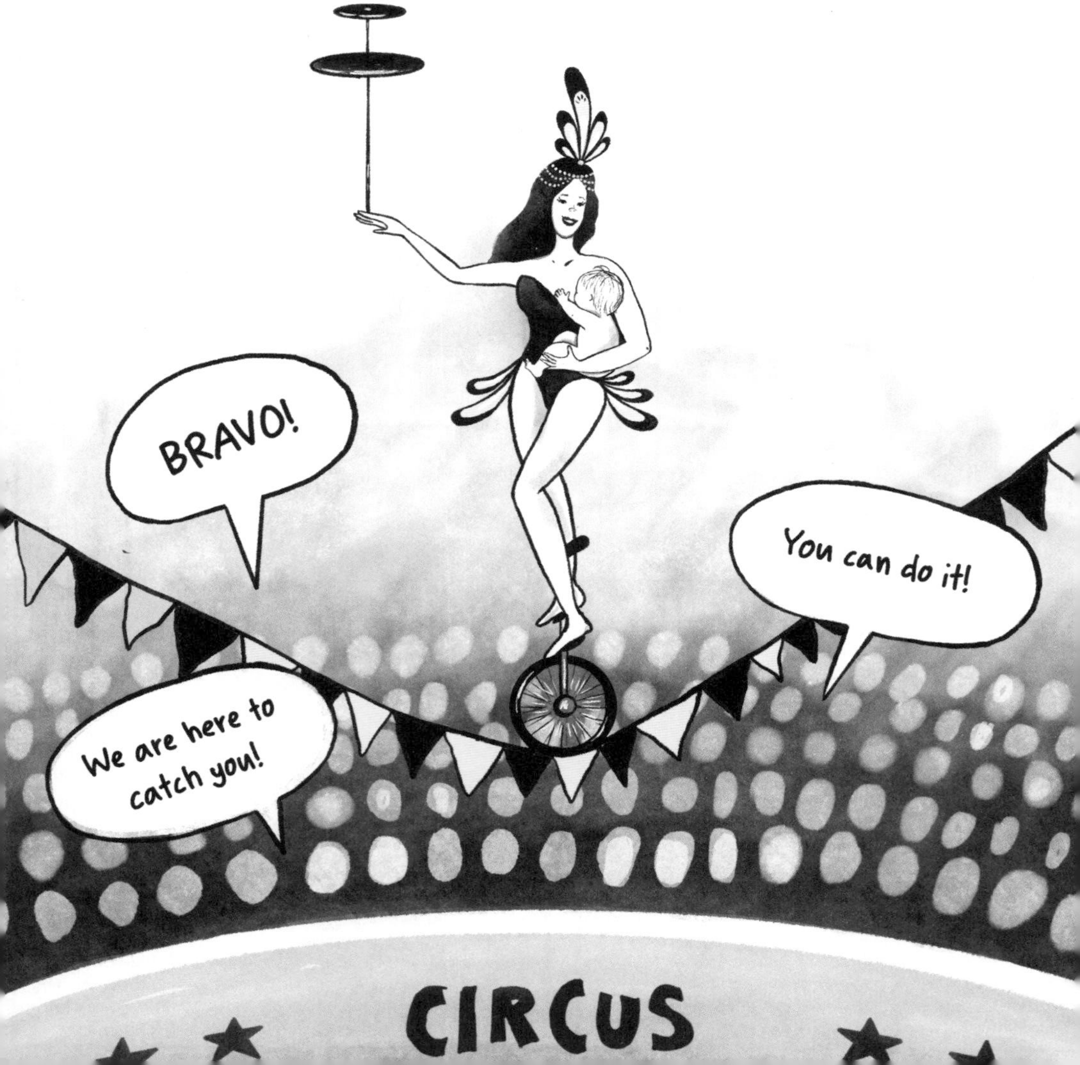
BRAVO!
You can do it!
We are here to catch you!
CIRCUS

This went on for about a month and a half until it became unbearable. We were a month into Covid lockdown, having to take care not only of a newborn but also my twelve-year-old brother, who was unable to go home because flights were grounded.

It was like prematurely launching into an emergency programme Parenting 2.0. Guy and I were home-schooling Oriel, my kid brother, from 9 A.M. till 4 P.M. every day. We had full-time help at home; Sangeeta would cook and clean, but we were still swamped with chores to share, groceries to order, finding inventive ways to channel the tween-ager's energy and getting through hourly baby duties. We couldn't find a moment to ourselves, to even shower or go to the bathroom sometimes, and every evening we would gather at the dinner table as though returning from battle, listening to the oblivious prattle of a twelve-year-old's bored mind while we gulped our food silently.

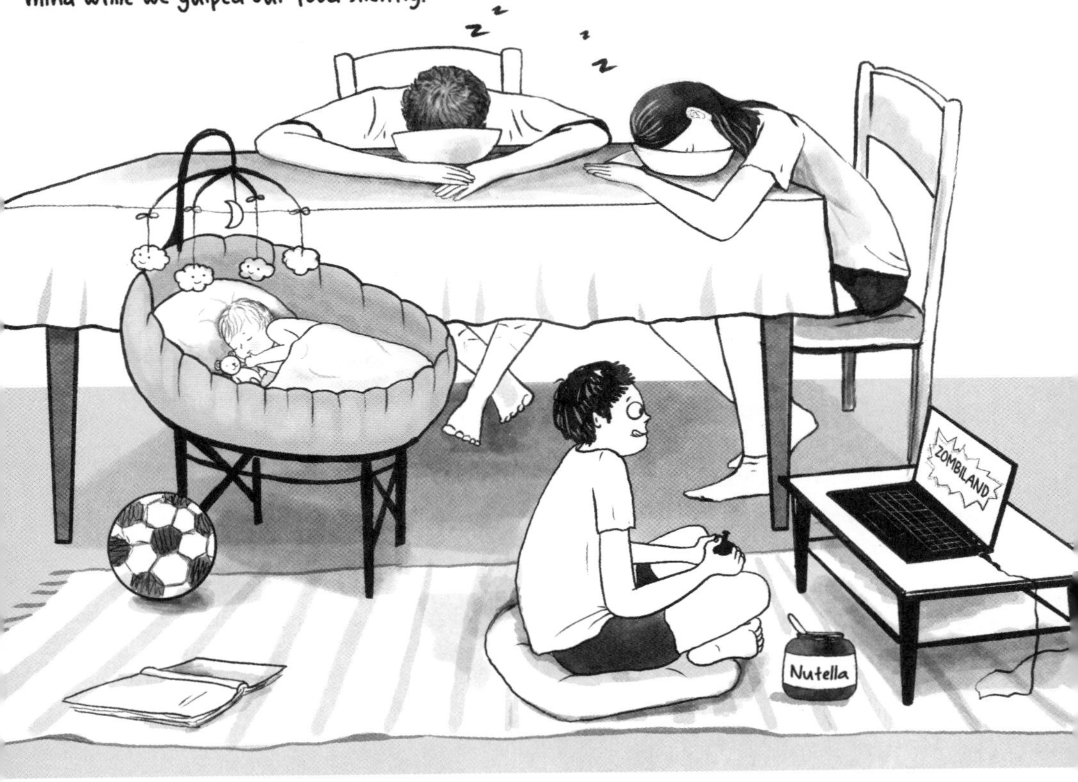

Z Z
Z Z
ZOMBILAND
Nutella

I think because of a combination of this pressure and the collective advice I gathered from friends with more than one child, through my paediatrician's encouragement, and through sheer luck, we found the resolve to change things. I dropped the night feeds, one at a time, week by week, using a technique that my paediatrician gently calls 'discouraging'. This basically meant anything from rocking Sappho back to sleep, to playing with her at odd hours of the night, to swinging her in my arms despite her high-pitched, heart-wrenching wails. 'Anything but the tit, just don't give her the tit,' I would repeat to myself over and over. So that by two months we had a baby that slept eight hours straight. A rare and enviable occurrence I tell myself, as I listen to friends who talk of interrupted nights at ten months or even two and a half years.

Now, of course, Sappho's blissful nights of sleep didn't last. There were bouts of sleep regression at six months when she had her first fever. Even at eight months, when she started teething, etc., but remembering our first few months with horror, there was always a sense of self-preservation we quietly persisted on, by gradually 'discouraging' her from getting up at night or by Guy shifting his work schedule to attend to the domestic pressures in the days when I hadn't slept. This makes me ask whether this erratic schedule that many people live with for months and years has only to do with choosing to breastfeed, or being unlucky, or also to do with a lack of support about what is correct for the whole family; the current trend tends to focus solely on what's best for the baby. I just cannot comprehend how this inhumane system of staying up at night is accepted as the norm, given a neat medical diagnosis like postpartum depression when often it is plain physical exhaustion, nor can I digest the amount of women who give up their work, or extend their maternity leave at their own expense, in order to service their baby at odd hours of the night while society does very little to support her, and I certainly don't think it's fair to call a woman who chooses work over staying at home with the kids 'career-oriented' and 'non-maternal'. If it hadn't been for the lockdown, I know that I would have been back to work after three months, taking Sappho with me on sets, leaving her with a nanny and pumped milk, only to see her late at night when she's sleeping. I also know that after a year of being at home. I can't wait to go back to work and yet I'm nervous about leaving Sappho in the hands of others who might not care as much about—say—her sugar intake.

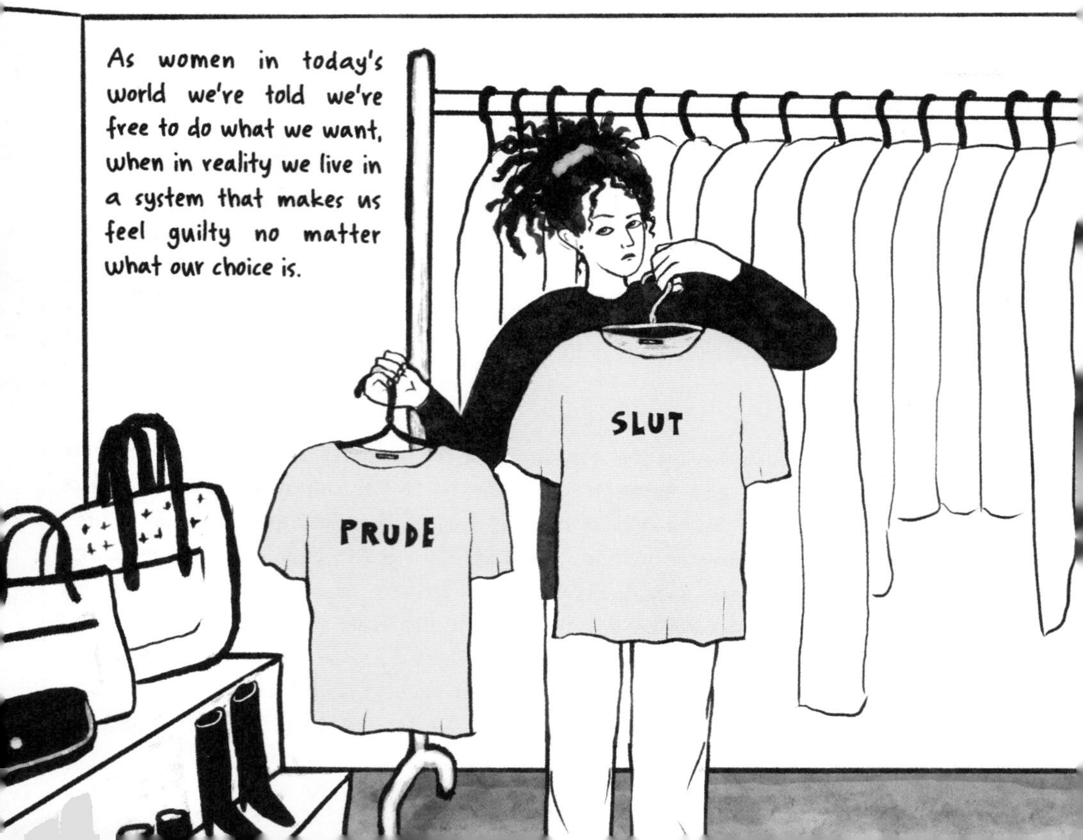
As women in today's world we're told we're free to do what we want, when in reality we live in a system that makes us feel guilty no matter what our choice is.
SLUT
PRUDE

I believe changing that is a question of reorganizing society, so that all workloads are shared between genders, and so that rest and play is valued and defended, just as we value and defend art or research. If Oriel wanted to play video games at night, he had to do the dishes, and let Sangeeta get some time off in the day. If Guy wanted to practise piano at the end of his day, he would need to bathe and put Sappho to sleep before that so that I could get a nap before night feeds. This was not a house where 'women nurtured and men worked', the roles were fluid and had to be in order to take on the mental and physical load of living at home all the time. The sad part is that in India, we still have many women living in 'lockdown' in their routine lives—they are at home, doing all of this work and there is no weekend break or financial compensation.

I spoke to a friend; she's a single mum and had a blooming career when she got pregnant, and felt like she was losing out on it all during early motherhood, as the lives of those around her continued to thrive and she was stuck at home, isolated and exhausted. She said that at least four people need to petition to have a child. Four primary caregivers. Four people who are hands-on, and there all the time. This existed in the time of extended families living together but often at the expense of loveless marriages and keeping up appearances; it also exists wherever there's a financial crunch and the elders of a family take care of the children because both parents work. But in a modern society, where we preach equality, choose who we love and praise individuality, is it possible to find a community that isn't born out of poverty, fear or religion? I do hope so. I know a friend who flew two continents away and spent three months living with his friends, a gay couple, when they adopted a baby, just to help out. Maybe it will be the LGBT community that will spearhead the movement of multiple nurturers. In Canada, it's illegal to pay for surrogacy, it's an act of altruism and so a long-term ongoing relationship with the surrogate is often an expectation and a reality. Starting in 2021, Finland will give each parent 164 days of paid leave, regardless of gender or whether they are the child's biological parent. Kim Brooks writes how those who have best managed to survive the recent pandemic from a psychological point of view are those who were already home-schooling, or living in communal housing situations, where the unpaid workload was distributed more evenly. I hope the rest of us can catch up with that kind of sharing.

SOCIAL ROLE MODEL

Perhaps the observation I've been most impressed with as a parent thus far, is that babies learn fast and accept change much better than most adults do. A mother once told me that the pain babies go through during teething would be intolerable for an adult without painkillers, and seeing Sappho go through serious contortions of her jaw and grabbing her ears as though trying to remove them, and imagining each sharp tooth bursting through the gum for the first time, I tend to believe her theory. And therefore, I tend to give more credit to my baby, in terms of what she can handle in life. The breastfeeding experience was tough, very tough in the beginning, but I realized that putting my baby through some discomfort was just part of the deal. That there's give and take, that you don't have to put up with an innocent tyrant, but rather, constantly compromise with a clever little human being.

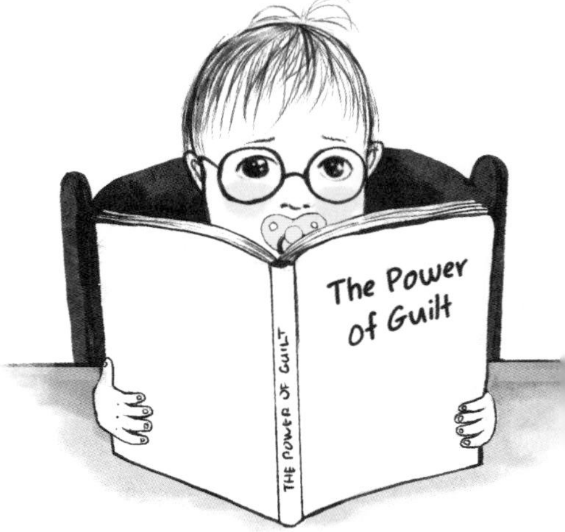
The Power of Guilt
THE POWER OF GUILT

There was this one day, around four months in, when Sappho just refused to drink from my right boob. This continued day after day until this right boob was suffering and engorged and needed to be pumped all the time and I wasn't willing to live with an unbalanced one-sided milk situation where I'd have to cope with a juicy watermelon and dried-up raisin, respectively. So I just didn't feed her. She reacted by screaming. These were deep, guttural, heart-wrenching screams that I ignored with a steely resolve while pretending to read my book.

After a while, still screaming, she started sending furtive glances my way, to see if she was getting my attention, and here I was, dying to react to the screams, but I didn't. I kept my eyes firmly on my book. I tried to feed her from the unfavourable boob again; she looked straight up at me and put her thumb in her mouth, as if to say, 'Fuck you, Mama.' I pottered around the room; her eyes followed me first with anger, then with weariness, and finally, after twenty minutes that felt more like a couple of hours, she looked at me with sad desire, hunger winning over her bullheadedness, and when I came over, she sucked voraciously from the less favourable boob like the grateful child of my dreams.

At first, the drama was so intense it was almost unbearable and made me feel terribly guilty but after a few times, after realizing that she wasn't going to die of starvation if I delayed a feed by half an hour, I saw that we could both get what we wanted. A relieving sip from the bloated boob before moving to her favourite boob, where she eventually fell asleep with a smile and a dribble of milk on her cheek.

I've been wondering where this 'mom guilt' comes from. Sure, it comes from hearing your baby cry and not understanding why, but I also think it's enhanced by the 'mother instinct' myth that is prevalent in society.

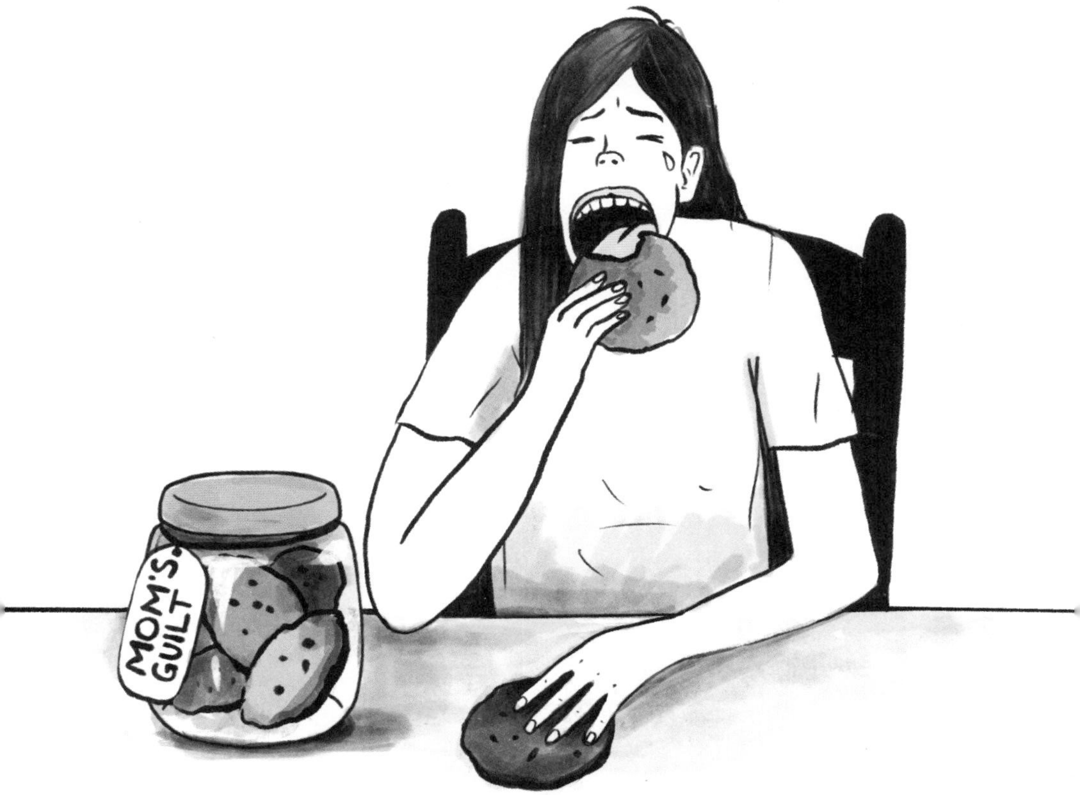
MOM'S GUILT

Mother Dairy, Bonne Mama, Mothercare are just a few examples of household brand names that seem to assume it's primarily the woman's job to bring up a child. And if a child misbehaves, adults often turn to the mother for answers. When I was breastfeeding, and overwhelmed with a tough day, I would sometimes drink a beer to wind down and I remember a mother friend raising her eyebrow at that. Whenever Sappho has a fever, Guy invariably asks me where the thermometer and baby crocin are, and I of course always keep these things stocked up and functioning because God forbid there's an emergency and I'm not prepared. It doesn't seem to occur to him that he should do the same.

I realized over the first year after birth how important it was to create a space of my own, separate from my baby, even if I was at home all the time because of Covid. I'll elaborate on this in Chapter 8. For now, just know that this guilt, if undealt with, can get in the way of enjoying some of the most precious times you'll have with your child, a time that you will never get back. Like in every relationship, this one too, has its give and take. We all know that babies take plenty in the first few months after birth, but, given a chance, they are incredible givers too.

Everything in this journey isn't about compromise, there is the pay-off. Mine happened at about week nine. It was a huge relief to see that Sappho understood there was a face attached to this boob. It was mid-afternoon, she was closing her eyes and opening her mouth as usual, waiting for the magic tit with ever-flowing milk to just find her lips. I happened to cough and she looked up at me, her eyes wide at first with the 'how dare you disturb my bliss' look, after which she returned to the tit, then again stopped and looked up at me and smiled as she drank. She pressed herself closer and held my boobs a little with her hand as if to say, 'Thanks, this is grand.' This is the reward. This is golden. Never mind the fact that her first words are all different versions of my partner—dada, papa, baba, abba—this is a real moment of our connection, of dance. We locked eyes and felt each other's heartbeats while we shared the warmth of our closeness. She could sense my discomfort when she latched wrong and realigned herself as I moved into a more comfortable position. We shuffled and jiggled, moved away and came closer. And this dance continued to grow over the next few months. Because as I got hold of the different positions during breastfeeding, I realized this didn't have to be just time to stare at the wall and be bitter about what I was missing out on.

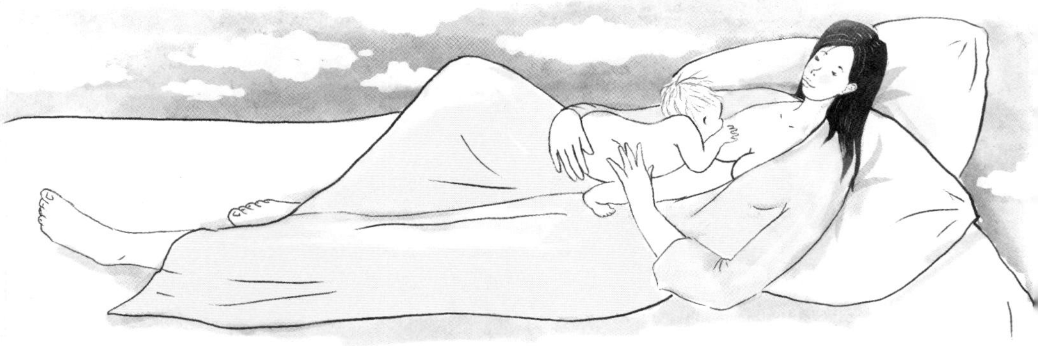

It was also a time to play, tickle and giggle. A time to let go of all the day's anxiety and be in the moment. A time to discover ways that could be comfortable for both of us, so I could read or work while she sucked and gurgled. A time to sing to her while she murmured with pleasure, a time to dream-feed while both of us closed our eyes and fell into pillows of love.

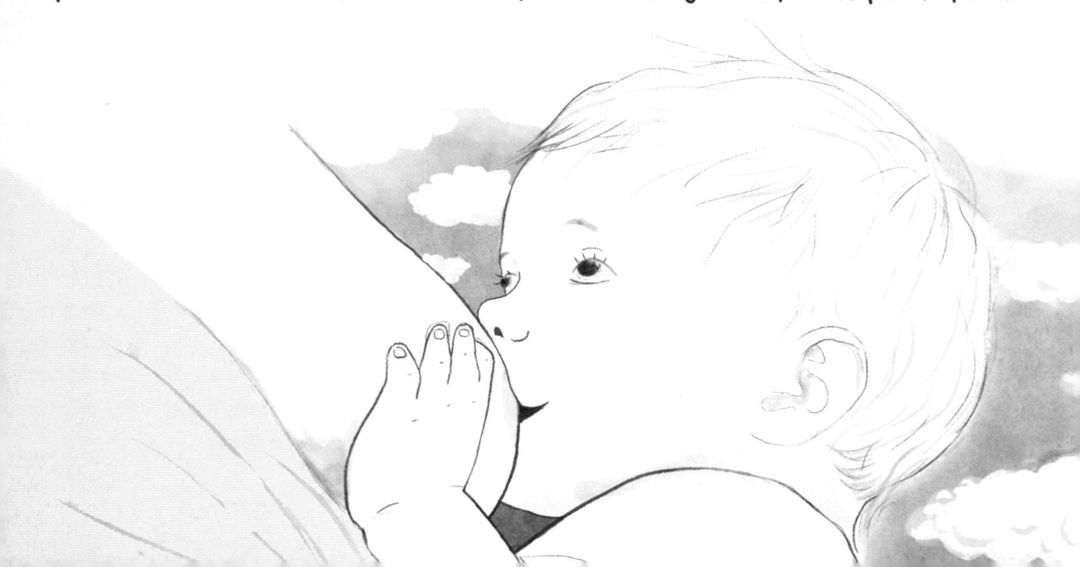

Here's a little lullaby I wrote for Sappho after a very long, tiring day. I've added chords for the uke and notes in case you want to learn it, and don't forget to add your child's name in the space.

Le Jardin de la Vie

On s'reveille quand le soleil sourit
Les moineaux se font leur nids
Les fleurs poussent et Sappho aussi
On s'reveille dans le jardin d'la vie

On s'balade, les garcons les filles
On s'dit bonjour, on fait des amies
On marche, on grimpe, on tombe aussi
On tourne en rond dans l'jardin d'la vie

L'enfant grandit et touche le ciel
Elle traverse la terre, la lune, la mer
Elle danse, elle rit, elle pleure aussi
Elle trouve son chemin dans l'jardin d'la vie

On ralenti et on vieilli
On vieilli et on oublie
On s'dit au revoir quand vient la nuit
Et on s'endort dans l'jardin d'la vie...

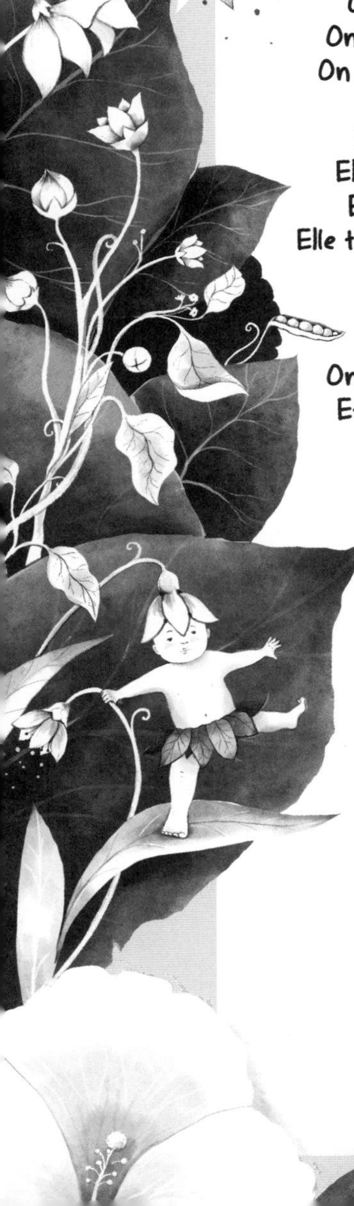

The Garden of Life
(translation)

We wake up when the sun smiles
And the sparrows are making their nest
The flowers grow and also,
We wake up in the garden of life

We wander around, both boys and girls
We say good morning and make friends
We walk, we climb, and we also fall,
We turn in circles in the garden of life

The child grows up and touches the sky
She crosses the earth, the moon, the sea
She dances, she laughs and she also cries,
She finds her way in the garden of life

We slow down and we get old
We get old and we forget
We say goodbye when the night arrives
And we fall asleep in the garden of life...

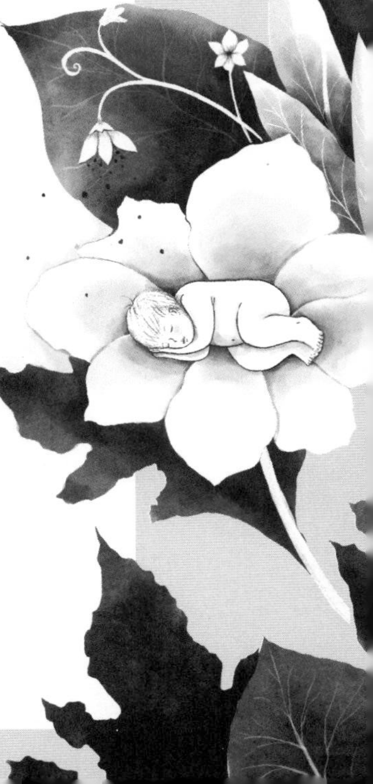

Le Jardin de la Vie

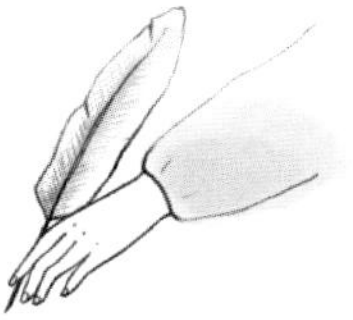

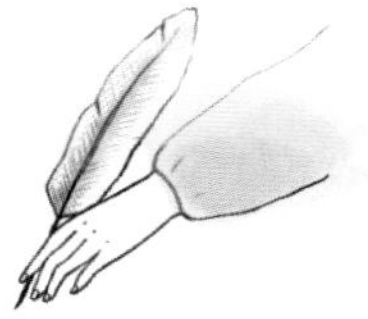

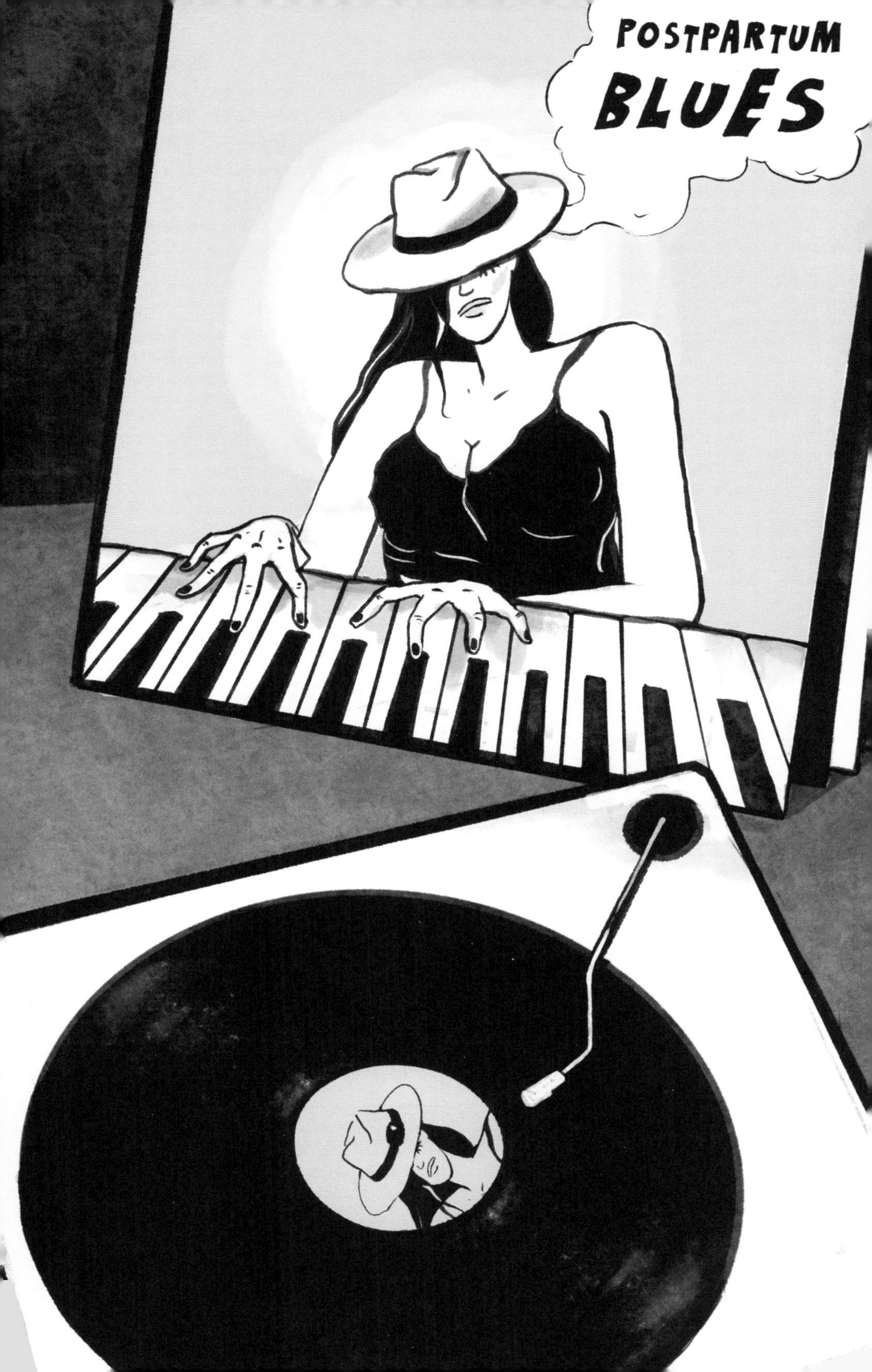
POSTPARTUM
BLUES

From the very first few weeks of pregnancy right through to when Sappho was a year old, I struggled with my sense of self, with knowing who I was, and what I wanted, outside the role of motherhood. When you have a baby, the sense of self goes away for a while. You don't know at the time that it's a transient stage. You roll your eyes at the serene mother-in-law who says, 'Suffering is just part of the process', you want to vomit—literally—when you read that 'creating life is a God-given gift only women have the privilege to experience'. Instead, the motivation to get out of bed every day becomes a twinkling light in the distance. Early motherhood is more like experiencing a permanent state of heavy drunkenness, making it impossible for you to think straight or keep your balance.

When you had a sense of self

Having control over your body and your emotions.

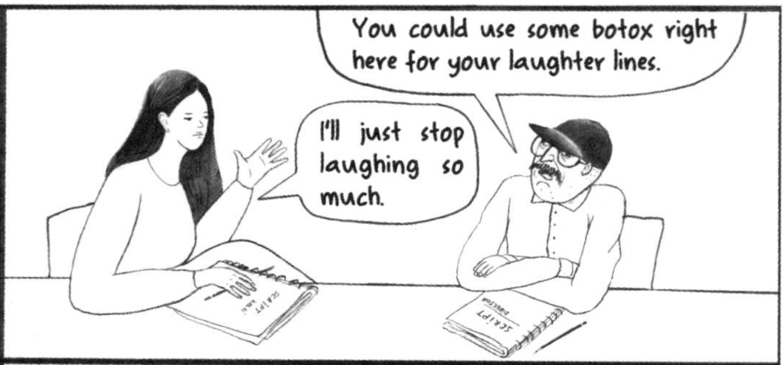
You could use some botox right here for your laughter lines.
I'll just stop laughing so much.

Fighting for your political and social standing in the world.

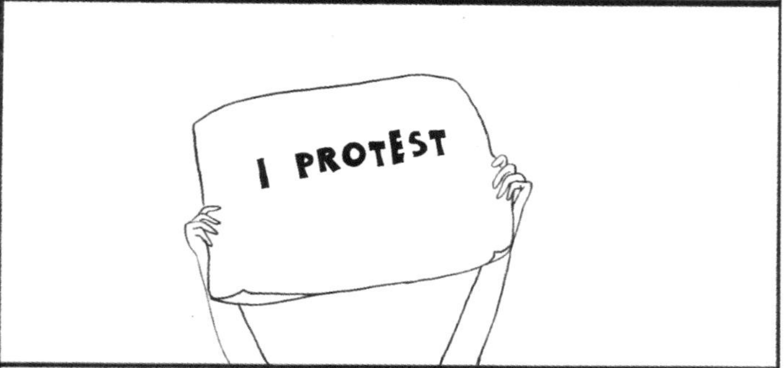
I PROTEST

Getting alone time.

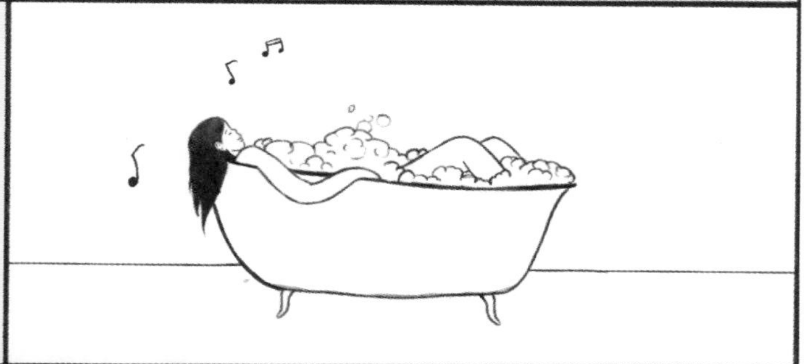

Having a sense of achievement from your work.

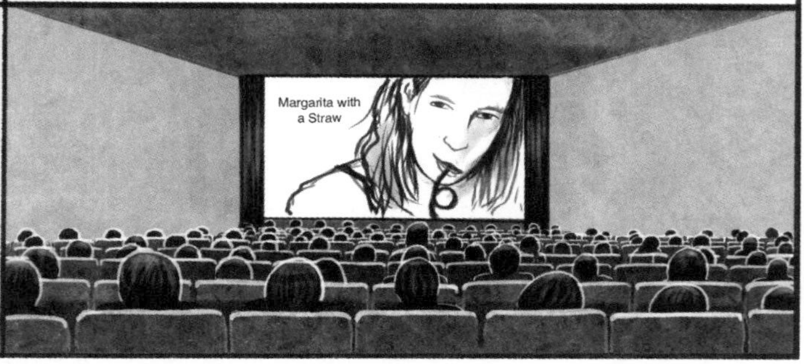
Margarita with a Straw

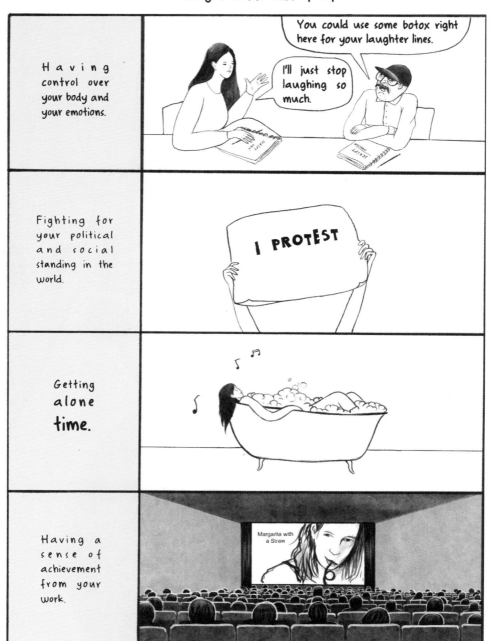

As your senseless self

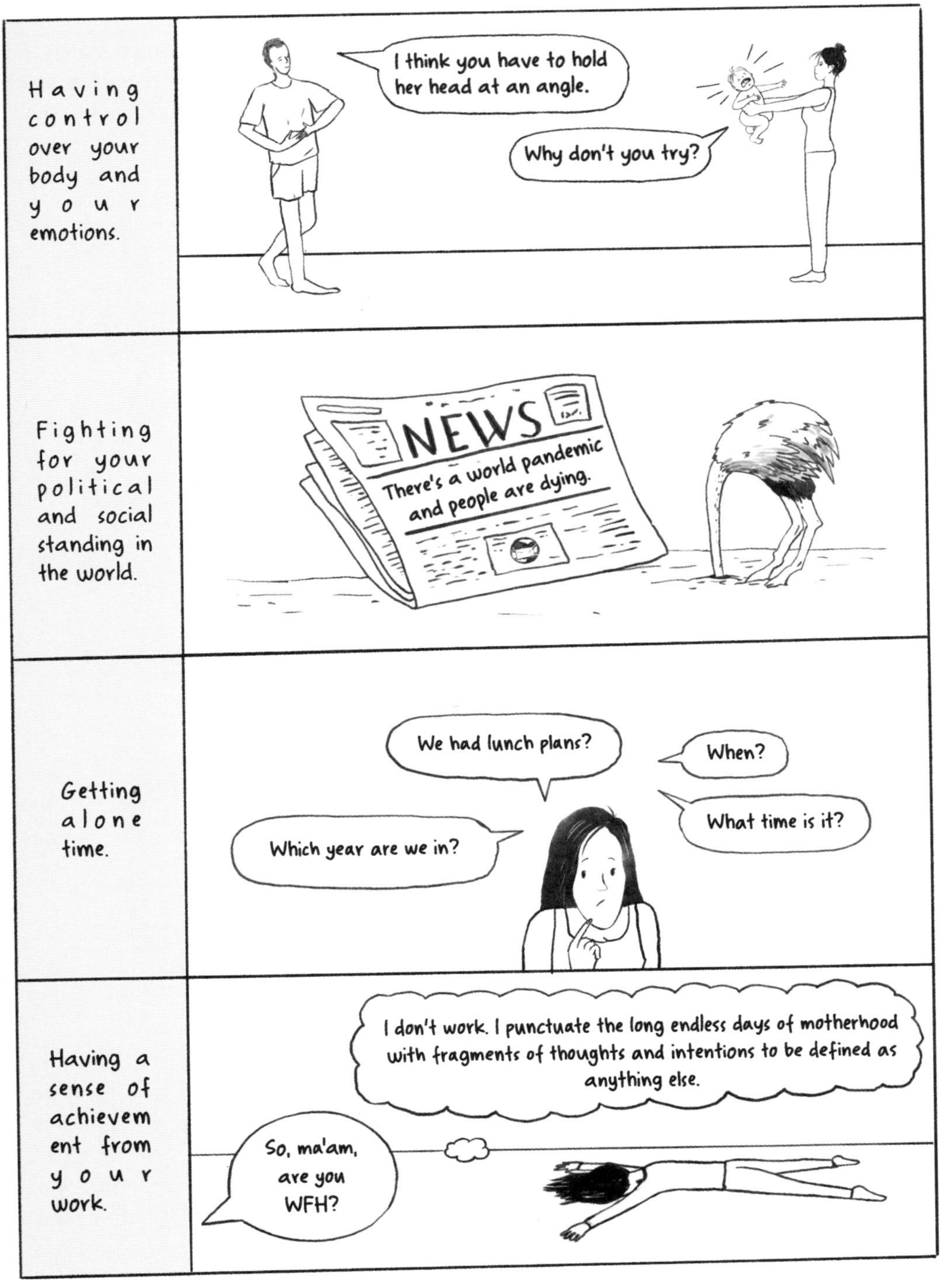
Having control over your body and your emotions.
I think you have to hold her head at an angle.
Why don't you try?
Fighting for your political and social standing in the world.
NEWS
There's a world pandemic and people are dying.
Getting alone time.
We had lunch plans?
When?
What time is it?
Which year are we in?
Having a sense of achievement from your work.
I don't work. I punctuate the long endless days of motherhood with fragments of thoughts and intentions to be defined as anything else.
So, ma'am, are you WFH?

One of the biggest things I suffered post birth was having a brain like Swiss cheese. I would get up to do something and forget why I got up. The simplest tasks would go by, interrupted by my wandering mind or my wailing baby and everything just felt unfinished.

I don't know what people hold on to during such times, but for me it was one person. Someone I barely knew. I had met her once, early in my pregnancy, when I was looking for a place that would encourage a natural birth, and chanced upon Birthvillage in Kerala through a friend. I didn't end up going to Kerala for logistical reasons

BIRTHVILLAGE
KERALA

DISTANCE   1300 km

TRAVEL TIME   24 hours

GPS

But I did end up staying in touch with Reba, a doula who worked with them, and she made sure she stayed in touch with me after my birth. As is often the case with depression, I didn't really feel like taking the proactive decisions to make myself feel better, by talking to someone, getting help, getting check-ups and tests, or joining a group—all these seemed like acts of moving giant boulders, and instead I retreated into my confused and exhausted mind looking for a place to put my thoughts to rest.

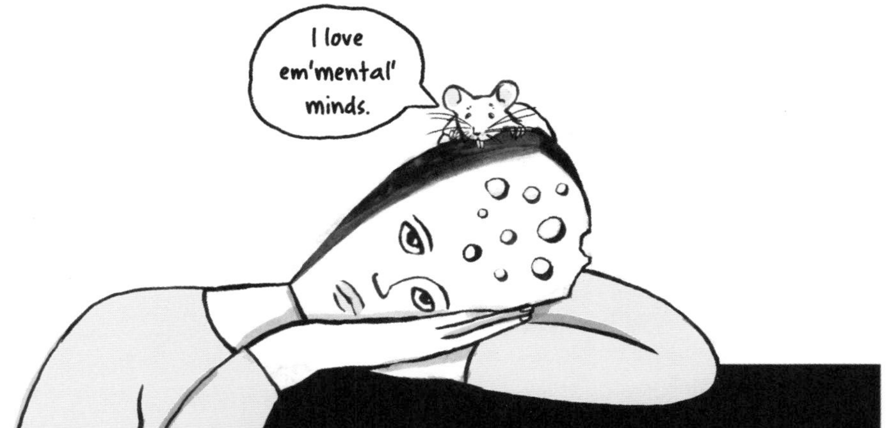
I love em'mental' minds.

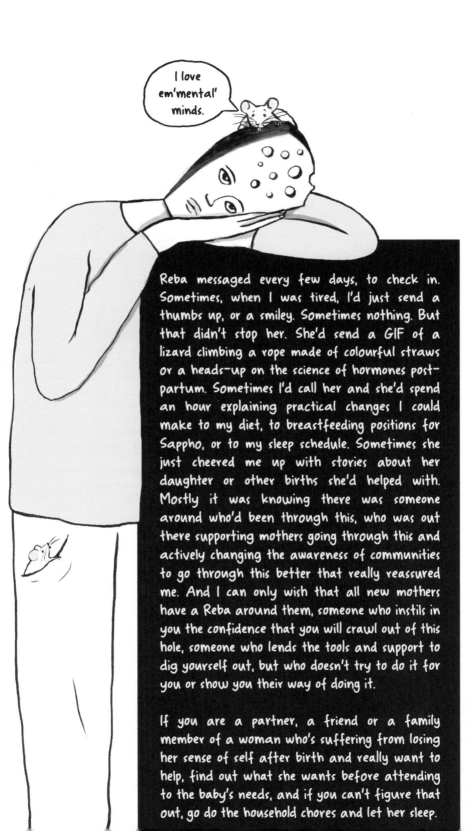

Reba messaged every few days, to check in. Sometimes, when I was tired, I'd just send a thumbs up, or a smiley. Sometimes nothing. But that didn't stop her. She'd send a GIF of a lizard climbing a rope made of colourful straws or a heads-up on the science of hormones post-partum. Sometimes I'd call her and she'd spend an hour explaining practical changes I could make to my diet, to breastfeeding positions for Sappho, or to my sleep schedule. Sometimes she just cheered me up with stories about her daughter or other births she'd helped with. Mostly it was knowing there was someone around who'd been through this, who was out there supporting mothers going through this and actively changing the awareness of communities to go through this better that really reassured me. And I can only wish that all new mothers have a Reba around them, someone who instils in you the confidence that you will crawl out of this hole, someone who lends the tools and support to dig yourself out, but who doesn't try to do it for you or show you their way of doing it.

If you are a partner, a friend or a family member of a woman who's suffering from losing her sense of self after birth and really want to help, find out what she wants before attending to the baby's needs, and if you can't figure that out, go do the household chores and let her sleep.

This job—and let's be clear, the first months after birth are a job and not so much a celebration of life; the daily routine, the frequent feeds, the hourly diaper changes, the minute-by-minute caregiving and the incessant sleep deprivation make it a job like no other—is not meant to be done alone. Or with just a caregiving partner for that matter. The village theory proves to be true, it takes a whole community to satisfactorily share the exhaustive work of taking care of a newborn, so that a mother can recuperate not only from the insane physical trauma of birthing, but also from the emotional and mental toll it takes on the good part of a year of her life.

But the way the world currently works, this more-than-a-full-time job, falls mostly on the mother, and the work she does remains invisible to society, quickly forgotten by her community, and often, she shoves the trauma aside herself to catch up with her previous life. Studies have shown that 38 per cent of women who suffer from postpartum depression experience chronic symptoms and ongoing depression, and that is indicative of how the problem is often not dealt with at the time, allowing it to resurface through future experiences of stress.

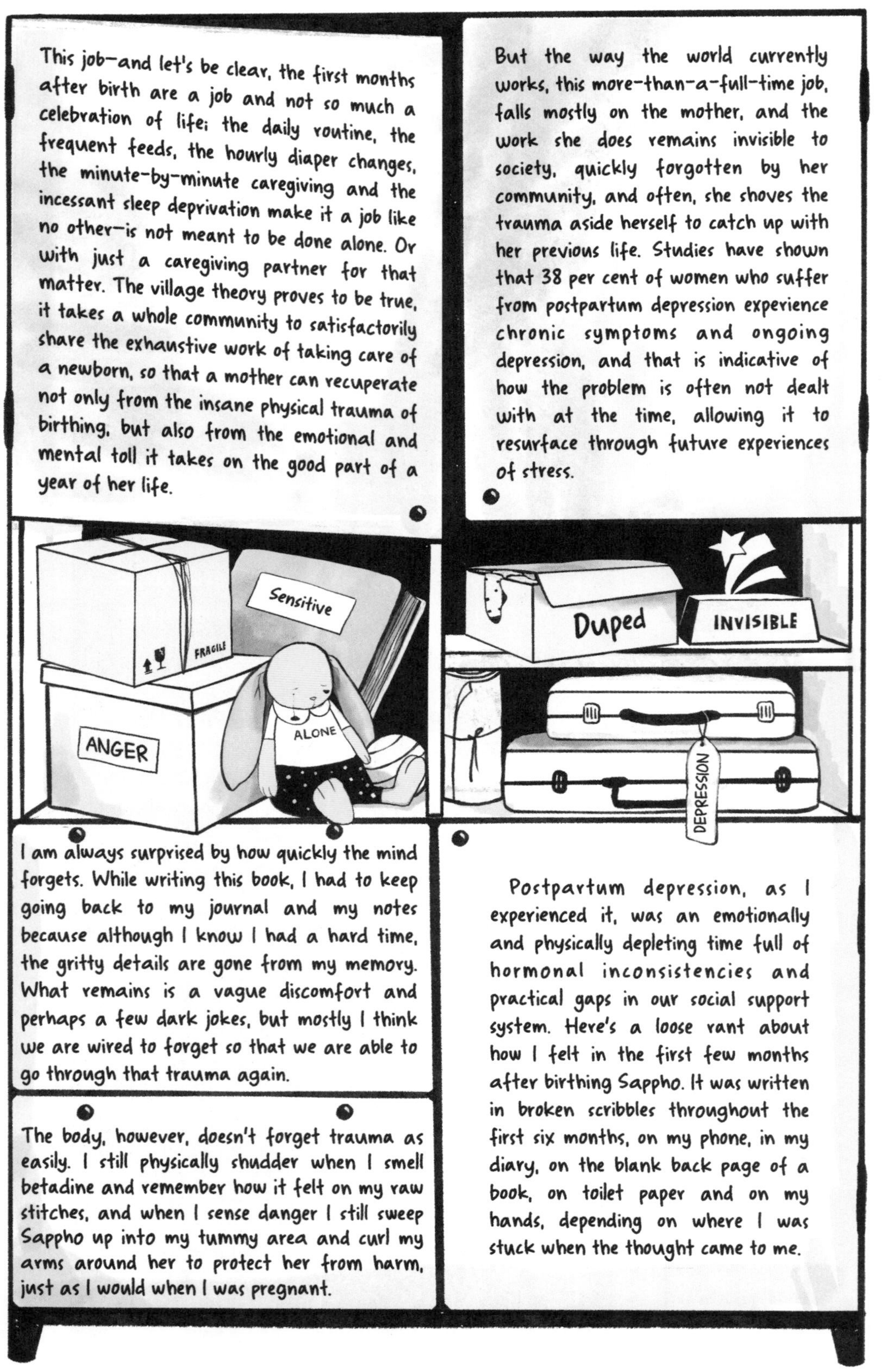
Sensitive
FRAGILE
ANGER
ALONE
Duped
INVISIBLE
DEPRESSION

I am always surprised by how quickly the mind forgets. While writing this book, I had to keep going back to my journal and my notes because although I know I had a hard time, the gritty details are gone from my memory. What remains is a vague discomfort and perhaps a few dark jokes, but mostly I think we are wired to forget so that we are able to go through that trauma again.

The body, however, doesn't forget trauma as easily. I still physically shudder when I smell betadine and remember how it felt on my raw stitches, and when I sense danger I still sweep Sappho up into my tummy area and curl my arms around her to protect her from harm, just as I would when I was pregnant.

Postpartum depression, as I experienced it, was an emotionally and physically depleting time full of hormonal inconsistencies and practical gaps in our social support system. Here's a loose rant about how I felt in the first few months after birthing Sappho. It was written in broken scribbles throughout the first six months, on my phone, in my diary, on the blank back page of a book, on toilet paper and on my hands, depending on where I was stuck when the thought came to me.

im OK I'm 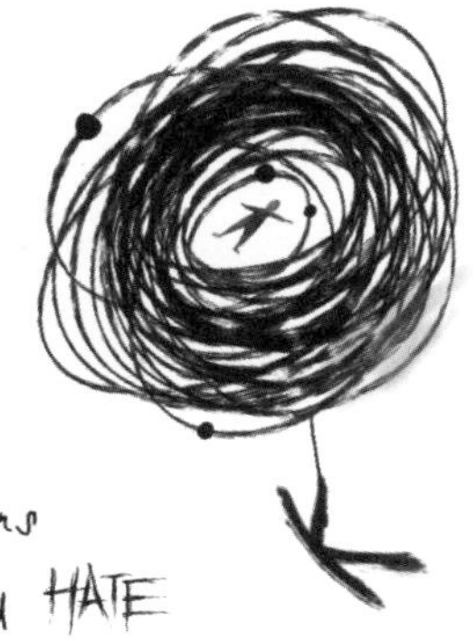

I'm OK

I'm OK
with warring the ups and downs
And making peace with ♡ (LOVE) and HATE
I'm OK with facing the fact
that nothing is ever
going to be the same again.
I'm OK with messssss
With moving to the floor,
With leaving things for tomorrow,
Or the day after or . . .

I don't know

When she's old enough for college
and walking out the main door.

I'm OK with clutter,

With not being able to articulate what is the matter.
I'm OK with piles of plates at the end of the day and we've
run out of eggs and butter in the morning and how we mutter
to each other about who's done more and who's slept less in a
house where we count points for how much we suffer.
I'm OK with being pissed off. Really pissed off
With anyone trying to tell me how this is done.
I'm OK with being pissed on.
Regularly.
By my newborn.

Oh.

And.

I'm OK with shit

I don't mean figuratively. I mean literally.

I'm OK with the shit my daughter flicks on my forehead
with her 5-mm toenail in a ritual reflex of arms and legs
Which I'll just wipe away along with whatever little sense of decorum I have left.
I'm OK with regular fights and sulks with my man
And quick hugs and make-ups before getting on with our baby's next demands.
I'm OK with the pleasure of twenty-minute naps replacing long, lazy afternoons of sex and desire.

I'm OK with
the efficiency with which one can do anything with two hands
when one has been one-handed for most of the day,

one-handed texting one-handed eating one-handed grabbing

for any kind of order or routine in my somnambulistic

state of wandering,

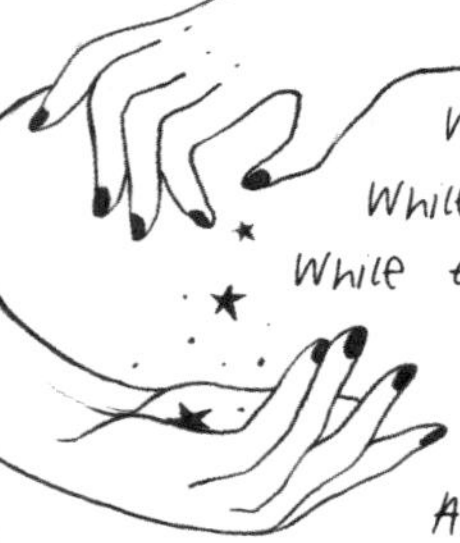

While the other hand holds,
While the other hand carries,
While the other hand is numb,
As she hangs off a
shoulder or a nipple
And my mind folds
and ripples

At the thought of offhanded titles like
'maternity leave'. As though we get to 'leave'
anywhere, any time for any moment,

As though this weren't a full-time job

and more demanding than anything

you've ever dreamed.

I'm

I'm OK to scoff at sentimental write-offs like maternal instinct, as though instincts were clean, clear-cut and cheery Instead of raw, twisted and messy. I'm OK with my amygdala — that's the part of the brain responsible for pleasure, fear and addiction — being wide open for the rest of my life, for being sentenced to a lifetime of anxiety for every move my child makes for the rest of her life. I'm OK with strangers who haven't spent a week with me but offer advice on how to handle this existential boulder. With three sentences and a shrug of the shoulder. I'm OK with exhaustion and the idea that there is no day or night, that we are meant to be wolves howling at the moon or rats looking for midnight snacks, that the cracks in my head are a place for the sun to come in And that eclipses exist to hide the imperfections of my worn-out skin. I'm OK with questioning life and the meaning of things, and allowing for the vulnerability of death to enter in. I'm OK to check her breathing, over and over, my finger near her nostrils, a manic minute-by-minute thing. I'm OK to shudder and respect the grandness of nature and accept that I've fallen madly in love with a stranger.

K

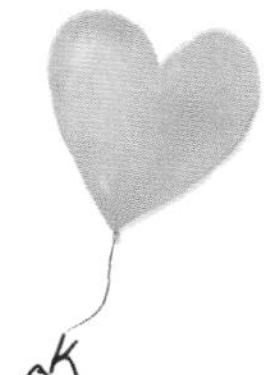

And I'm OK with love beyond description.
Love that overrides pain and prescriptions.
Love that makes me sing to her at odd hours of the night.
Love that hangs on to the creases between her little fingers.
Love that makes me cry
with all my might.
I'm OK with oxytocin levels shooting up to the point of irrationality
with welcoming skips in my heart along with holes in my memory.
I'm OK with being impatient and snappy at changing a fifth nappy
while cooing and awwing at her cuteness simultaneously.
I'm OK with living in constant contradiction;
with being a tit, an it, a source of milk to searching, suckling lips.
With being Mother Mary cradling her divine incarnation
or Durga with eight arms and multitasking through every situation,
I'm OK to invoke the wrath of Ma Kali and stick out my tongue at
uninformed judgements from those who've never tried.
I'm OK with lying about having to go to the toilet, just so I can be alone
for a moment,
just so I can burst into tears
or get a moment of privacy,
or splash cold water on the flames of my inadequacy.

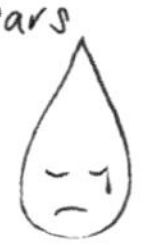

I'm OK with wanting to get away from the sound of incomprehensible wailing,
of seeing my partner deal with
it and walking away while she
kicks and screams.

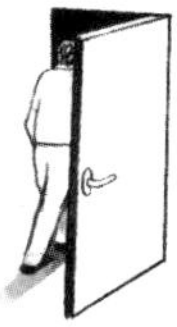

I'm

with an
identity
crisis
that
makes me
struggle
with
ambition and jealousy.

I'm OK with breast pumps,
bottle feeds,
daily heartbreaks
and not being able to
please everybody.

I'm OK
with asking
family,
friends,
doctors,
therapists,
nannies,
neighbours
and
traffic cops
to understand me.

I'm OK
with being late.
With taking a breath.
With just hanging on by a thread
or a couple of minutes sleep
knowing I'm nothing
but a small cog
in evolutionary biology.

I'm OK with not being 🙁K

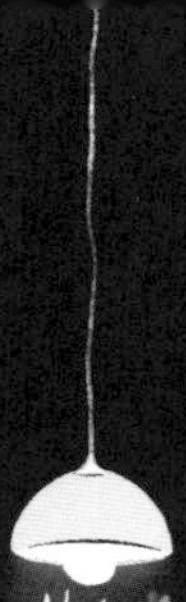

Not
being a
supermom.
Not wearing my
heels or my make-up.
Not doing the housework
and the career without a
hiccup. I'm OK with staying
home and reinventing the world
with her eyes, eyes that programme
everything from scratch and don't yet
know how to discriminate or divide. I'm OK
hanging out with someone whose curiosity can
save the world. I'm OK with remapping, readjusting,
reworking and receiving. I'm OK with speckles of sun
on my face in the early sunrise, and gurgle sprinklers
and tummy ticklers and butterflies on my cheeks.
I'm OK with waking up from nightmares where my baby dies
and seeing that she's doing just fine. I'm OK with fear and
fragility being a daily part of how we survive. I'm OK with feeling
like I'm speeding down a highway while being chased by a hurricane
sticking my head out the window and looking back at my life upturned and
unrecognizable and thinking I'm the luckiest person alive.
I'm OK with lying here in the dark and counting sheep for eternity...

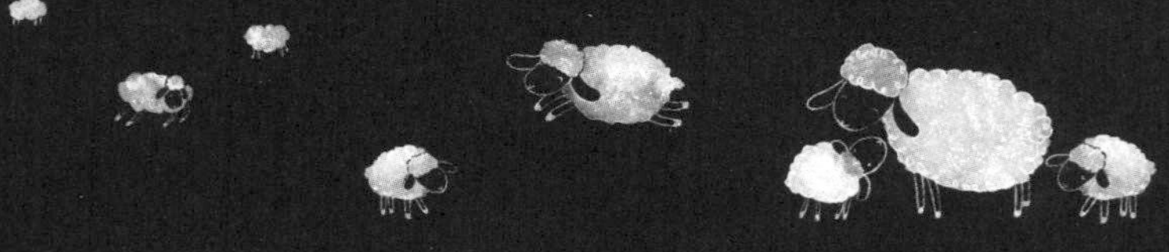

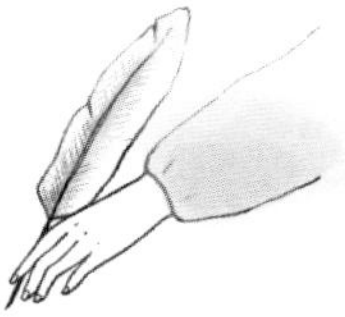

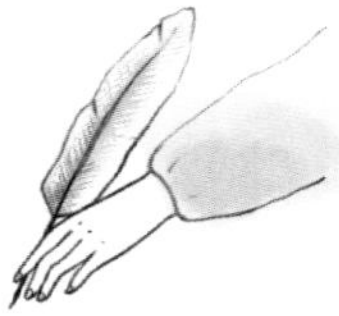

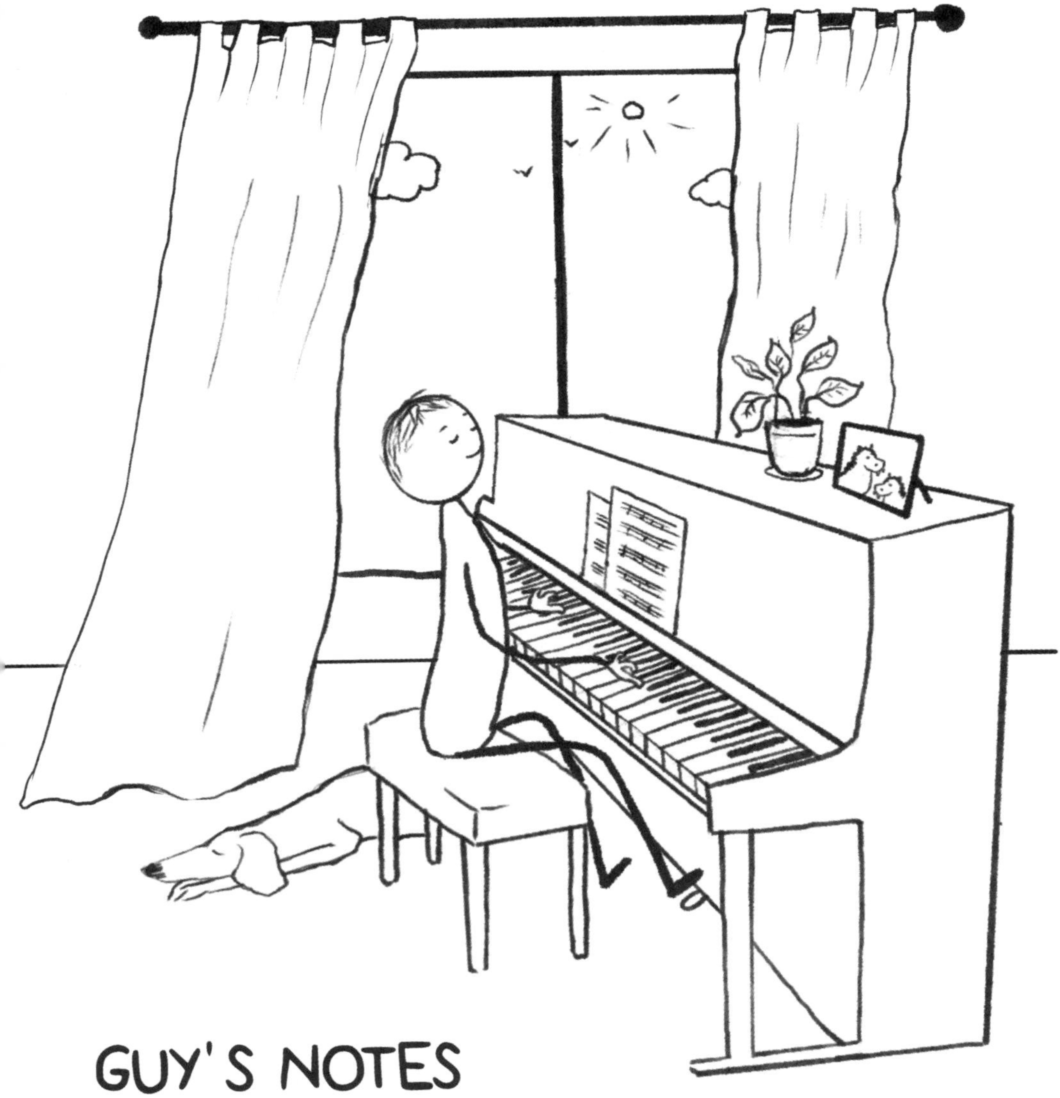

GUY'S NOTES

*This chapter was written by my partner.

(Just some context. Guy is a music teacher, composer and curious creature. He was a fairly self-sufficient, settled and single forty-year-old when I met him, and having spent the last seventeen years in Jerusalem in the same apartment, he suddenly moved to India with a piano and a dog.

I know, right? A flute and a cat would have been easier, but hey, that's love for you.

And then, well, among other things, we made a baby together...)

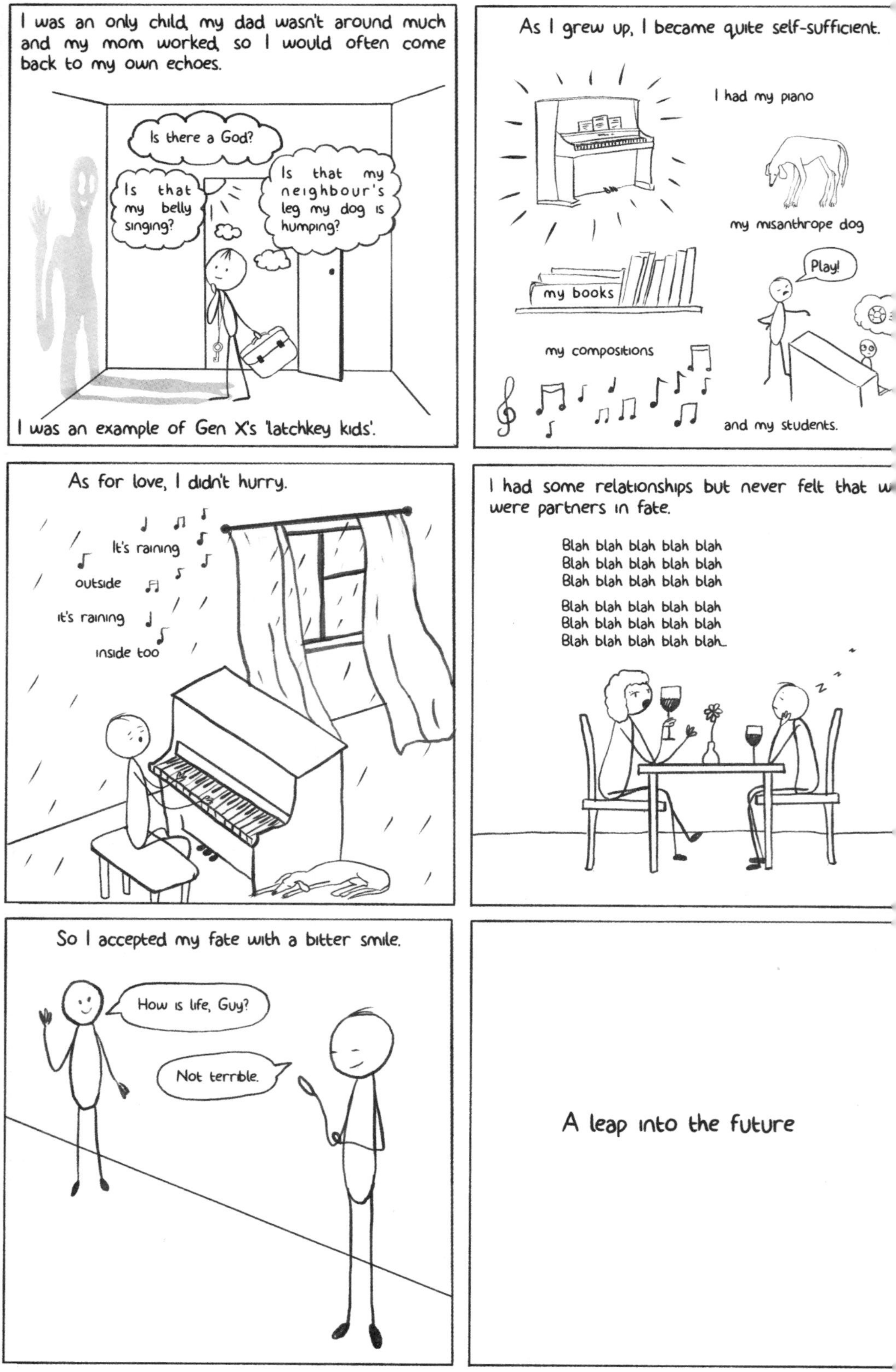
I was an only child, my dad wasn't around much and my mom worked, so I would often come back to my own echoes.
Is there a God?
Is that my belly singing?
Is that my neighbour's leg my dog is humping?
I was an example of Gen X's 'latchkey kids'.
As I grew up, I became quite self-sufficient.
I had my piano
my misanthrope dog
my books
Play!
my compositions
and my students.
As for love, I didn't hurry.
It's raining
outside
it's raining
inside too
I had some relationships but never felt that w
were partners in fate.
Blah blah blah blah blah
Blah blah blah blah blah
Blah blah blah blah blah
Blah blah blah blah blah
Blah blah blah blah blah
Blah blah blah blah blah...
So I accepted my fate with a bitter smile.
How is life, Guy?
Not terrible.
A leap into the future

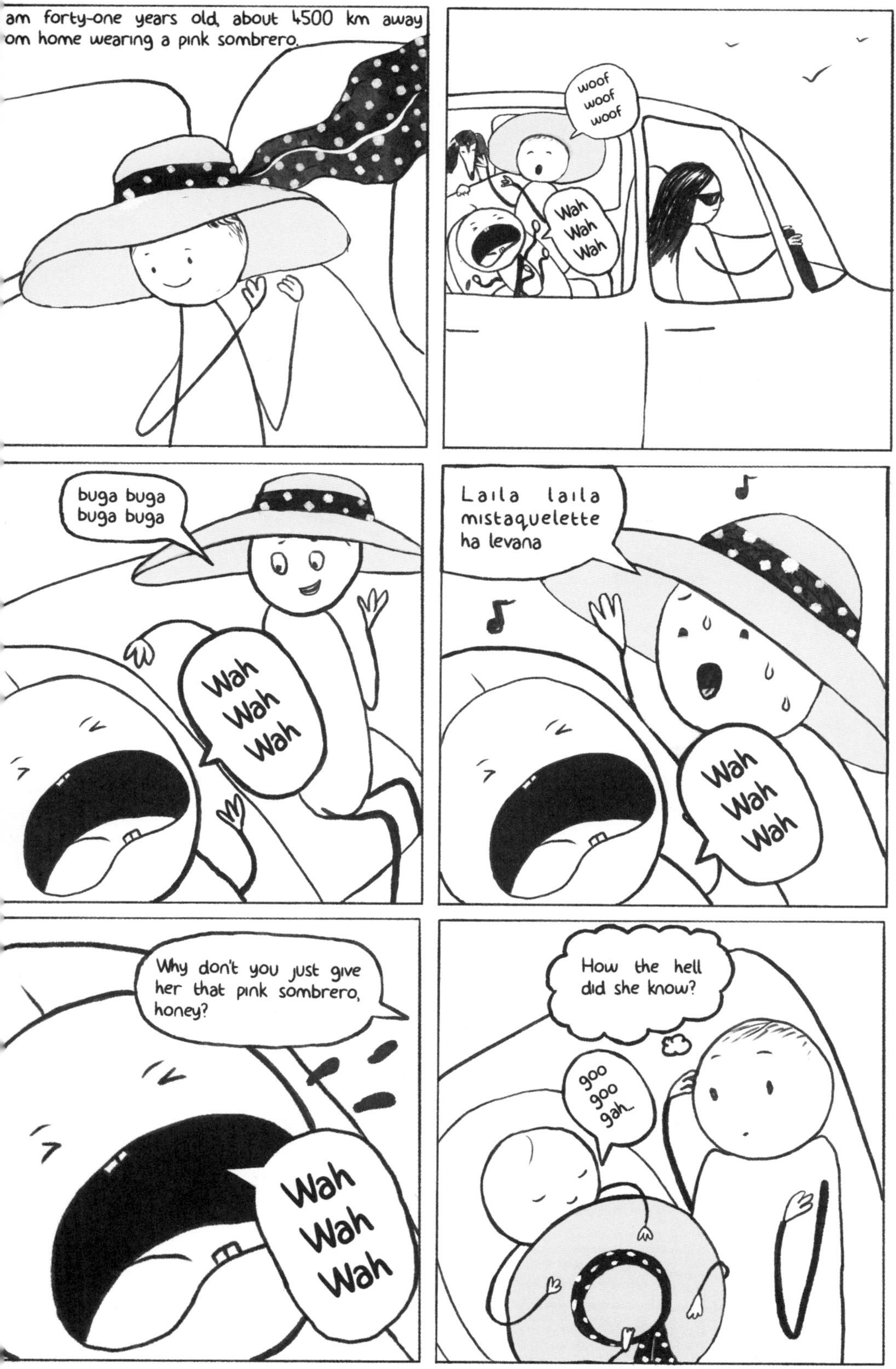
am forty-one years old, about 4500 km away
om home wearing a pink sombrero.
woof woof woof
Wah Wah Wah
buga buga buga buga
Wah Wah Wah
Laila laila mistaquelette ha levana
Wah Wah Wah
Why don't you just give her that pink sombrero, honey?
Wah Wah Wah
How the hell did she know?
goo goo gah...

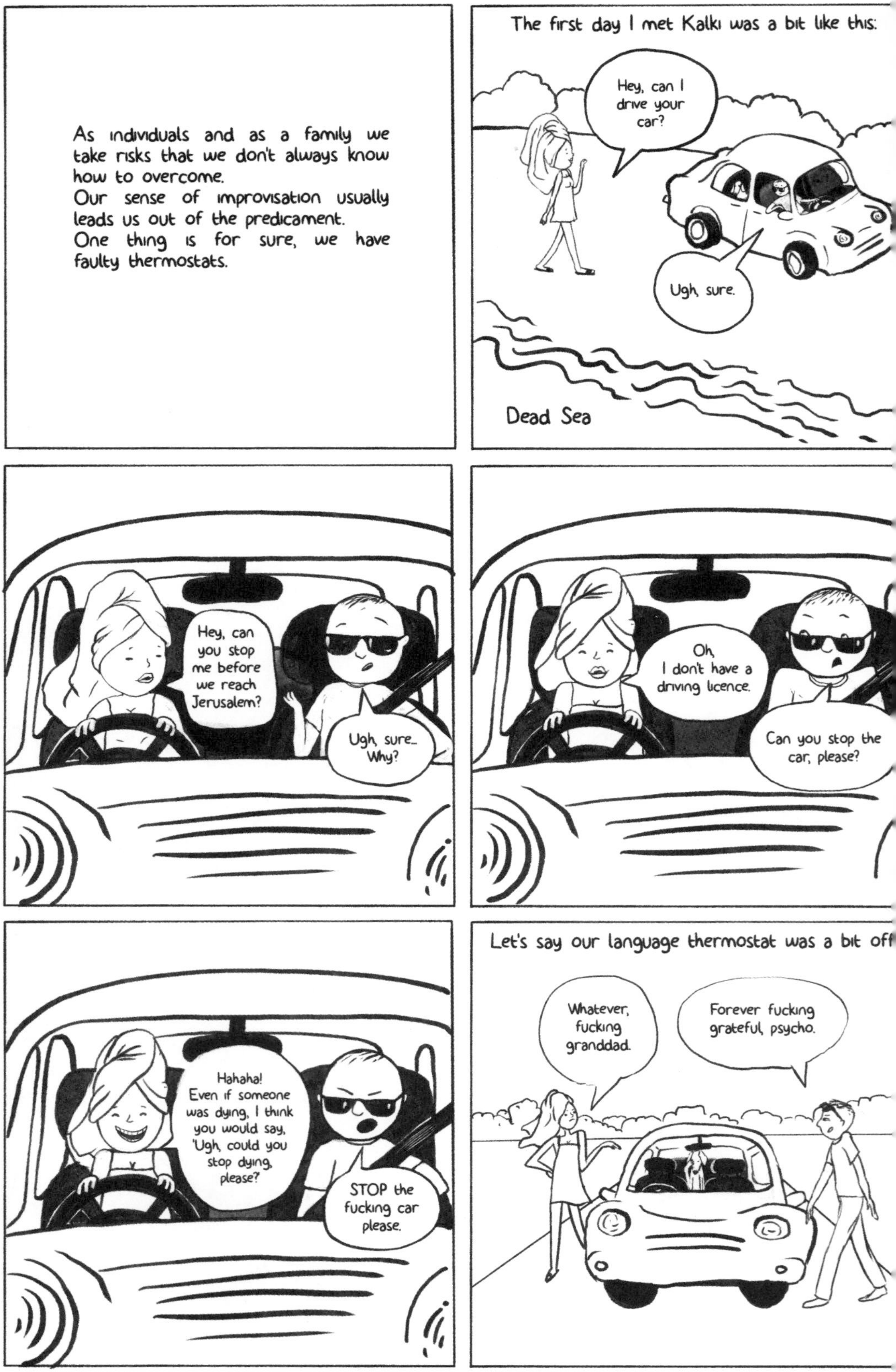
As individuals and as a family we take risks that we don't always know how to overcome.
Our sense of improvisation usually leads us out of the predicament.
One thing is for sure, we have faulty thermostats.
The first day I met Kalki was a bit like this:
Hey, can I drive your car?
Ugh, sure.
Dead Sea
Hey, can you stop me before we reach Jerusalem?
Ugh, sure... Why?
Oh, I don't have a driving licence.
Can you stop the car, please?
Hahaha! Even if someone was dying, I think you would say, 'Ugh, could you stop dying, please?
STOP the fucking car please.
Let's say our language thermostat was a bit off
Whatever, fucking granddad.
Forever fucking grateful, psycho.

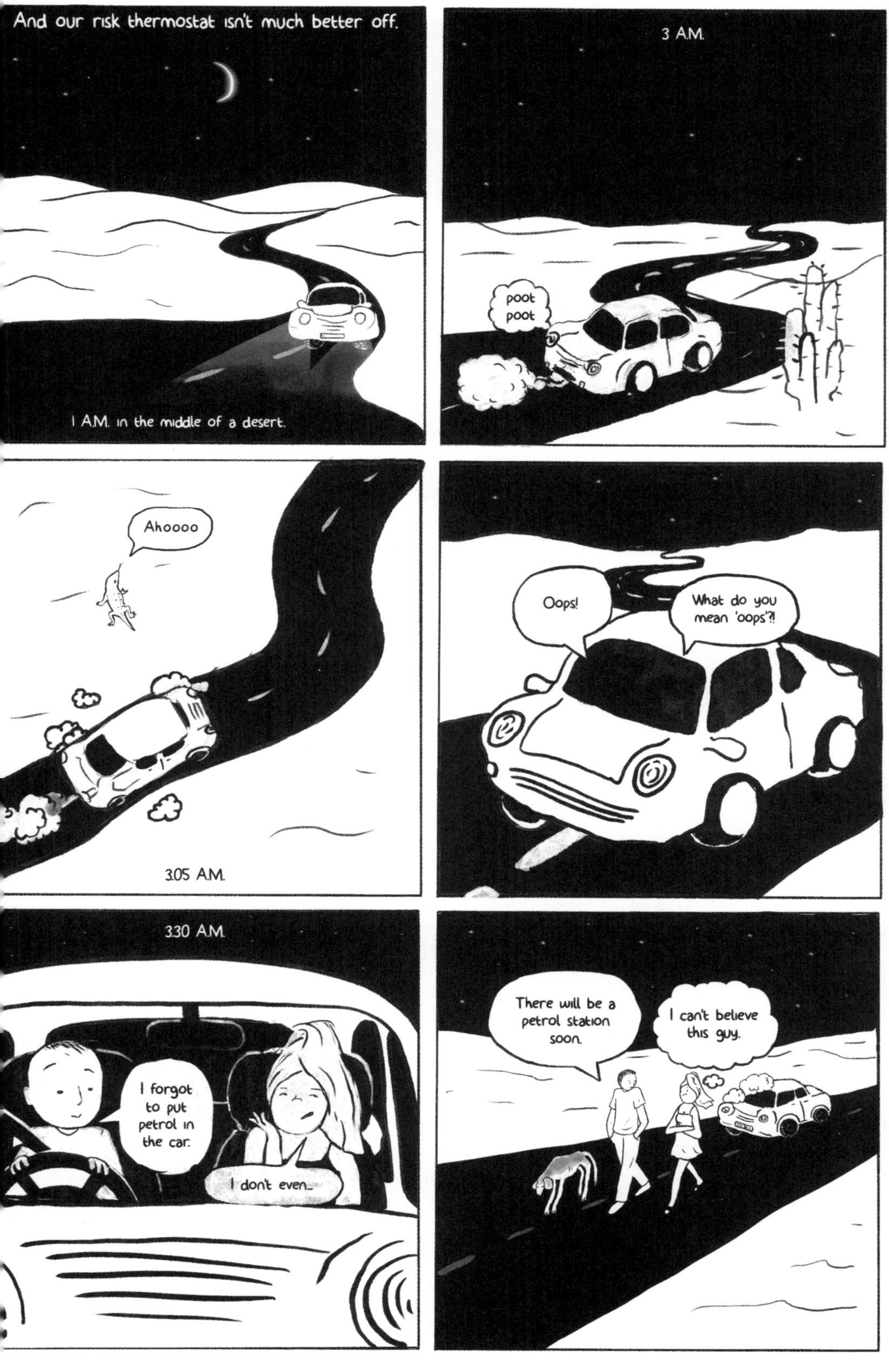

And our risk thermostat isn't much better off.
I A.M. in the middle of a desert.
3 A.M.
poot poot
Ahoooo
3.05 A.M.
Oops!
What do you mean 'oops'?!
3.30 A.M.
I forgot to put petrol in the car.
I don't even...
There will be a petrol station soon.
I can't believe this guy.

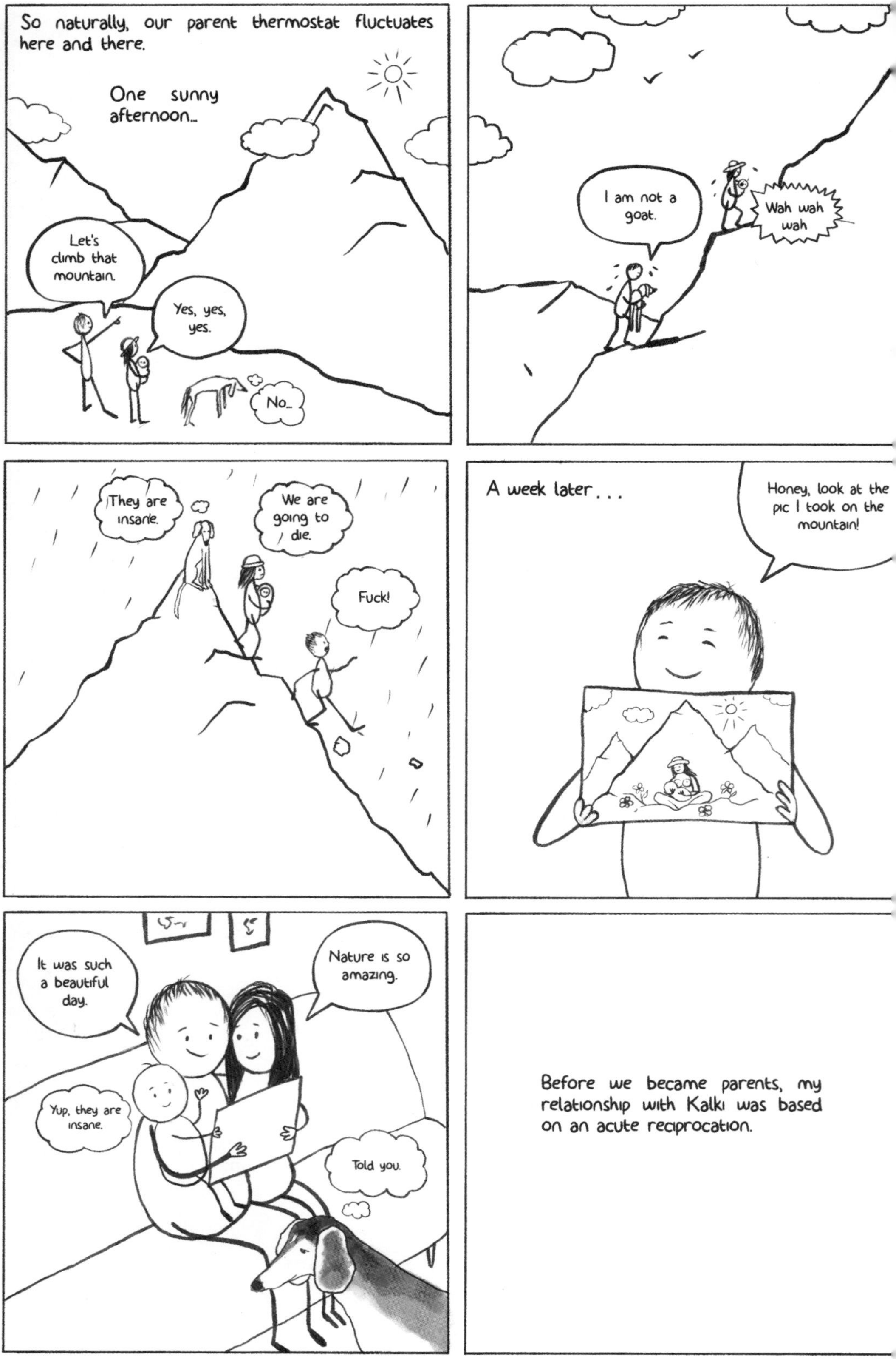
So naturally, our parent thermostat fluctuates here and there.
One sunny afternoon...
Let's climb that mountain.
Yes, yes, yes.
No...
I am not a goat.
Wah wah wah
They are insane.
We are going to die.
Fuck!
A week later . . .
Honey, look at the pic I took on the mountain!
It was such a beautiful day.
Nature is so amazing.
Yup, they are insane.
Told you.
Before we became parents, my relationship with Kalki was based on an acute reciprocation.

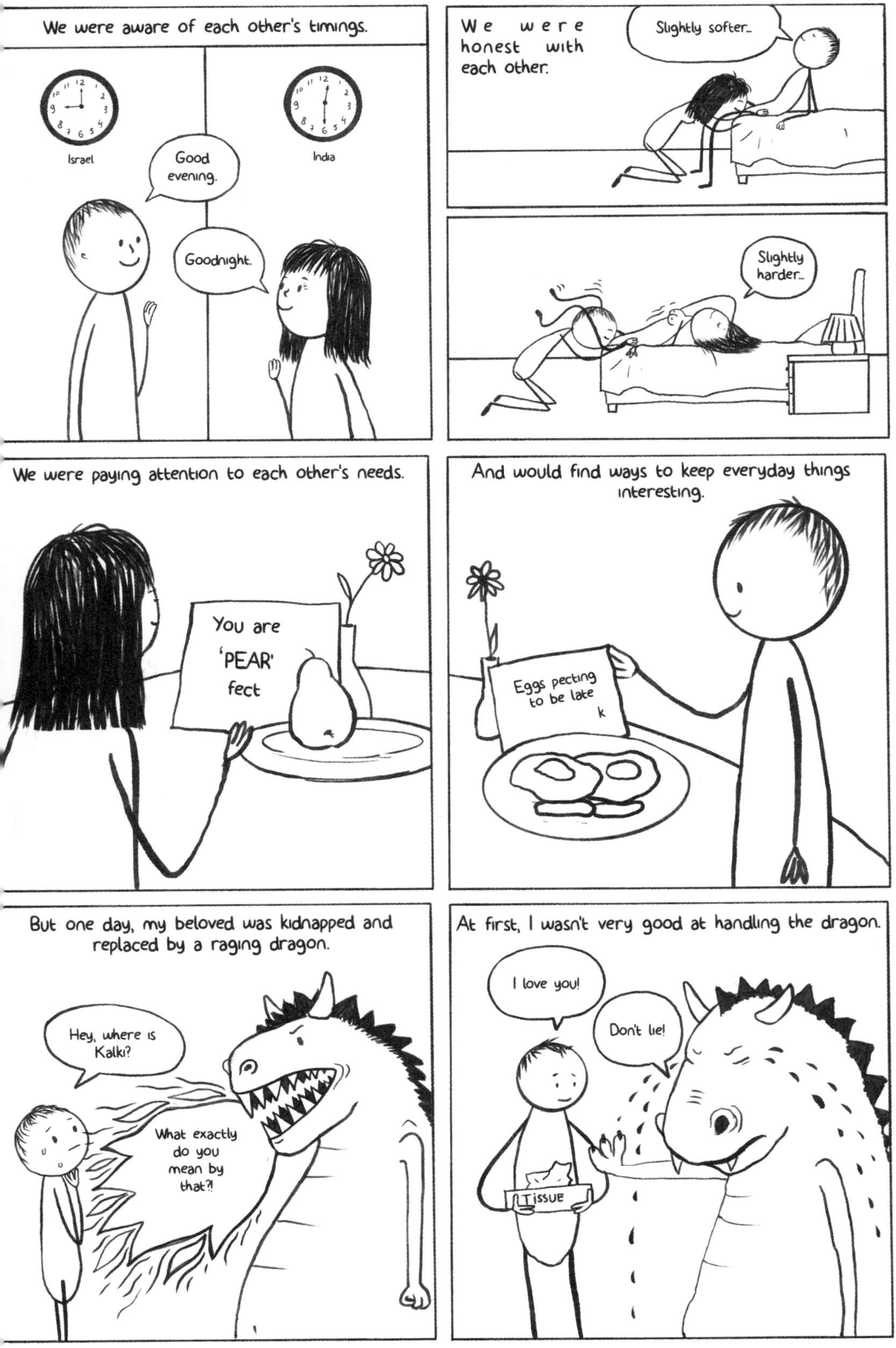

We were aware of each other's timings.
Israel
India
Good evening.
Goodnight.
We were honest with each other.
Slightly softer...
Slightly harder...
We were paying attention to each other's needs.
You are 'PEAR' fect
And would find ways to keep everyday things interesting.
Eggs pecting to be late
k
But one day, my beloved was kidnapped and replaced by a raging dragon.
Hey, where is Kalki?
What exactly do you mean by that?!
At first, I wasn't very good at handling the dragon.
I love you!
Don't lie!
TISSUE

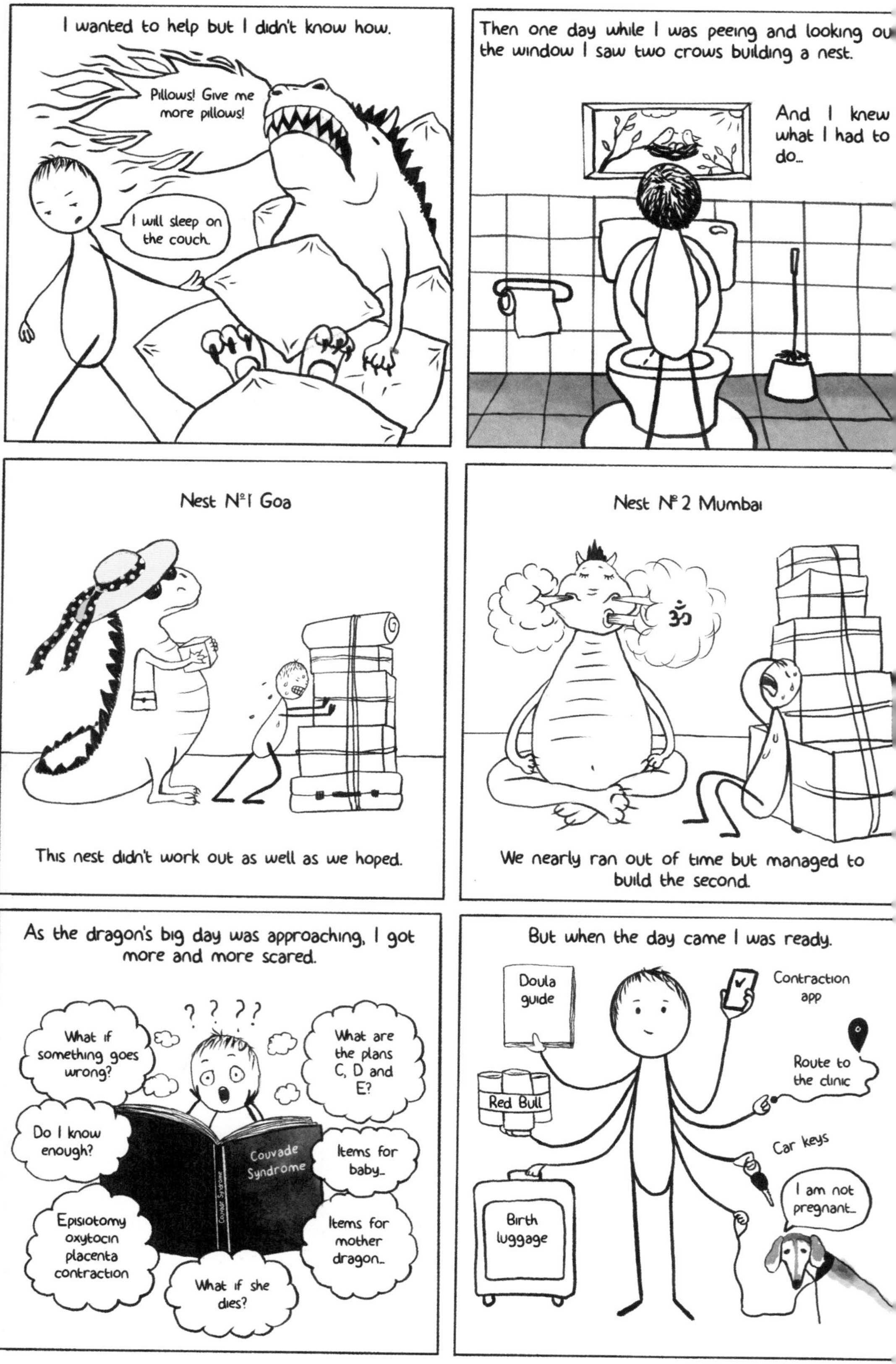
I wanted to help but I didn't know how.
Pillows! Give me more pillows!
I will sleep on the couch.
Then one day while I was peeing and looking ou the window I saw two crows building a nest.
And I knew what I had to do...
Nest №1 Goa
This nest didn't work out as well as we hoped.
Nest №2 Mumbai
ॐ
We nearly ran out of time but managed to build the second.
As the dragon's big day was approaching, I got more and more scared.
? ? ? ?
What if something goes wrong?
What are the plans C, D and E?
Do I know enough?
Couvade Syndrome
Items for baby...
Episiotomy oxytocin placenta contraction
Items for mother dragon...
What if she dies?
But when the day came I was ready.
Doula guide
Contraction app
Route to the clinic
Red Bull
Car keys
I am not pregnant...
Birth luggage

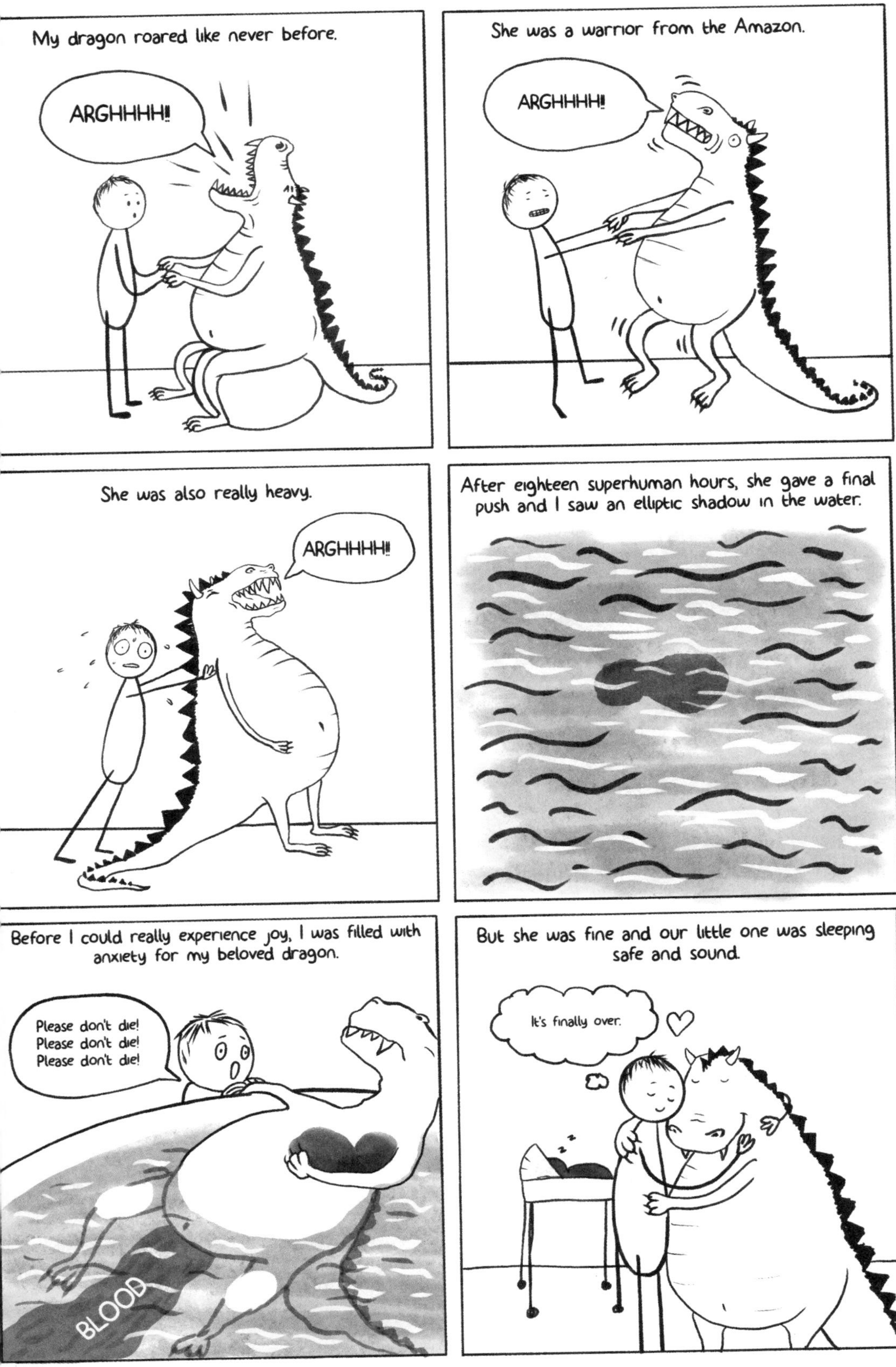
My dragon roared like never before.
ARGHHHH!!
She was a warrior from the Amazon.
ARGHHHH!!
She was also really heavy.
ARGHHHH!!
After eighteen superhuman hours, she gave a final push and I saw an elliptic shadow in the water.
Before I could really experience joy, I was filled with anxiety for my beloved dragon.
Please don't die!
Please don't die!
Please don't die!
BLOOD
But she was fine and our little one was sleeping safe and sound.
It's finally over.

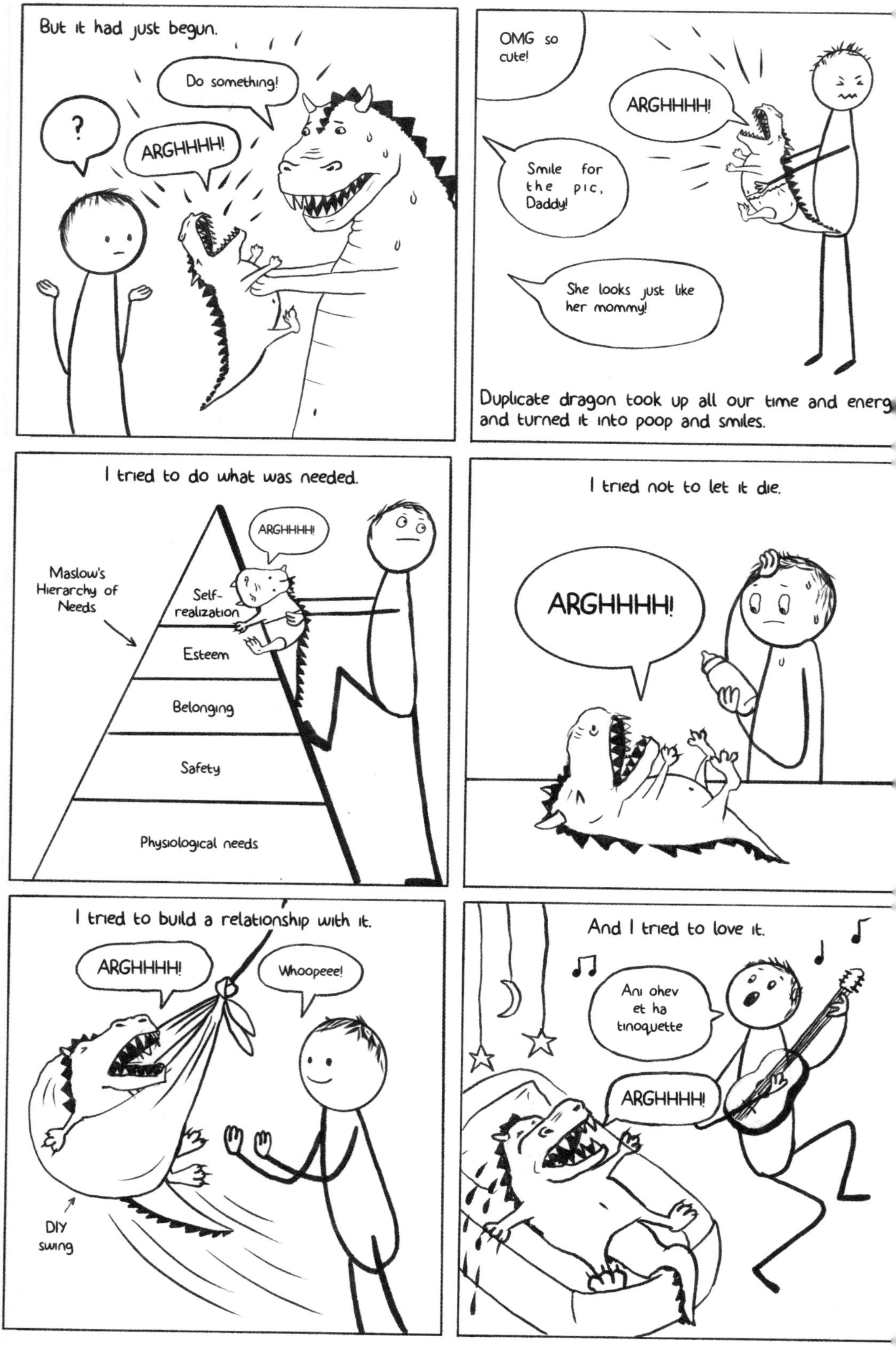

But it had just begun.
?
Do something!
ARGHHHH!
OMG so cute!
ARGHHHH!
Smile for the pic, Daddy!
She looks just like her mommy!
Duplicate dragon took up all our time and energ
and turned it into poop and smiles.
I tried to do what was needed.
ARGHHHH!
Maslow's Hierarchy of Needs
Self-realization
Esteem
Belonging
Safety
Physiological needs
I tried not to let it die.
ARGHHHH!
I tried to build a relationship with it.
ARGHHHH!
Whoopeee!
DIY swing
And I tried to love it.
Ani ohev et ha tinoquette
ARGHHHH!

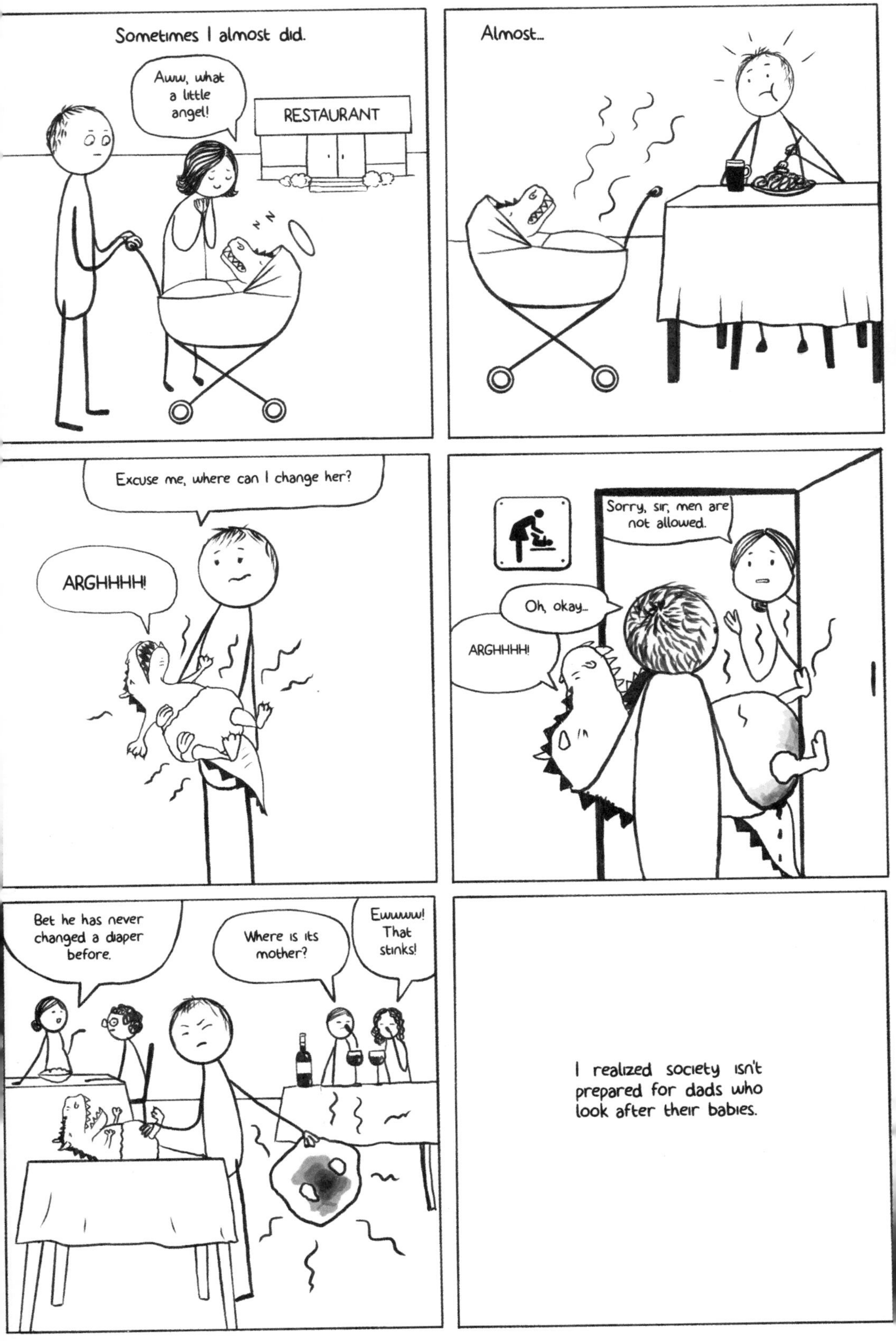
Sometimes I almost did.
Aww, what a little angel!
RESTAURANT
Almost...
Excuse me, where can I change her?
ARGHHHH!
Sorry, sir, men are not allowed.
Oh, okay...
ARGHHHH!
Bet he has never changed a diaper before.
Where is its mother?
Ewwww! That stinks!
I realized society isn't prepared for dads who look after their babies.

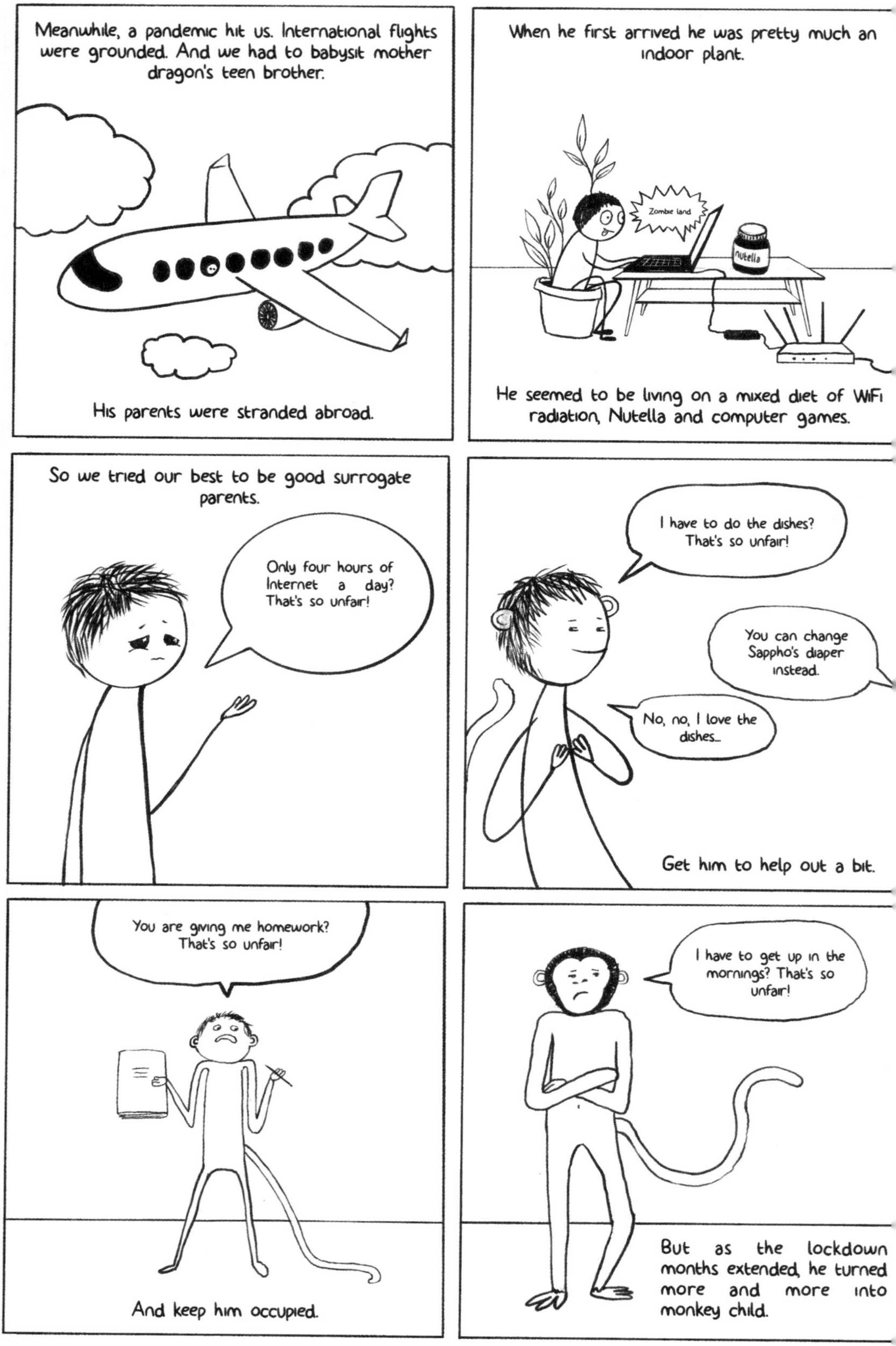
Meanwhile, a pandemic hit us. International flights were grounded. And we had to babysit mother dragon's teen brother.
His parents were stranded abroad.
When he first arrived he was pretty much an indoor plant.
Zombie land
nutella
He seemed to be living on a mixed diet of WiFi radiation, Nutella and computer games.
So we tried our best to be good surrogate parents.
Only four hours of Internet a day? That's so unfair!
I have to do the dishes? That's so unfair!
You can change Sappho's diaper instead.
No, no, I love the dishes...
Get him to help out a bit.
You are giving me homework? That's so unfair!
And keep him occupied.
I have to get up in the mornings? That's so unfair!
But as the lockdown months extended, he turned more and more into monkey child.

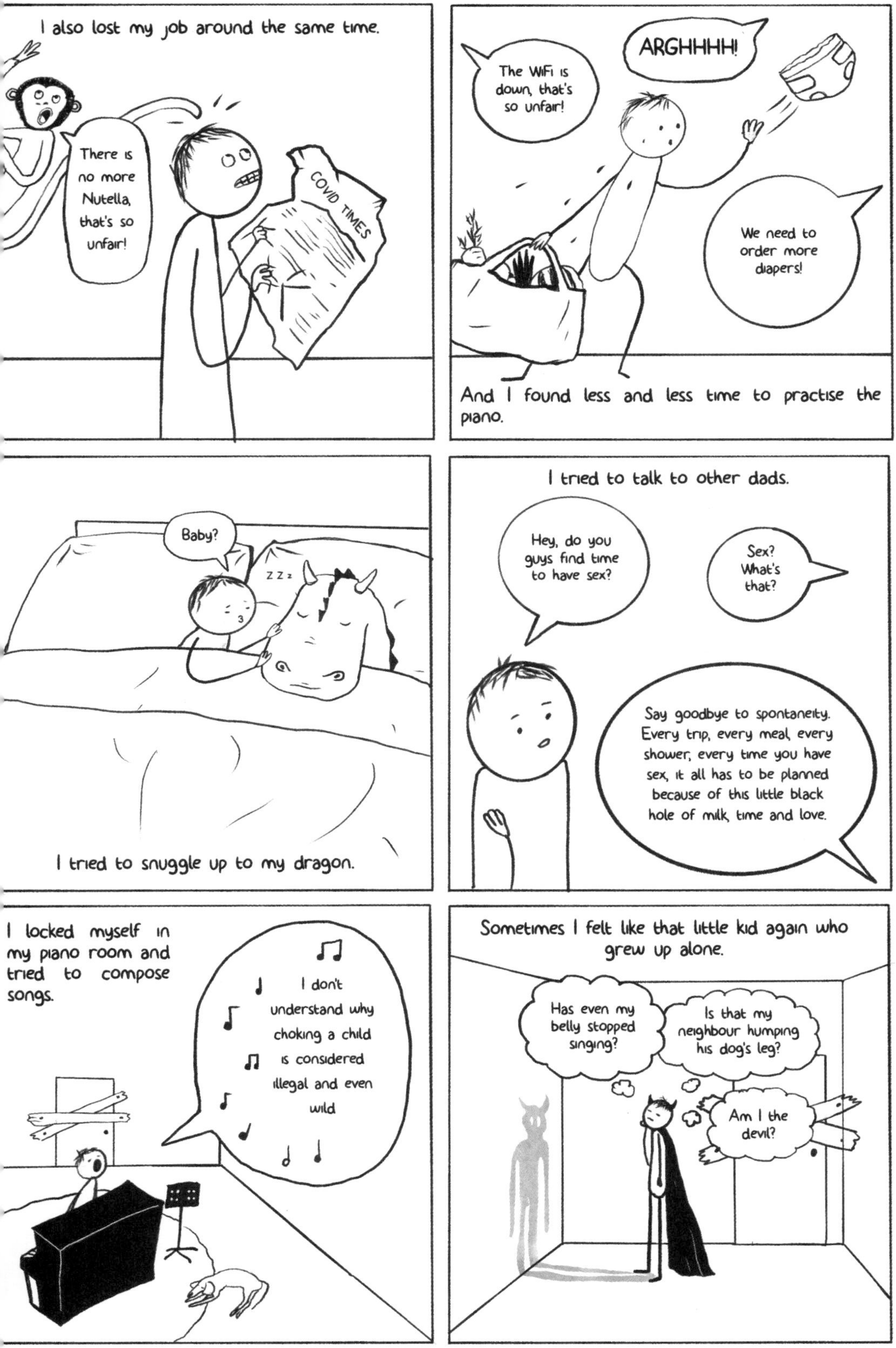

I also lost my job around the same time.
There is no more Nutella, that's so unfair!
COVID TIMES
The WiFi is down, that's so unfair!
ARGHHHH!
We need to order more diapers!
And I found less and less time to practise the piano.
Baby?
Z Z z
I tried to snuggle up to my dragon.
I tried to talk to other dads.
Hey, do you guys find time to have sex?
Sex? What's that?
Say goodbye to spontaneity. Every trip, every meal, every shower, every time you have sex, it all has to be planned because of this little black hole of milk, time and love.
I locked myself in my piano room and tried to compose songs.
I don't understand why choking a child is considered illegal and even wild
Sometimes I felt like that little kid again who grew up alone.
Has even my belly stopped singing?
Is that my neighbour humping his dog's leg?
Am I the devil?

I really struggled with myself during this time.

TT isn't even exercise!

It is for my wrists.

We are going to exercise.

Like, I remember wanting to let off some steam one day.

The kid was pretty good for a twelve-year-old.

YAY!

Nice smash, monkey child!

But then I lost to a neighbour kid Min, who could beat me with his weaker hand while texting on the phone.

But you said you wouldn't smash! That's so unfair!

HA HA HA! Too bad, kid! Life is unfair!

And then I took it out on monkey child.

I am not proud of myself.

Nothing...

What happened?

Monkey child must have felt lonely too.

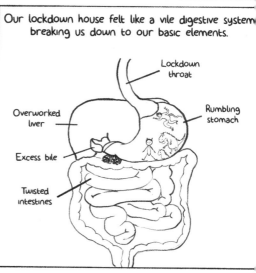

Our lockdown house felt like a vile digestive system breaking us down to our basic elements.

Lockdown throat

Overworked liver

Rumbling stomach

Excess bile

Twisted intestines

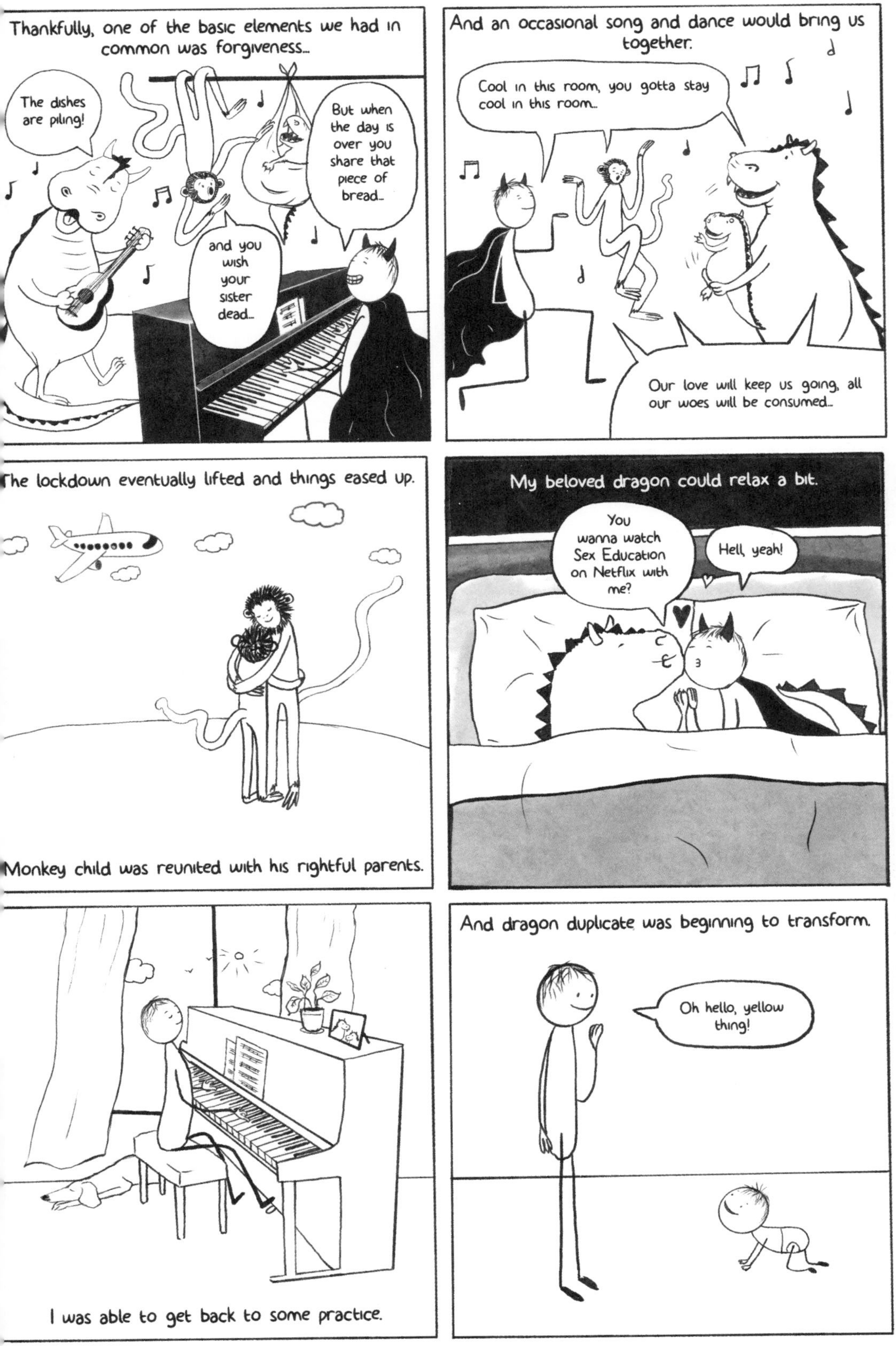

Thankfully, one of the basic elements we had in common was forgiveness...
The dishes are piling!
and you wish your sister dead...
But when the day is over you share that piece of bread...
And an occasional song and dance would bring us together.
Cool in this room, you gotta stay cool in this room...
Our love will keep us going, all our woes will be consumed...
The lockdown eventually lifted and things eased up.
Monkey child was reunited with his rightful parents.
My beloved dragon could relax a bit.
You wanna watch Sex Education on Netflix with me?
Hell, yeah!
I was able to get back to some practice.
And dragon duplicate was beginning to transform.
Oh hello, yellow thing!

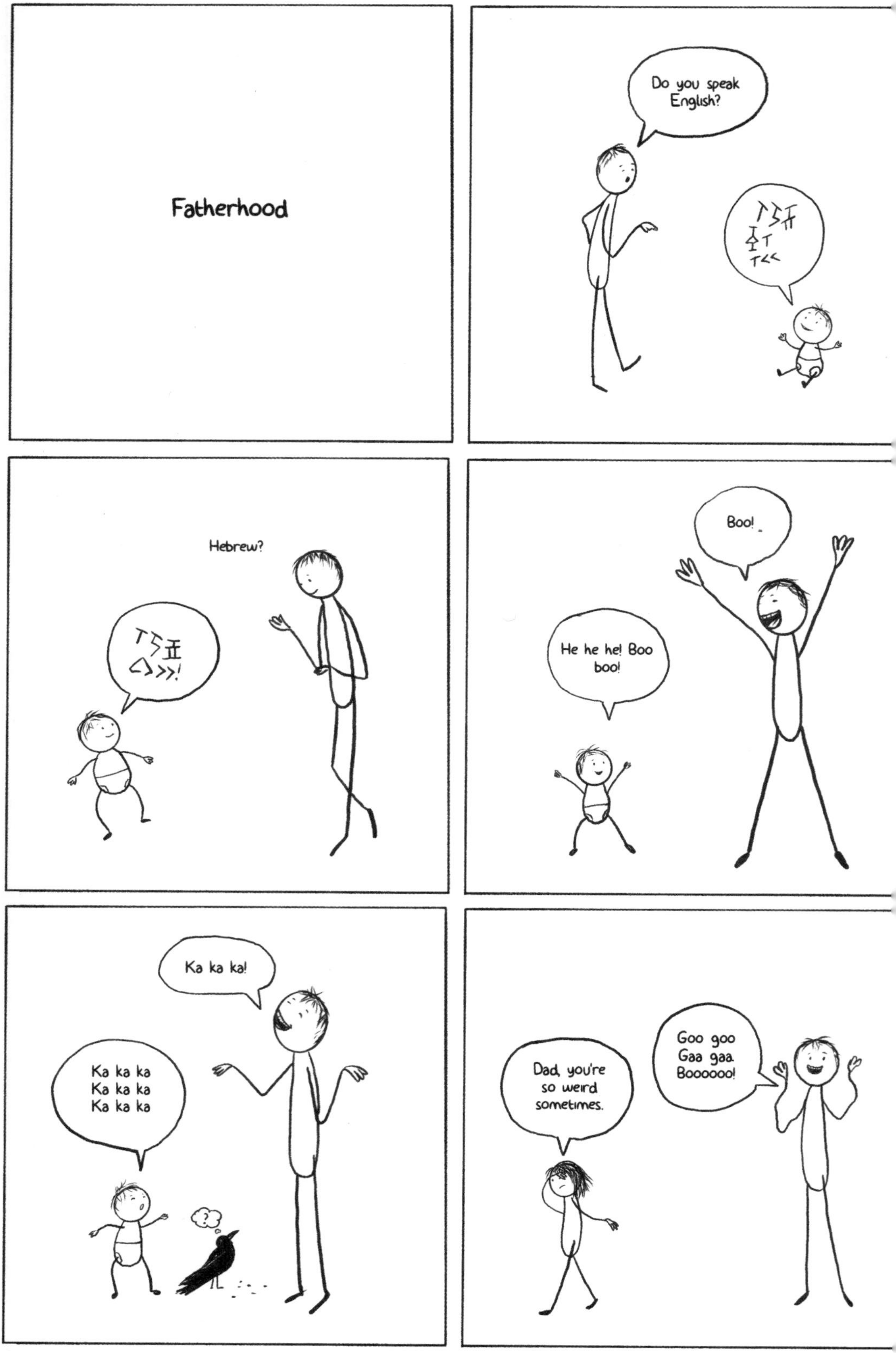
Fatherhood
Do you speak English?
Hebrew?
Boo!
He he he! Boo boo!
Ka ka ka!
Ka ka ka Ka ka ka Ka ka ka
Dad, you're so weird sometimes.
Goo goo Gaa gaa. Boooooo!

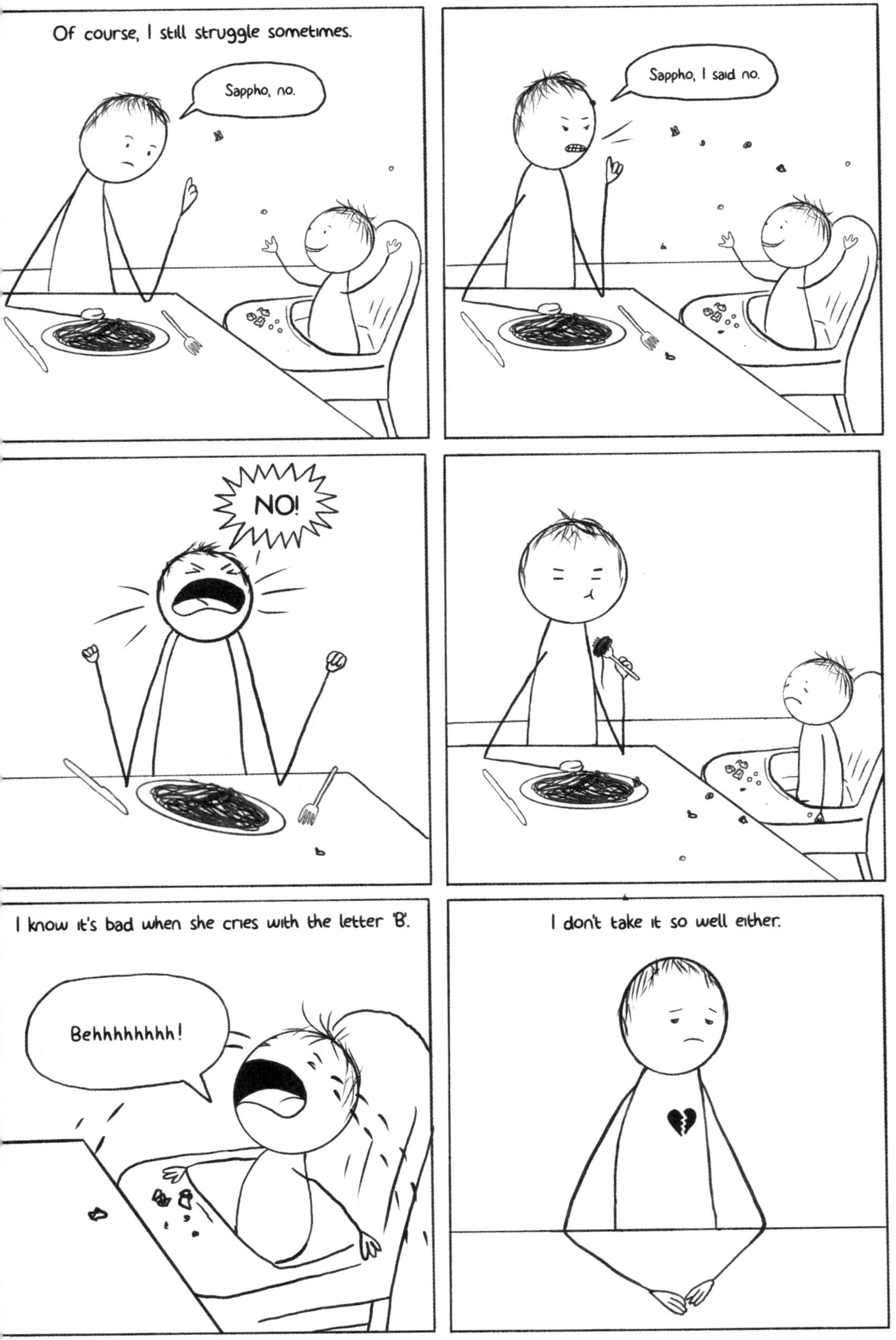
Of course, I still struggle sometimes.
Sappho, no.
Sappho, I said no.
NO!
I know it's bad when she cries with the letter 'B'.
Behhhhhhhh!
I don't take it so well either.

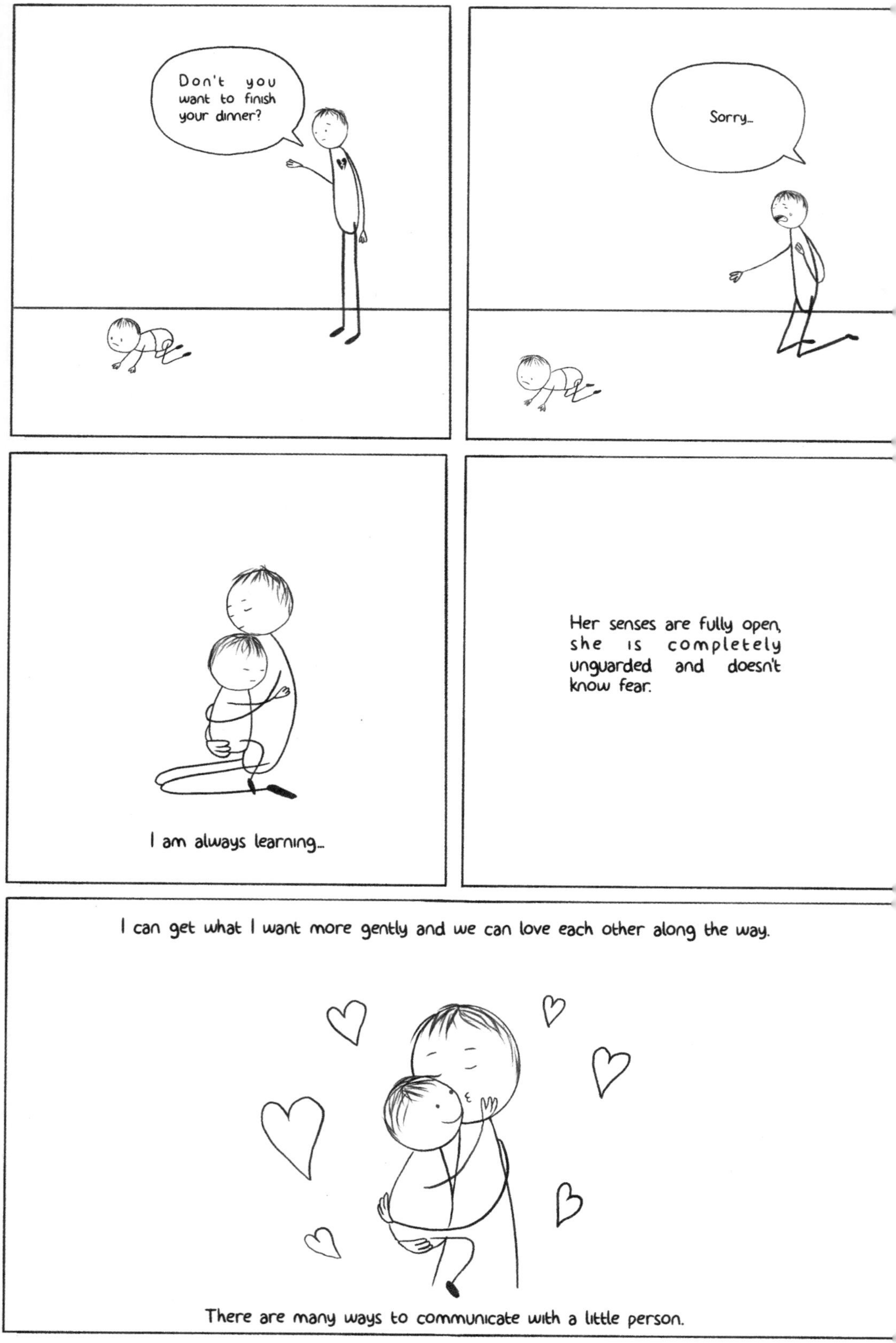

Don't you want to finish your dinner?
Sorry...
I am always learning...
Her senses are fully open, she is completely unguarded and doesn't know fear.
I can get what I want more gently and we can love each other along the way.
There are many ways to communicate with a little person.

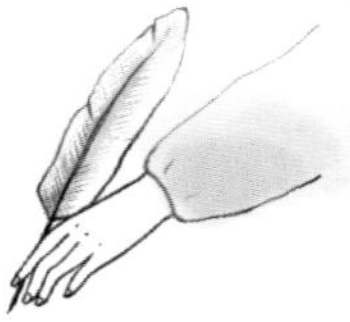

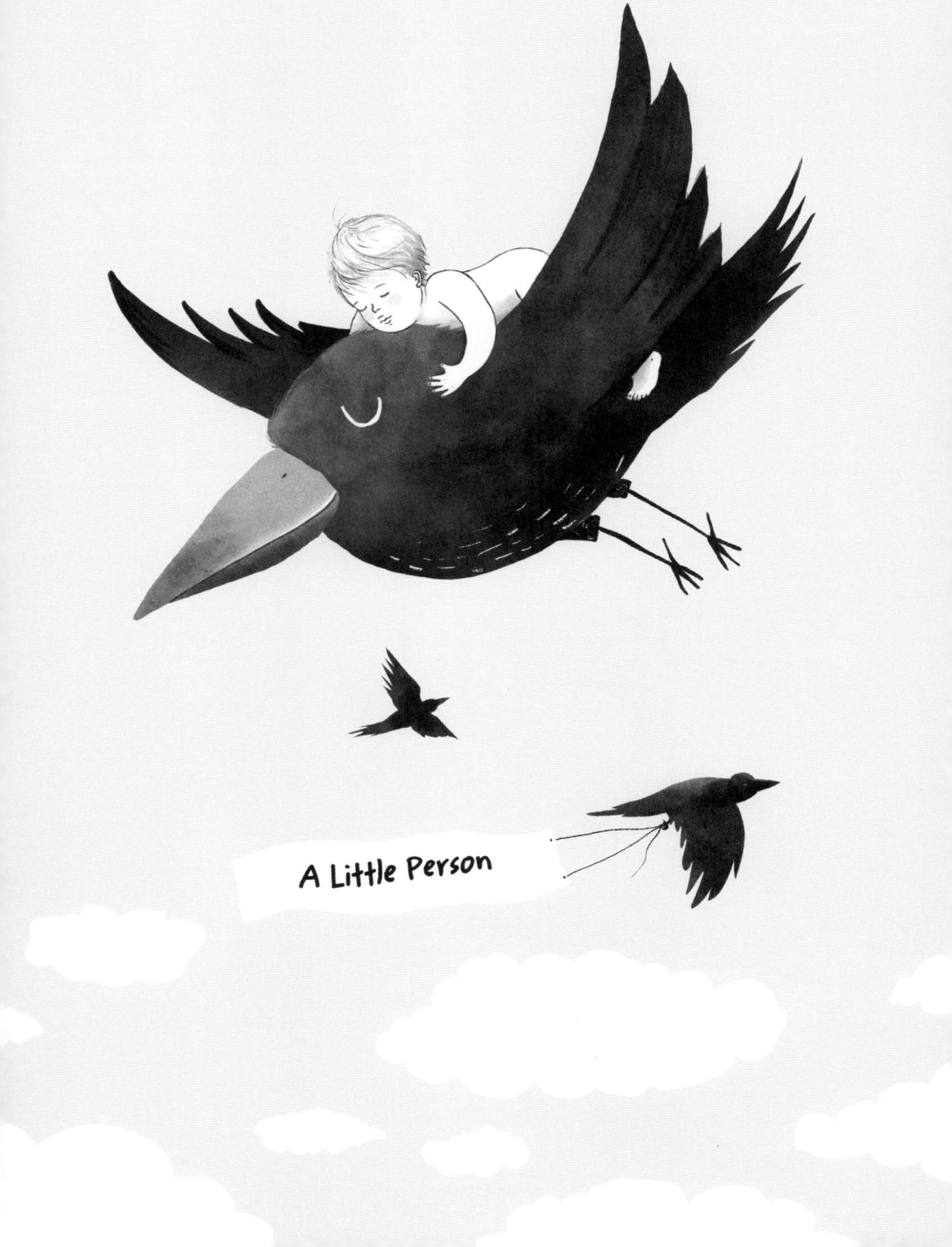
A Little Person

I'm really too new at the parenting game to know what to write here. I've tried to begin this chapter several times and each time stopped and deleted it because I realized I'm in my own infancy of motherhood and my relationship with Sappho will unfold over many years. So I've mapped out this chapter on the 'little person' much like this year—as unknown and unresolved fragments of a new landscape.

She wasn't here a year ago and now she takes up most of our time, thought and energy. Who is this person? Where did she come from? Does she already have her personality ingrained in her system or are we going to shape it?

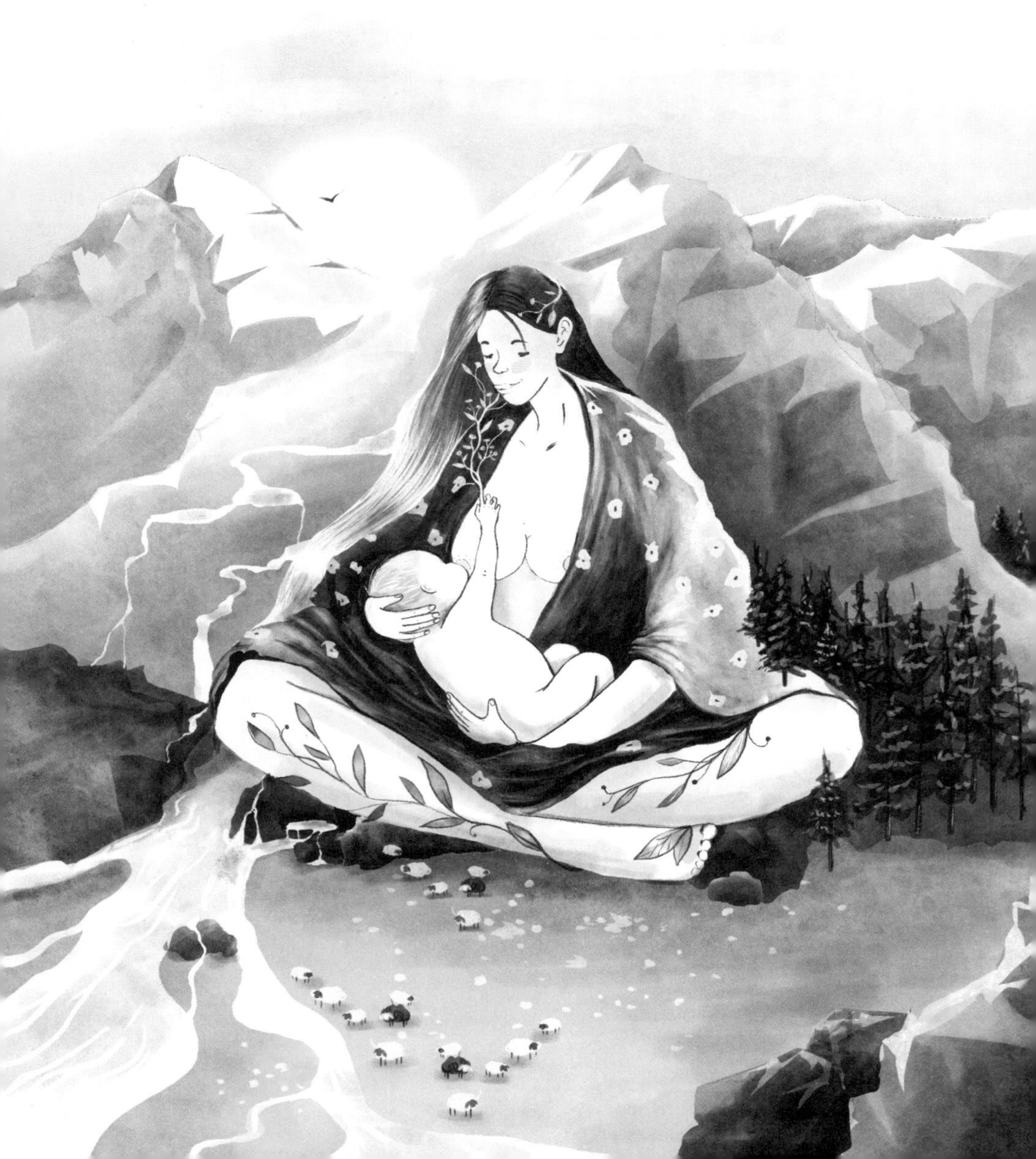

I remember referring to Sappho as 'the baby' for the first few months. I'd say, 'I need to feed the baby' or, 'Can you change the baby's diaper', and I rarely used her name. Only when she was around six months did I frequently address her as Sappho, because she started becoming a little person by then.

And what a relief that was. Because in the first few months, you really are groping in the dark; you have no idea what you're doing, no matter how much you might have prepped for this big moment. You're putting in this immense effort to just keep this baby alive, you're talking to her all the time, explaining new words and experiences, you're singing to her to put her to sleep, you're entertaining her with funny faces and silly sounds and you really have no idea if any of that is registering or having an effect. And then one day, she gives you her first smile, or her first intent of wanting something by pointing to it, or she just gets off the bed and starts walking like she's been doing that all along. These transitions were constant during the first year; one minute I would be dealing with a babbling, indecipherable creature and the next with a real little person capable of independent thought, armed with opinion and temperament. These moments are what I assume parents are talking about when they say, 'It's magical' or, 'There's no other happiness that can be compared.' Because all these broken parts you've been struggling with come together to form pieces of a puzzle that fit quite perfectly together.

All those moments of her babbling to a blank wall were practice for words, or her deadly, unimpressed stares when we were clowning around for her was her brain computing and registering new ways of behaviour. We realized, as the year plodded along, that there was a lot going on in terms of learning and feeling inside Sappho, even when she was not yet able to express it outwardly. And while we were still taking photos of her adorable sleeping faces, she was quietly developing a sense of humour or an ear for music.

Raising our voice at Sappho has never really worked. Perhaps because it's not something we do in our daily lives, putting it on for her comes out as artificial and she simply doesn't take us seriously.

I remember when Sappho started sticking her finger into plug points. We would keep shouting, 'No!' She would pause for a second, smile and then keep going towards it. So then we would pick her up saying, 'No, no, no, nooo!', and put her in 'prison'—her crib—for some time. She didn't stop reaching out for plug points every chance she could, until one day she reached the plug point and stopped. She looked back at us, smiled and started wagging her index finger from side to side, humming 'No no no no nooooo' in the same sing-song tune that Guy used on her. The game had changed and we wardens were just beginning to learn the rules. Now the inmate was not interested in the plug as much as she was interested in getting our attention. Since she wouldn't touch the plug, we were not allowed to put her back in prison.

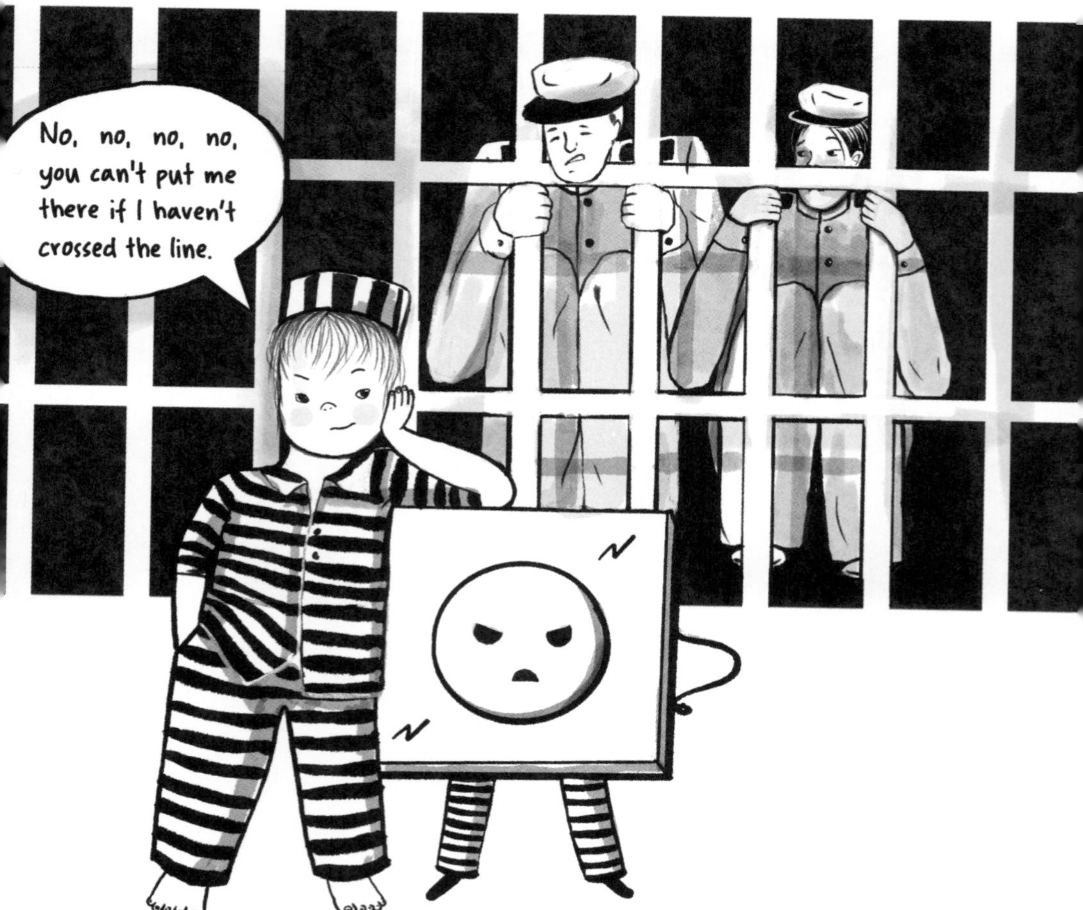
No, no, no, no, you can't put me there if I haven't crossed the line.

Now we sing the 'no no no noooo' song back and forth to each other for many things, knowing that 'no' doesn't mean 'no' as much as a trade-off, and it seems to be working just fine. (Although I know this too shall pass.)

I've never been great at ignoring her cries, even when I know they're exaggerated for the purpose of attention. I'm getting better at sifting between tantrums and genuine tears, but I usually have to leave the room, or sometimes even the house, so as not to react to her. Guy tends to be firmer and even lighter about it. He can make fun of her while she's wailing and eventually she does stop, and crawls towards some dust particle or pigeon feather like nothing ever happened. I usually feel a little silly for taking everything to heart, but I selfishly enjoy being the one she wants pressed against her when things get dire.

One day, on my first full day away from her, when I had a 9-to-9 shoot, I called Guy, saying I'd be half an hour late because I was stuck in traffic. I heard Sappho's blood-curdling screams in the background, and even Guy, who is usually calm in the face of her lamentations, said, 'I don't know what to do.' So I stepped out of my car, and ran approximately 2 km between cars and broken pavements to catch a rickshaw ahead of the bottleneck and reach Sappho a mere fifteen minutes earlier than I would have otherwise. She put her head on my chest and held on to my sweaty T-shirt for the rest of the evening.

I'm not sure what this says about my parenting style, but I do know that I still have some kind of inexplicable unseen visceral cord attached to her, one that can't be surgically cut. In a documentary I watched on Netflix called Babies, research has shown that the mother's (or the primary caregiver's) amygdala opens up significantly after birth and stays that way for the rest of her life. This means that there's a part of your brain that becomes permanently dedicated to worrying about your child. I'm finally able to understand why my mother still calls me to ask if I've had my vitamins at age thirty-seven, or checks if I've used the loo before leaving on a long trip. While I want to be 'cool' about things with my daughter as she grows up,
I think I am always going to have
the urge to fly across cities
when I hear her crying
on the phone.

YEAR 2060

We speak to Sappho in many languages. I speak to her in French, Guy, in Hebrew, Sangeeta, our cook, and lately her nanny at shoots, Julie, both speak to her in Hindi. In our social lives and between Guy and me, she hears English. I suppose we've overwhelmed her a bit because the first language she seems to have picked up is Crow. For most of her eleven-month life, she's had a crow waking her up in the mornings outside our window and so she responds to my 'bonjour' with 'ka ka ka'.

KA-KA-KA!

Bonjour!

She's also learnt to pant to signify Kiara and pictures of dogs but she barks to signify other dogs, which makes sense because Kiara is mostly a painting, as is so often the case with royal Salukis. She seems to have an inbuilt ultrasound system similar to a dolphin's high-pitched call although she hasn't been exposed to any dolphins as far as we are aware. She can repeat a note from the piano with perfect pitch. In fact, she seems to be copying sounds from all over, her two lips vibrating to make a scooter-like sound, the creaking-of-a-door sound, going up and down a musical scale like a voice warm-up and a pop sound like a bubble gum bursting. Despite the fact that she hasn't uttered a single comprehensible human word except when imitating us, she succeeds in expressing what she wants, doesn't want, and what she's feeling and thinking quite often. She has one breathy 'o' for when she's excited and another deeper one for when she's hurt. I mean emotionally hurt. When it's physical pain, it's a loud yelp. Maybe because I'm an actor and always looking for ways to communicate an emotion, I'm finding her languages fascinating because they remind me of how everything around us helps us emote, how the body itself can emote according to the stimuli around it. Feeling hot can change the way we breathe, make the voice raspier and drier; a loud noise can make us stressed and our muscles tense up. Once again in the programme Babies * they speak of an experiment where children younger than twelve months are able to recognize different monkeys by their facial features individually, and not just as one species, and they lose this ability as the brain starts prioritizing complex human interactions. Although I'm looking forward to Sappho developing complex human interactions, it seems to me that as we grow up we begin discarding a sensitivity to the space around us in an attempt to become more 'civilized' and more acceptable to our social community. I'm kind of hoping that Sappho doesn't lose these other sounds as words take form, so every once in a while I greet her with, 'Ka ka ka.'

....

* (I don't know what it is about this very science-y documentary that gets me excited but here I am, spending all my energy on a baby, and then when I'm exhausted and put her to sleep at night, I go and look at more babies on my screen.)

As I find myself in conversations with other, more experienced mothers about alternative forms of education like home-schooling and community activities, or I listen to how they couldn't get admission in this or that school, I become quietly attentive. I seem to be so far from that phase of reaching out into the 'real' world. Because of Covid, and new viruses sprouting everywhere, I have been in the 'bubble' phase for longer than expected, at home giving Sappho milk and attention. The first year has been about ensuring this little person's survival and paying attention to her early development. Mostly, I'm ensuring her survival.

Actually, Sappho seems to be developing quite well on her own. I can leave her at a safe distance on a patch of grass in the garden or in her room with a bunch of differently textured blunt objects and she'll touch, eat, smell and make sense of them. I just have to pull the occasional worm out of her mouth. Things are calm for now, we no longer need full-time help, we sleep seven hours most nights, and Sappho and Kiara are developing a strong friendship based on searching for crumbs. I'm thankful for this time and I'm starting to enjoy neatly scheduled days—mornings to write, afternoons at the park, dinners as a unit of four.

I often go to sleep with my phone switched off and a smile on my face. But from time to time, I panic. My shooting schedules are about to get very busy. I will need to start depending on others and trusting the world around me with my daughter, and frankly, I'm worried. I look around me and see the hierarchy at the park; kids with parents get priority on the swings over kids with nannies. A rowdy three-year-old whacks Sappho on the head; he is immediately violently grabbed by an adult and given a slap. At no point is there an attempt to get the two of them to face each other again. What have we been teaching our children? To live in separate spaces and learn to say, 'This is mine', to grow up competing with each other instead of getting along with each other?

I try to imagine a scenario where the two kids are given a chance to work it out...

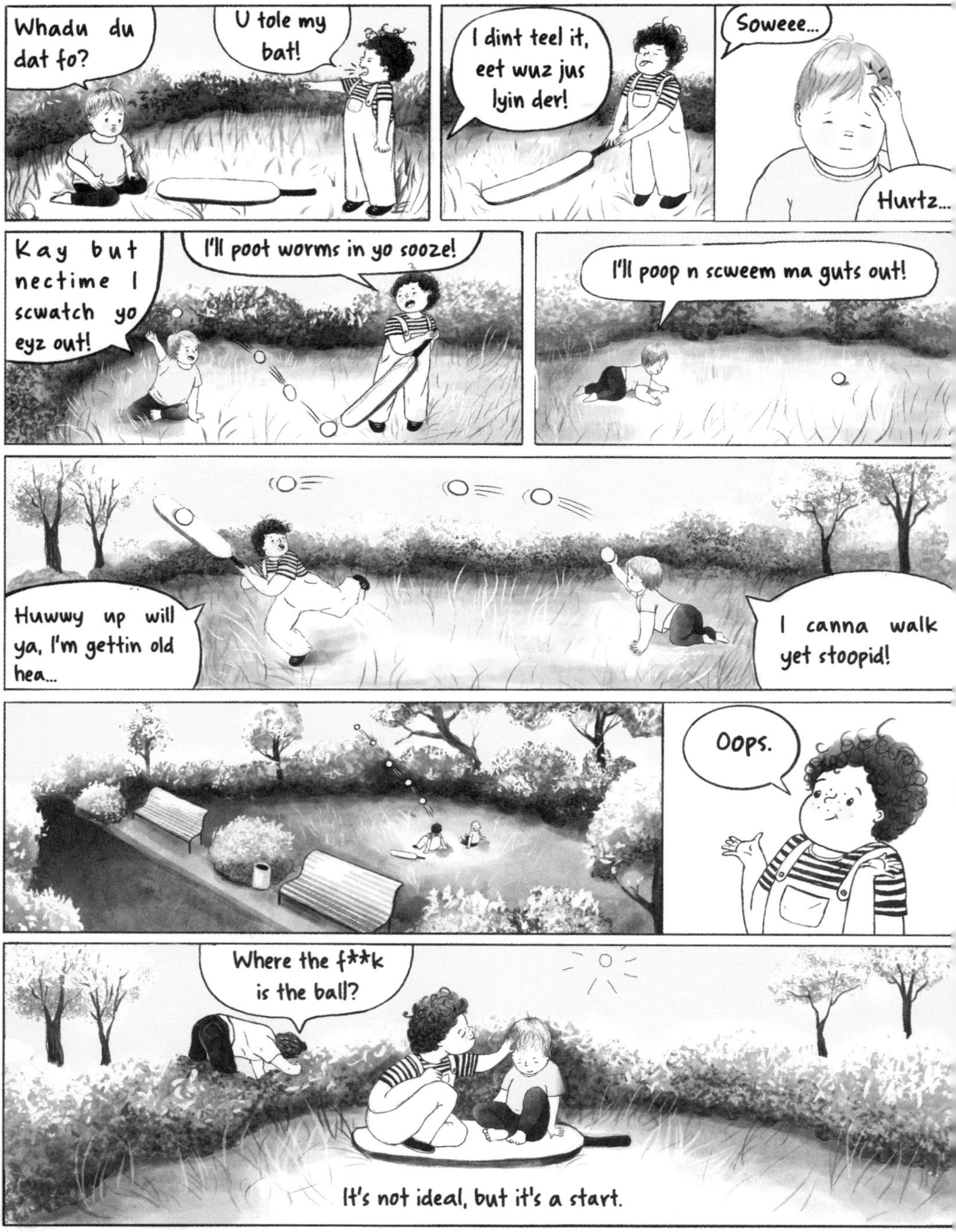
Whadu du dat fo?
U tole my bat!
I dint teel it, eet wuz jus lyin der!
Soweee...
Hurtz...
Kay but nectime I scwatch yo eyz out!
I'll poot worms in yo sooze!
I'll poop n scweem ma guts out!
Huwwy up will ya, I'm gettin old hea...
I canna walk yet stoopid!
Oops.
Where the f**k is the ball?
It's not ideal, but it's a start.

The first three years of a child's life are the most critical in shaping their brain architecture according to a study by *UNICEF*. This will impact the way they think, what they prioritize, and how they feel about almost everything they later experience. And considering this impact, the social set-up seems to indicate serious mismanagement as a species, bringing to light the fact that we've centred our existence on careers and self-preservation rather than community-building and shared knowledge.

The recent Covid pandemic in 2020 has helped reveal these gaps in our system. Research in American homes has shown that, of the more than 1 million workers who exited the labour force in September, 8,65,000 were women. Many lost unemployment insurance because they 'chose' not to return to work, even if they had no real choice because they had no childcare.

As always, women bear the brunt of a false system of equality that is based on individual success rather than human development as a whole. The fact is that we have a broken system, where we run around juggling between daycares and nannies and preschools, getting the 'best' we can afford, too afraid to really look into or question these institutions lest the responsibility falls on us to change things.

My best friend is selling her cosy and newly decorated house to shift into another neighbourhood so her daughter can 'walk' to a school which prioritizes 'caring for the environment and being a good human being'. Guy and I have had extensive debates about moving to a country that promotes a more equal standard of living versus creating a community of friends and family to make this happen where we currently are. Overall, the world is not ready to take care of its little people and each of us is grappling with how best to compromise, as the pandemic forces us to take a closer look at our broken system.

In October 2020, after spending most of the year locked up in a two-bedroom Mumbai apartment with a teenager, a newborn, three adults and a dog, we finally braved the pandemic and travelled to south India to my mother's house in the countryside. Guy had a two-day journey with Kiara in the car since pets were still not allowed on flights, and I was travelling with Sangeeta and Sappho by plane.

I was so excited about getting out into nature but also extremely anxious about the travel risks and how Sappho would respond to this long day, a two-and-a-half-hour flight and a three-hour car ride. We got up very early to make sure nothing was forgotten; I spent the entire day holding Sappho close to me, making sure she didn't get her usual exploration routine of putting everything in her mouth, breastfeeding her for most of the flight and singing to her till she slept. Poor Sangeeta kept trying to relieve me of Sappho, but I was having none of it. Today I was going to be OCD-control-freak mom and everybody best social distance the fuck away!

As dusk arrived, exhausted but relieved, we took a walk in the coconut grove surrounding my mother's place. Sangeeta, a widow with a grown-up daughter of her own, my divorced mother, me, a new mother, and little Sappho, all in the arms of Grand Old Nature. Four women, three generations, between light and dark, moved as one. We didn't speak. The sound of owlets waking and our feet crunching through dry palm leaves was enough for our listening.

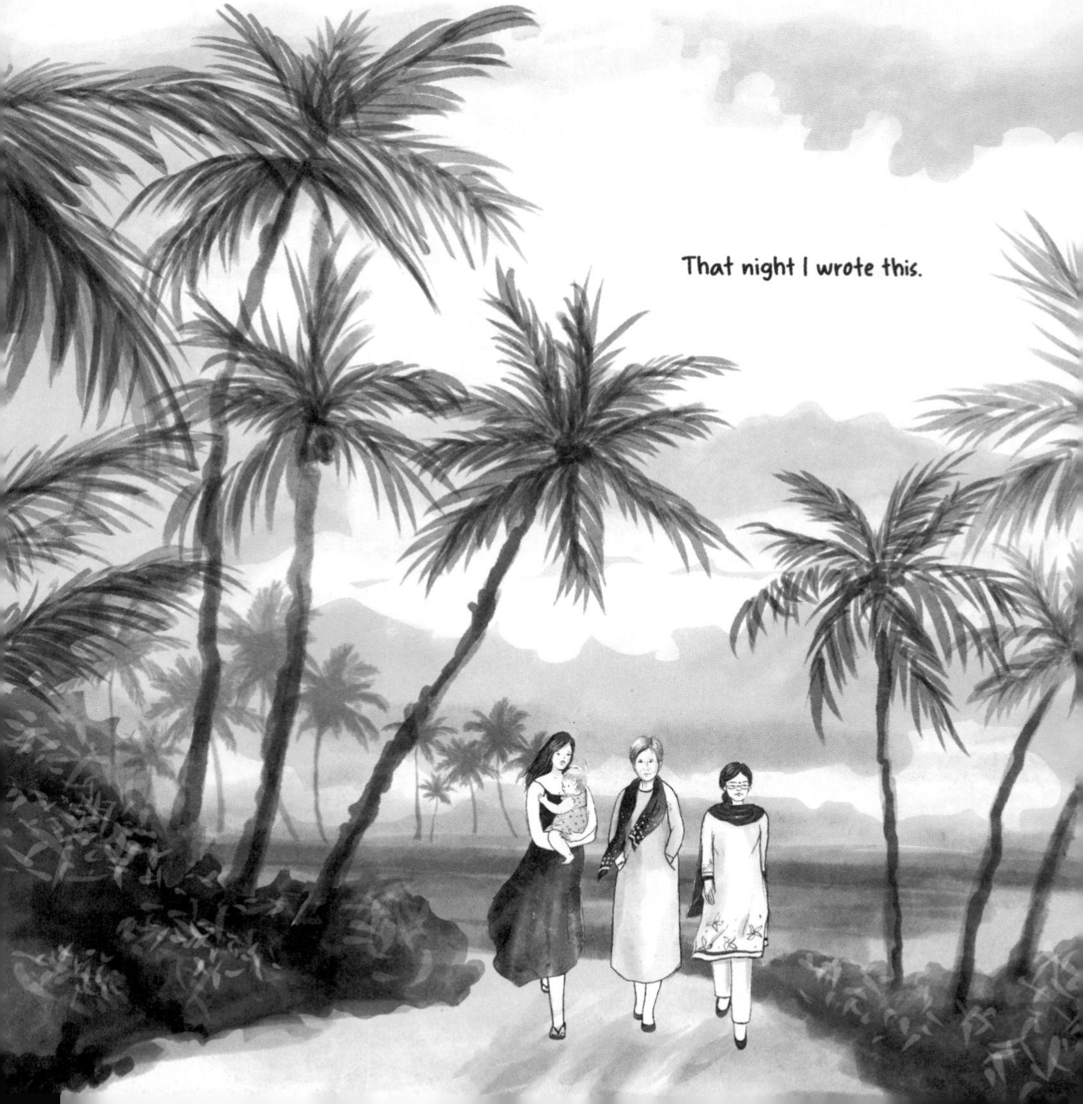
That night I wrote this.

There is no end to the gratitude I feel. Despite running on no sleep. Despite

rescheduling my life — or maybe because of it — this — this quiet walk at dusk,

between the trees, is the most satisfying experience I've had since she was born. At

this moment, I feel superhuman. I can do anything. I hold her in the palm of my

hand, and though I'm shivering with exhaustion I have no doubt that this is where I

want to be. To face fear, to finally tackle it directly, not just in the mind, but

physically and emotionally is the only way to move forward. To love someone is to be

careful around them in every moment, even in moments of exasperation or resentment,

to tolerate those feelings without letting them overtake you. And then — then to be

loved in return, with all your imperfections. To be loved in this way, this heroic way.

There's nothing I can't do for her, she believes, and her belief reinforces my

confidence. And I am not alone, there are many like me, and we'll tell each other

of our battles, compare scars, and learn to love again. The birthing process taught me

there's more power and more healing capacity in me than I had ever imagined. I can

go on, simply live, another day will break through and I will fight or wade or glide

through it. But I am grateful, to myself, to her, to us. To the calm after the

storm, to the joy of sharing warmth between other living things, to time stretching

out like a long night of sleep.

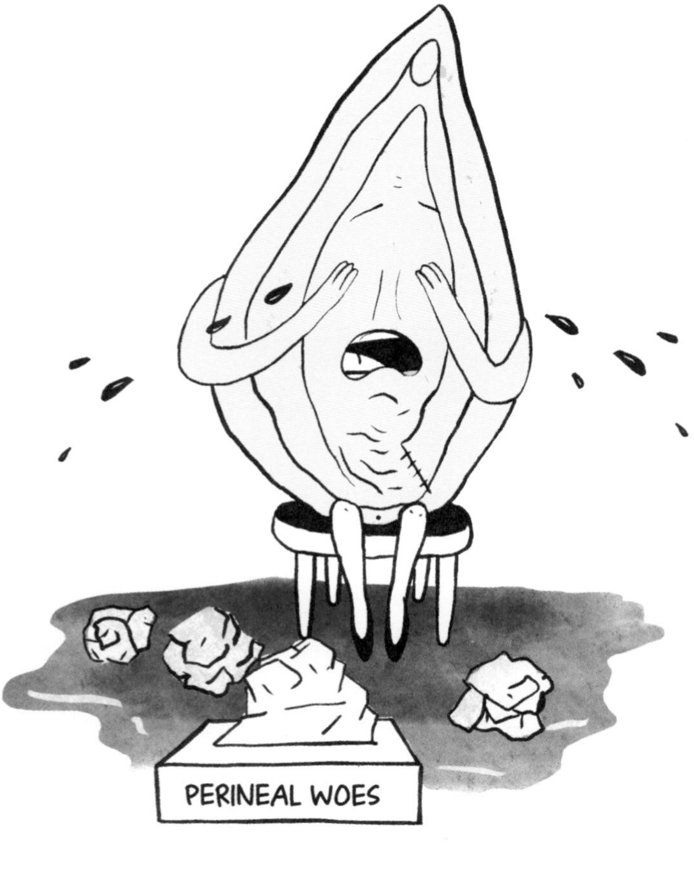
PERINEAL WOES

So the thought of having sex after my vagina had dilated 10 cm, was torn at the perineum, had been stitched up, had required application of calendula, betadine and anaesthetic gel twice a day while I was bleeding for four weeks straight just didn't occur to me. I don't think I looked at my partner in any remotely lustful way for months, despite his tenderness, and if he had any desire for me, he certainly kept it discreetly tucked away behind a shower curtain. As far as I was concerned, I was never going to have sex again. I had enough trouble just maintaining my daily personal hygiene. If I could find the time to poop, between the feeding and diaper changes, and getting the house sorted, I was terrified to do so because of haemorrhoids that would peek out of my arse at the slightest effort of pushing. I couldn't sit cross-legged for the first few weeks or get back to exercising as it could undo the stitches and I'd feel the skin stretching and tearing at the slightest effort. When I had to medicate and wash my vagina every day, I would take long deep breaths to calm my shivering fingers and the tension between my legs. When Guy tried to touch me, I felt like a goldfish flinching in a bowl when a cat tries to paw at it, each time narrowly escaping disaster.

It was only after three months that I started considering the possibility of a sex life again, worrying more than desiring, trying more than enjoying, and generally making a desperate attempt to remember that there was more to our relationship than discussing to-do lists. The first time we had penetrative sex, or tried, it felt like a thousand needles were poking me all around my vagina. We tried again, and again, only to find that with each attempt we became more tense and quicker to give up. It didn't help that there was so little leisure time between domestic chores, caring for our baby and managing sleep. It didn't help that my body was all out of whack and I didn't feel beautiful or desirable, or that I would spend my bath time cleaning the shower drain blocked by severe hair fall caused by breastfeeding. As the months lengthened, and the discomfort between my partner and me grew, I began to wonder if our relationship would slowly simmer into a stereotype of lifelong fidelity. A future filled with a friendship that grows stronger, and a love that endures even when the flames have long died out. My body was still a little loose and bulgy around the middle, my boobs were leaky and changing size on a daily basis, I hardly had time to bathe, let alone the energy to wear pretty clothes or make-up, and my underarm hair had grown longer than Guy's. I was a different person and I couldn't remember who I was before or how I could get back to her.

And here's the thing. Guy seemed just the same. He was light on his feet, dark with his jokes and hard in the mornings. I don't think I've ever been so jealous in our relationship, and I mean, we were in a lockdown, we met nobody. But I felt jealous. Like a teenager. If Guy liked a picture of a beautiful girl on Instagram, I felt rejected. If I suspected him of masturbating in the shower, I felt betrayed. I simply hadn't been this vulnerable in my body before; physically, I had always been quite fit, and here I was unable to get back to my headstand or the wheel stretch in yoga, unable to zip my high-waist jeans. And mentally, I didn't know day from night, who I was and who I'd be. I had only the present to contend with, and presently I felt old.

This was not the kind of old where you look in the mirror and notice dark circles. Feeling old is something you come to terms with if you work in front of the camera over an extended period of years, the extreme close-up where you notice every new wrinkle magnified in a way you wouldn't otherwise, the director asking the cinematographer to 'brighten up' the face. You know that your eyes do the talking, you're able to pull yourself out of it, tell yourself there's more to acting than the physical. This was not that kind of old; this was not just about my physical appearance, it was about my mind not responding to me. It was an old that sat deep inside my stomach and told me I was incapable and broken and couldn't be fixed.

So I turned to the only thing I knew could comfort me. → RESEARCH

83 per cent of new parents experienced a moderate to severe crisis in marriage during the transition to parenthood.

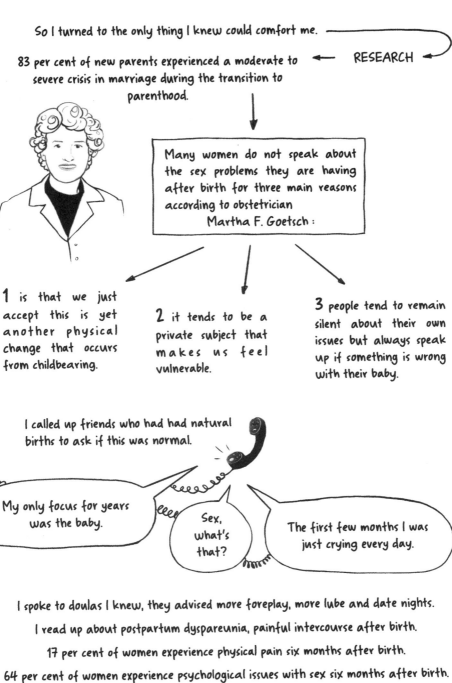

Many women do not speak about the sex problems they are having after birth for three main reasons according to obstetrician Martha F. Goetsch:

1 is that we just accept this is yet another physical change that occurs from childbearing.

2 it tends to be a private subject that makes us feel vulnerable.

3 people tend to remain silent about their own issues but always speak up if something is wrong with their baby.

I called up friends who had had natural births to ask if this was normal.

My only focus for years was the baby.

Sex, what's that?

The first few months I was just crying every day.

I spoke to doulas I knew, they advised more foreplay, more lube and date nights.

I read up about postpartum dyspareunia, painful intercourse after birth.

17 per cent of women experience physical pain six months after birth.

64 per cent of women experience psychological issues with sex six months after birth.

Breastfeeding lowers estrogen. Low estrogen levels means less vaginal lubrication, and can lead to fatigue, excessive sweating and even depression.

Breastfeeding also delays your menstrual cycle (mine only resumed after six months).

It seemed like my hormones were geared towards nurture and my body was telling me, you're not quite ready for reproduction just yet.

I called up my gynaecologist, and told her I was unable to have sex without pain way beyond the six-week mark. At the check-up she pointed out that new scar tissue had formed farther into my vagina. My skin had 'healed aggressively and excessively' from the rawness of giving birth, hence the entrance to my vagina was actually smaller than before giving birth.

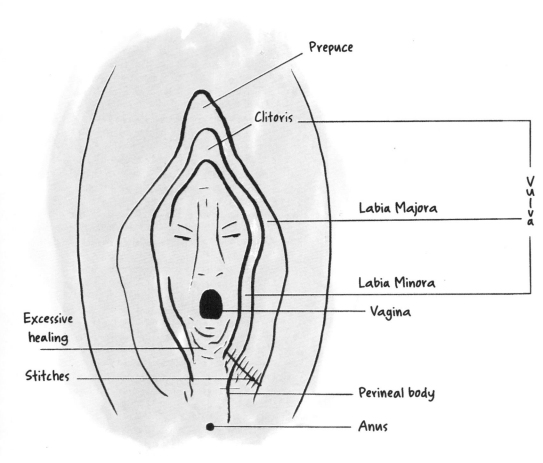

Prepuce

Clitoris

Labia Majora

Labia Minora

Vulva

Vagina

Excessive healing

Stitches

Perineal body

Anus

Great, so now I had a bunch of physical and hormonal symptoms to back up my death-to-sex mood. Why was I still feeling empty and hopeless?

I suppose I just wasn't ready to accept that my relationship and my body could not be what it used to be. I mean, I wanted to be full of passion, full of spirit and spontaneity but instead I was going to sleep at 8 P.M. in full pyjamas and an eye mask, while Guy read his book next to me and patted my head absent-mindedly. This was not acceptable. I. Sorry. We. We were going to work at it, schedule it, make it happen. I will C-O-M-M-U-N-I-C-A-T-E with my partner after the instructions of so many articles I'd read by googling sex after baby. So we bought an assortment of lubes, I was on Zoom calls with my therapist regularly, and my partner and I were doing a lot of scheduled cuddling and scheduled talk about cuddling, all to no avail.

Of course now it's clear to me that my businesslike approach to the whole thing was working against me and that aside from the physical problems, this was a problem of leisure. My therapist asked me in one of my sessions when the last time I did nothing for three hours was. 'Three hours?!' I exclaimed. 'I'm lucky if I get half an hour to shower or nap.' I was feeding Sappho every three to four hours, so the time between that was spent in little half-an-hour spells of eating, napping or finishing chores. At the time I couldn't separate my physical traumas from my emotional ones. I couldn't tell myself that my body will heal with time, that I need to be patient, that I need to let go a little. Instead, everything was on a tightly wound-up string that could snap at any point. Six months after I'd given birth I still wasn't able to masturbate, and it wasn't for lack of private time. I just didn't get any pleasure from being alone, I was afraid to face myself minus the mother role and peer into the broken bits and pieces of my previous life, and I realized that my creativity seemed to suffer from it too. Since I didn't allow myself time to do 'nothing', I didn't allow myself to daydream, I didn't let my mind wander, and I stopped defending my sense of space.

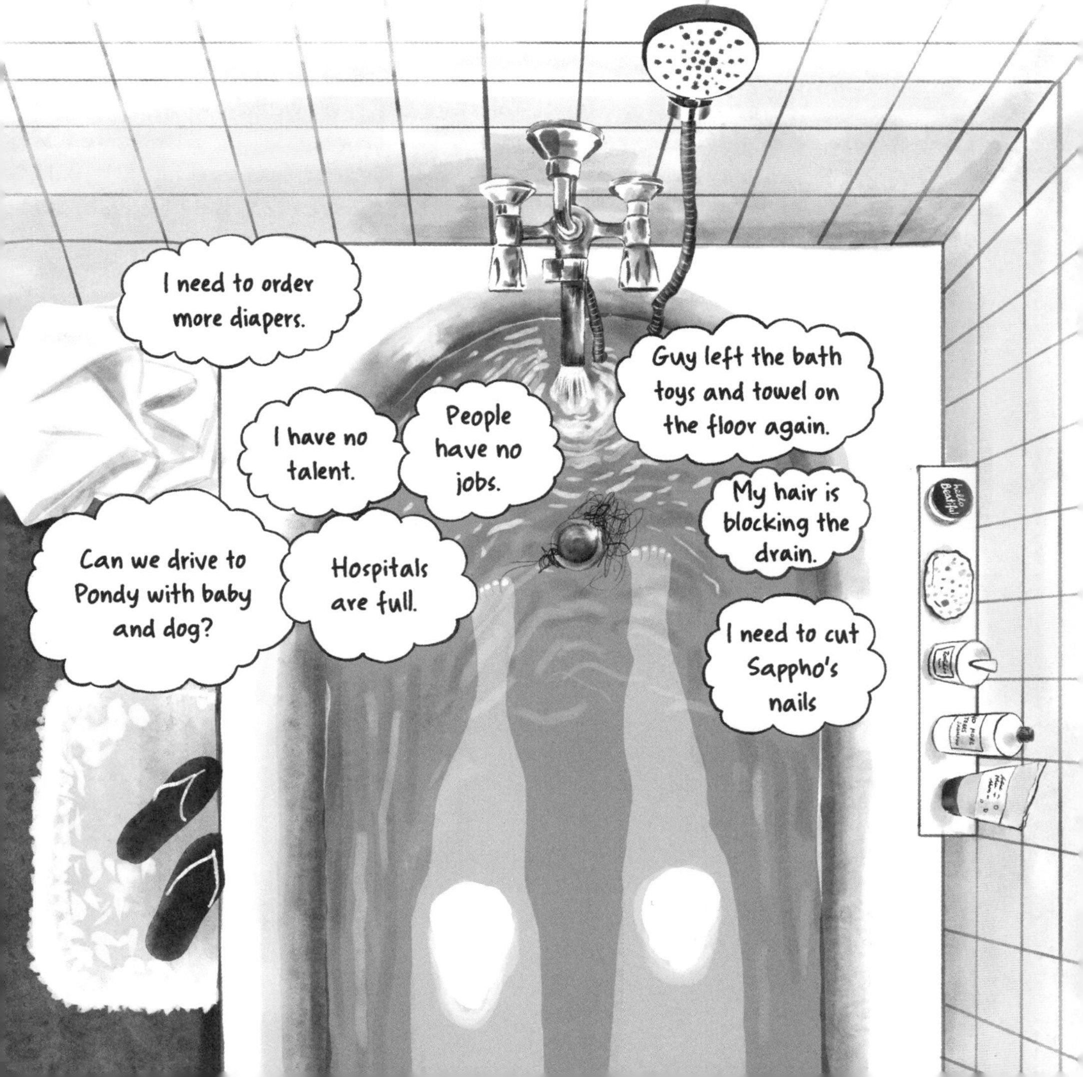

I need to order more diapers.
Guy left the bath toys and towel on the floor again.
I have no talent.
People have no jobs.
My hair is blocking the drain.
Can we drive to Pondy with baby and dog?
Hospitals are full.
I need to cut Sappho's nails

On the contrary, I started spending more and more time with Sappho, even when Guy was on duty. I chose to hang out with them, instead of sitting with myself to work, or write or simply enjoy the alone time. I stopped writing in my journal, I didn't take care of my physical appearance and my workouts were like a hamster in a tunnel, just something I had to rush through to get to the other side. I even started resenting my partner's private time and his ability to hang out with himself and create good music. All my sense of belonging came from Sappho, from caring for her and worrying about her, and that was the tempting thing to do. It was easy to slip into this mother's role so fully that I forgot myself. Here was this bright, shining, smiling little girl every morning, waking me up and wanting my love, only mine, and I could forget a world of problems in her company and feel complete in her presence.

Then there was the network of mothers my age, you know, people you make friends with because you need a play date for your child? And many of them seemed perfectly happy in this new role. Phrases like, 'Isn't this the best thing that happened to you?' or, 'Don't you feel you were born to be a mother?' made me quiet. I would respond with a quick nod, avoiding eye contact, because how could I burst this person's bubble and say, 'What are you talking about? It's a fucking nightmare'. The one time I did laugh and say, 'I have to keep reminding myself that this is the best time of my life', the sarcasm was completely ignored and my mother friend responded with a sweet, 'Yes, we're so blessed.' There are few safe spaces for mothers to talk about the difficulties and failures they might experience because we're under a kind of collective pressure to assume this role naturally. And well, for some, maternal instinct slowly grows on us over time, like a Jane Austen novel. We pretend we're happy until we really are happy.

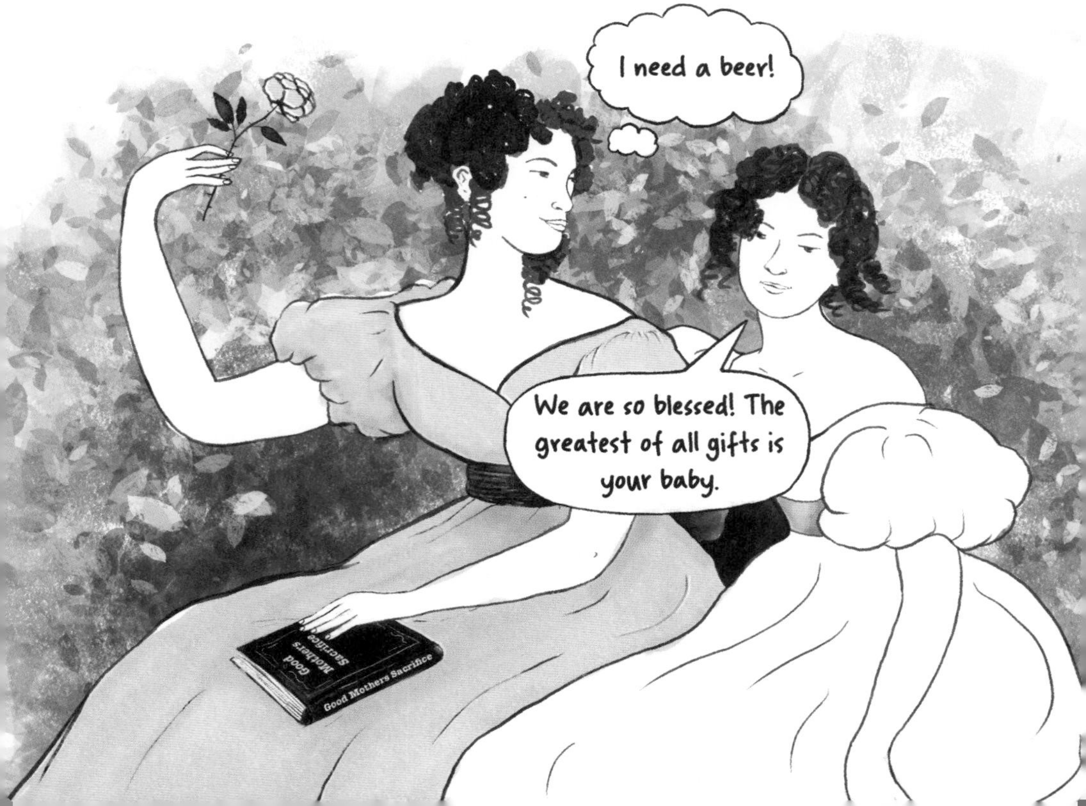
I need a beer!
We are so blessed! The greatest of all gifts is your baby.
Good Mothers Sacrifice
Good Mothers Sacrifice

This is nothing new; most of the women from my mother's generation were geared to sacrifice themselves for their children, only to find themselves oppressively dependent on that nurturing or struggling to let go in their later years. As children leave home, 'Mothers are left with a sense of emptiness, as the duty from the past two decades has suddenly ceased, leaving behind an incomprehensible amount of time and a gaping hole in their identities,' reads an article by Pooja Kini. And I know a large part of my relationship with my mother is fraught from this era of sacrifice. She's there dipping her biscuit in her tea, bitterly recounting the years she sacrificed for our upbringing and I'm trying not to burn the rice while Sappho crawls around my feet in the kitchen.

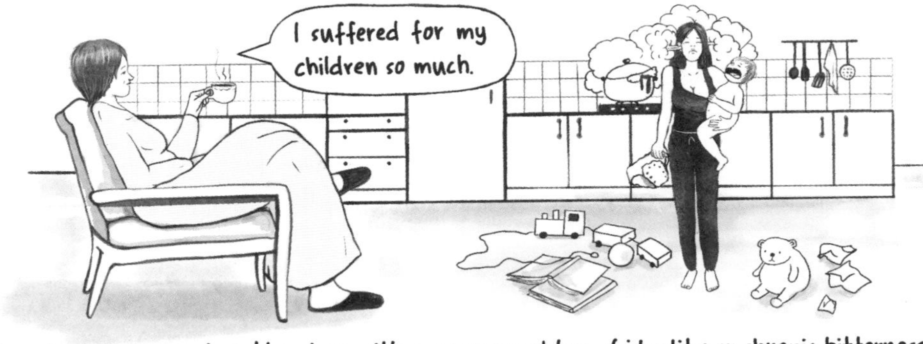
I suffered for my children so much.

If I continue this way, I could end up with a permanent loss of identity or chronic bitterness, I thought to myself. I could be stifling Sappho's sense of space, possibly depending on her for my needs. I have a fair partner, he nudged me to take time for myself and leave Sappho with him.*

I also mostly have childless friends, whose careers are bustling with travel, improvisation and creativity. They reminded me of who I am. An independent actor who thinks on her feet. So I began consciously stepping out of the house, for walks, cycling or small social gatherings (yes, I broke some social distance codes). And sometimes, I just paced an empty corridor with nothing to do and nowhere to go, forcing myself to look at the bits and pieces of the former me until slowly I began to pick up the pieces I liked. I ate cake, I drank beer and slept heavily, I let Guy worry about ordering more diapers, I doodled in pages of my journal when I couldn't find anything to write, I talked to my girlfriends, I let my mind wander, I picked up a monologue and learnt it just to remind myself I was an actor, I got dressed up and danced to loud music, and although there was no seeming correlation between these activities, they somehow helped collect my broken pieces and rework the puzzle of who I was. Eventually, these habits developed into better concentration, higher energy levels and a thirst for personal space. It was like looking into a broken mirror that had been glued back together, creating a complex mosaic of new angles and perspectives. As time passed, as I found myself healing in my head, gradually the problems in my body didn't seem so dreadful and irreparable, not for lack of dramatic physical troubles...

*.....................

Note: I carefully choose the word 'fair' as opposed to 'great' or saying I'm 'lucky'. It's not lucky or great to have a partner who participates wholeheartedly in bringing up a child. It is normal, and it is expected. Partners who choose to have a child are equally responsible for bringing them up. I can't even count the number of times when Guy has changed Sappho's diaper that I've heard a version of, 'Oh you're so lucky to have such a great partner', and not once when I've changed Sappho's diaper has there been a peep of the same complimentary comments said to him about me.

My perineal woes were far from over. Seven months after birth, I needed surgery to cut the extra scar tissue formation around my vagina. The extra skin would be stitched to either side of my vulva and I would need another four weeks of recovery. I was so reluctant to do this I even went to see another gynaecologist for a second opinion. The diagnosis was the same.

As an aside, it was interesting to note the difference in both the doctors' attitude to anaesthesia...

Should I go under full anaesthesia?

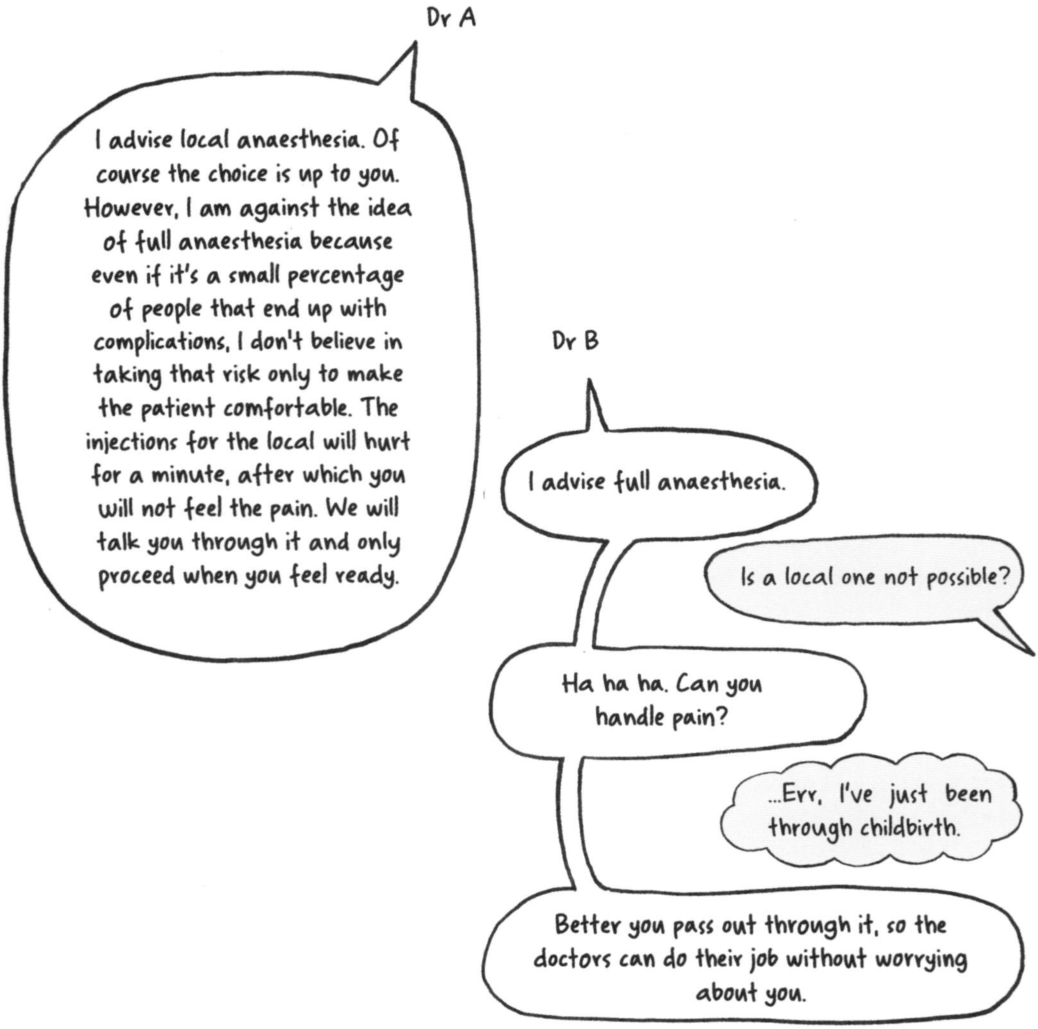
Dr A
I advise local anaesthesia. Of course the choice is up to you. However, I am against the idea of full anaesthesia because even if it's a small percentage of people that end up with complications, I don't believe in taking that risk only to make the patient comfortable. The injections for the local will hurt for a minute, after which you will not feel the pain. We will talk you through it and only proceed when you feel ready.
Dr B
I advise full anaesthesia.
Is a local one not possible?
Ha ha ha. Can you handle pain?
...Err, I've just been through childbirth.
Better you pass out through it, so the doctors can do their job without worrying about you.

I went for local. Not only because I thought I could 'handle pain' but because I wanted to be in the hands of someone who took the time to explain clearly to me how it could be and didn't just tell me how it is.

It was unpleasant to say the least, four hands stretching my vagina, the smell of something burning and the sound of a tiny electric saw. Being conscious through surgery, however small, is a surreal experience. To distract myself from the business down there, I started talking to the doctors and nurses about 'embroideries', an Iranian euphemism for stitching up women who've had sex to make them look like virgins before marriage. The fact that on this operating table we were kind of doing the opposite had some strange justice to it, we laughed. The procedure, physically speaking, was a quick and smooth one, but I remember getting home after the surgery feeling raw and dizzy, and as soon as I reached the bedroom I burst into tears. I felt like a piece of meat, like my sexuality had been stolen from me, like I would never be able to enjoy erotic penetration again. I texted my girls' group with vivid descriptions of my post-op vagina:

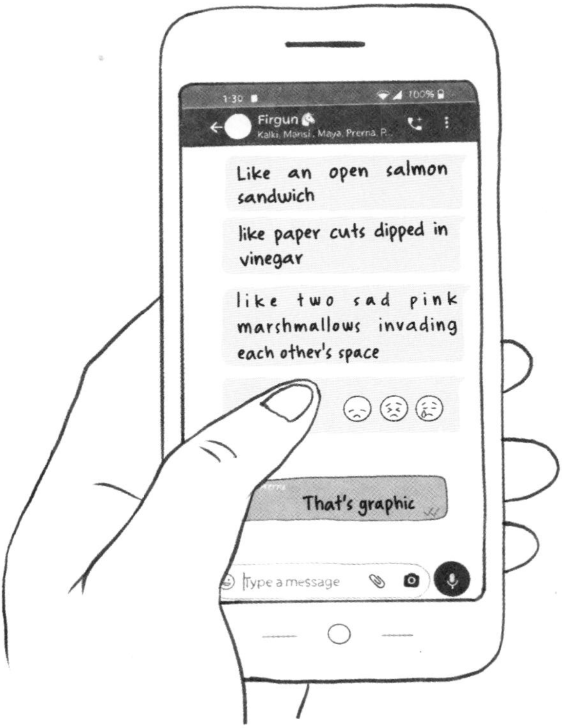
1:30
100%
Firgun
Kalki, Mansi, Maya, Prerna, P...
Like an open salmon sandwich
like paper cuts dipped in vinegar
like two sad pink marshmallows invading each other's space
That's graphic
Type a message

Even after healing well from this, a month and a half down the line, while we had taken advantage of one of Sappho's long afternoon naps to cuddle, things got exciting until when shifting positions I felt a sharp pain. The area around my perineum that had been stitched up at birth, gave way to a tiny tear. Again. I could have once again sunk into hopelessness and hatred towards my body but because I had worked on taking time out for myself, because I'd taken some load off of my mind, my body's wounds didn't upset me as much. I was able to recall how my body had recovered again and again from traumas I thought were irreversible, and as I closed my legs for a few more weeks of healing, I opened my heart to the flexibility of love.

If my vagina had a personality of its own (which she does) I would say she's really opened up this last year.

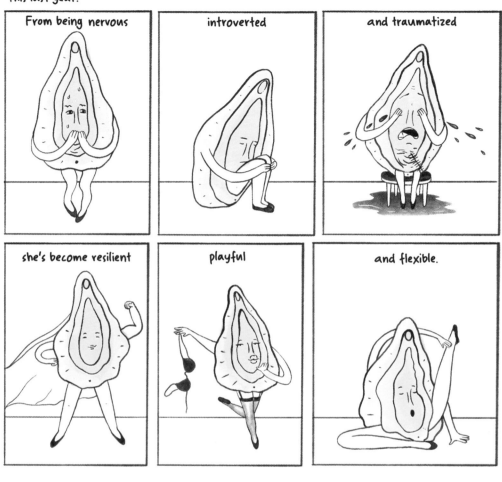

From being nervous

introverted

and traumatized

she's become resilient

playful

and flexible.

She's gained the confidence to take her time with things and let go of functionality for the purpose of curiosity.

Love wasn't just a feeling, it was also a state of mind, something I needed to make space for in my daily life by paying attention to my own needs and relieving myself of the mental pressures of motherhood. There was some kind of sense, even in the dull, tired routine of daily life. By being too tired to care, I would inadvertently end up paying attention to parts of me that were uncared for, my body's way of teaching me how to be easier on myself, my mind's way of delegating some of my worries and burdens to those around me, and letting go of control over my baby. My body and my mind needed the time to process things they'd never experienced before. Even in the hardest moments of pain and recovery, I was breathing, sometimes even laughing, and my heart was pumping blood into my veins. And needless to say, love found its physical expression again. First in short bouts over long interims, and eventually more often. One year down the line, postpartum sex, just like my postpartum body, sure isn't the same as it was before having a baby. Instead it's stronger, more attentive and more malleable.

2 A.M shopping list

- Maida - 1 kg

- Toor dal - 1 kg

- Brown rice - 2 kg

- Walnuts - 1/2 kg

- Chicken liver - 1/2 kg

- Eggs - 1 dozen

- Milk - 2 L

- Spare time - out of stock

- Sleep - wait-listed

- Self care - limited supply

- Sense of humour - 50 per cent sale

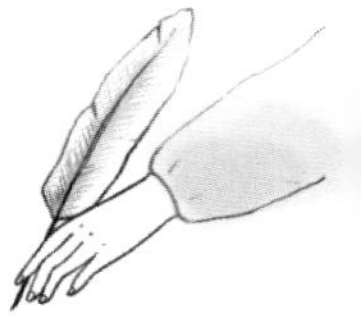

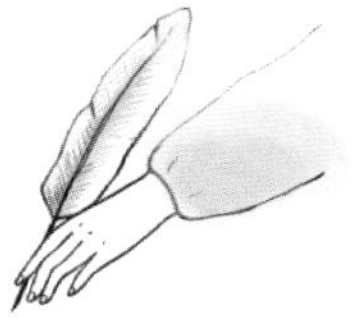

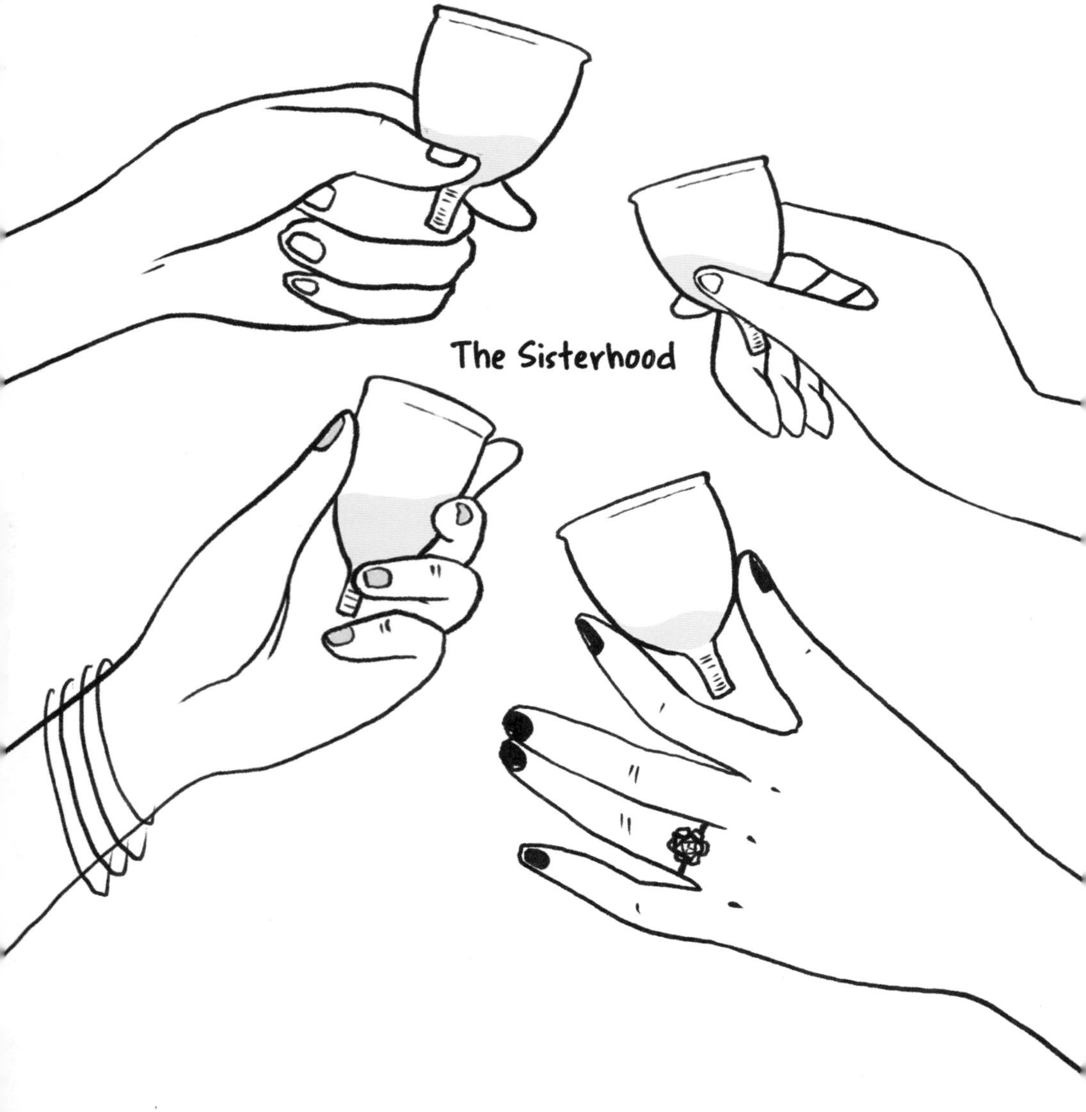
The Sisterhood

Dear New Mom,

As we reach the end of this book, I try to think about what to leave you with, since there is no end to this journey, and in fact, this is just the beginning. And I suppose what I have to share with you is the solace of the sisterhood.

When I was pregnant I had women who I'd never met before go out of their way to help me with infrastructure and community just because I voiced a problem or struggle I had. More than the practical help I've received, it's been their emotional connection that's pulled me through.
I wanted to share some of their stories with you because if it weren't for my interaction with them, I probably wouldn't have had the confidence to write this book. It was knowing that there are ordinary, everyday feminists all around me going through similar struggles that made me think, 'Me too!' The women I write about in this chapter are women I've been in touch with personally through my struggles with pregnancy and motherhood. They are upper-middle-class women who work and raise children, are roughly from the same generation as me, and live in different parts of the world.

I guess what I want to leave you with is that you are not alone, you are not the only one going through this. And many times you may feel guilty for complaining because someone (usually a man) will tell you something along the lines of 'get over it, everyone does it', or you'll feel inadequate because your mother and your mother's mother did it all, over and over again. But the truth is, we all have an elephant in the womb, so to speak, each of us is carrying different weight, in a different frame, at a different time, and no one but you should be able to say what that feels like.
While reading the next few pages, I hope you can take comfort in the fact that you're not alone and gain confidence from the solidarity of being in this together. And I hope you know that your story is worth telling, even when you are only telling it yourself.

Love, Kalki

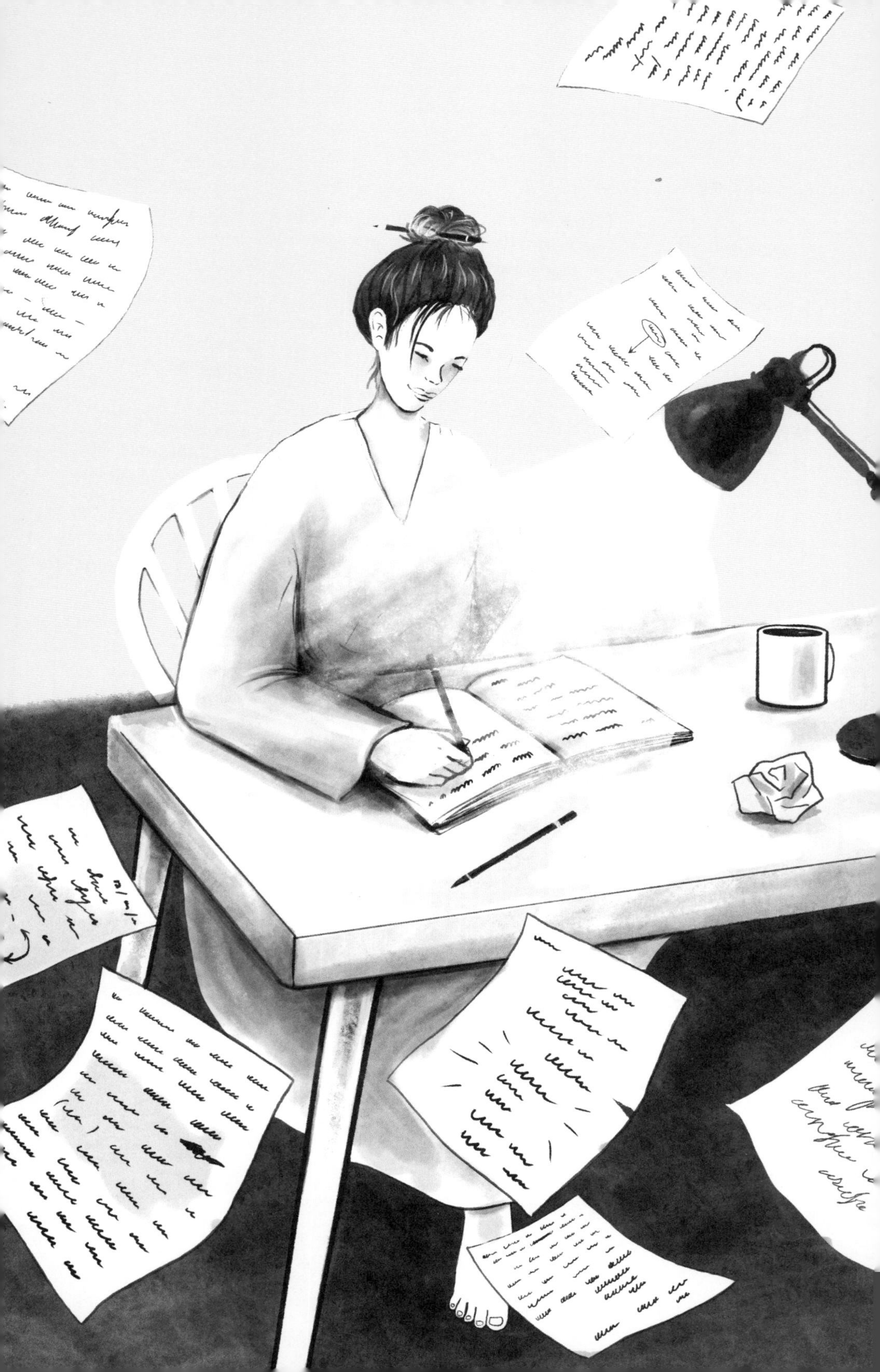

C lives in The Hague, Holland and works in immigration. She had badly wanted a natural birth. 'I was so prepped and at peace I was convinced I wouldn't feel pain,' she laughs. After two nights and two days of contractions, she had a C-section in a state hospital during the Covid lockdown. On the first night of contractions, she stayed at home because they were far apart. The next morning she went to the hospital because the pain was becoming intense. Without checking if she was dilated, she was told to go home because she was too 'calm'. She remembers feeling embarrassed for feeling pain and thinking, 'If these aren't contractions I don't know if I can survive the real thing.' The following day she went to see her midwife, who was shocked to see that she was already 6 cm dilated, C hadn't let out a moan for thirty-six hours because she had been told her pain wasn't real. She went straight to the hospital at 11 A.M. thinking, 'We'll be out by lunch.' But she was there till late that night and felt like she was 'leaving my body from exhaustion'. After 11 P.M. the doctors said it was time for a C-section since C was barely conscious at this point. After her baby girl was born, she says, 'They were more respectful then and made a big effort to keep me close to my baby.'

After the birth she was 'offended and surprised' at how people would ask, 'How is the baby?', without ever thinking to ask how she was. It was dehumanizing. 'I felt like I had moved mountains, but now I was just the carrier. I felt really, really sad.' She found it even more baffling that so many women who had previously given birth could dismiss a new mother while giving all the attention to a newborn. 'It's strange,' she goes on, 'I mean you wouldn't come by and visit someone you know has been sick and then just ignore them.'

The change she would like to see most in the world is more focus on what dads are going through—statistically 10 per cent of men go through postpartum depression, and she suspects her husband was one of them. When she confronted him, he admitted to hating the whole experience of early parenting, and they later realized he had a severe vitamin D deficiency. 'There's not much literature for dads, how he can prepare and what he can do. By saying men don't have a place, we're actually saying it's a woman's job to raise children.' She believes the involvement of dads needs to start during pregnancy, men attending prenatal birth classes and reading up on postpartum preparation. She overheard two women recently. One of them said, 'When I was giving birth my husband was watching TV,' and then both women laughed. C exhales deeply over the phone, 'What the fuck? This is not the 1930s, things really need to change, women need to stop saying men are good-for-nothings and men really need to grow a vagina and step up, not just to make it easier for mums but because they deserve that experience, they're missing out.'

R is mum to a twelve-year-old and lives in Bengaluru. At the time of her pregnancy, she had reached a point of saturation with hospitals because her father was ill for many years. 'You've just giving money and the person is getting sicker, and so I was looking for sustainable solutions in the health industry,' she says. Three weeks before her daughter was born, her mum passed away out of the blue from 'one of those hospital superbugs' she contracted while looking after her father in the hospital. This solidified her feeling of not wanting to give birth in a hospital, so she started looking for a doula, an old nurse, a midwife, or just about anybody who would help her give birth at home. She couldn't find anyone. Ten days before she gave birth, she came across Laura Shanley concept of 'free birth' or unassisted birth. R wrote to her and Laura replied the next day. This gave R the confidence to go ahead with birthing at home, with her husband. When I asked her if she was scared, she said, 'There was rising anticipation but no fear. My only doubt was how will I know when to push.' When the time came, she knew, she says, because, 'I felt the uterus pushing, I felt it in my body, like a rubber band being pulled tight, I put my fingers in my vagina and felt her hair, I gave two pushes, reached down and pushed my vagina tissue aside and cleared space for her.' I still find it difficult to understand where her strength came from and when I ask her she simply says, 'Every pregnant woman gets the kind of birth she needs.' She said her birth led her to becoming a doula and preparing other women for birth. When I ask her if she thinks we should do away with hospital births altogether, she says no, she sees a future where doctors and doulas work together to practise healthy births without routine interventions as the way forward. After a pause, she concludes, 'Midwifery is not the solution, the empowered woman is the solution.' Since R's daughter (E) is now twelve, we spoke more broadly about her upbringing, which was considerably unconventional, even by my standards. R decided not to put E in school or give her any structured learning until very recently. When E was seven, R and her husband taught E the alphabet because they were 'worried'. She showed interest in it for about two weeks, after which they let it go. At the age of ten, E started to read and also kept a journal, and when I try to wrap my head around how that happened with no formal education, R answers, 'We're surrounded by data all the time and we take it in, learning happens through observation not teaching, I don't know how else to explain it.'

While parents all over the world are grappling with online teaching and home-schooling post Covid, I ask her how she found time to work through the years while having her daughter at home all the time. Her husband also works from home, she told me, and they lived in a large community complex with sports grounds and plenty of nature. 'My biggest ally was the outdoors, I knew she was safe and there was endless stimulation there.'

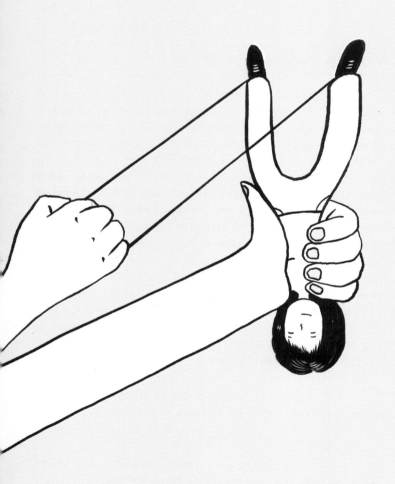

'When I got pregnant, it really took me by surprise,' says K, 'because the pregnancy part, I'd heard, was the easy part.'

K is an actor living in Mumbai who spent most of her second trimester in bed because her amniotic fluid was 50 per cent of what it should be. She said that this time at home was quite miserable because, 'Everyone else's life went forward and I was missing out. I was not mentally prepared that it was temporary. I also had some sort of itching disease (Pruritic Urticarial Papules and Plaques of Pregnancy, PUPPP), my whole body was itching all over and I had to be put on steroids.'

When she gave birth, she considered a natural birth because her sister had done that, but eventually, she opted for an epidural after her mother told her, 'If you had a tooth extraction, would you not use anaesthesia?' Two minutes after the epidural, she dilated the whole 10 cm, and three pushes later, her baby was out. 'It was so good I wanted to name my son Epidural!' she laughs.

About the experience of becoming a mother, she says, 'The amazing part everybody tells you about, but the hard stuff nobody talks about.' She had a terrible time breastfeeding; she wasn't producing enough milk and her nipples were chapped and bleeding. She had to wear nipple shields and she found it exasperating that everybody, including her husband, would give her advice about latching. She also felt as though her body had betrayed her; she couldn't lift her legs in her first yoga class after birth. 'All the nutrition in your body is going to your baby and you feel like a host.' When she decided to shift to formula after three months, she felt a conflicting mix of guilty relief and rejection.

When I ask her what got her through it all, she says, 'A sense of humour, learning how to roll cigarettes I couldn't smoke, and well, sheer strength of character.' She feels as a society we need to normalize the hardships of pregnancy and parenting. 'We should be able to say that they [babies] get on our fucking nerves.' And when I ask her what it would be like to give birth again knowing what she knows, she says, 'I'd be better at it the second time around, more in charge, more confident.'

She chuckles and adds, 'I'd kill it.'

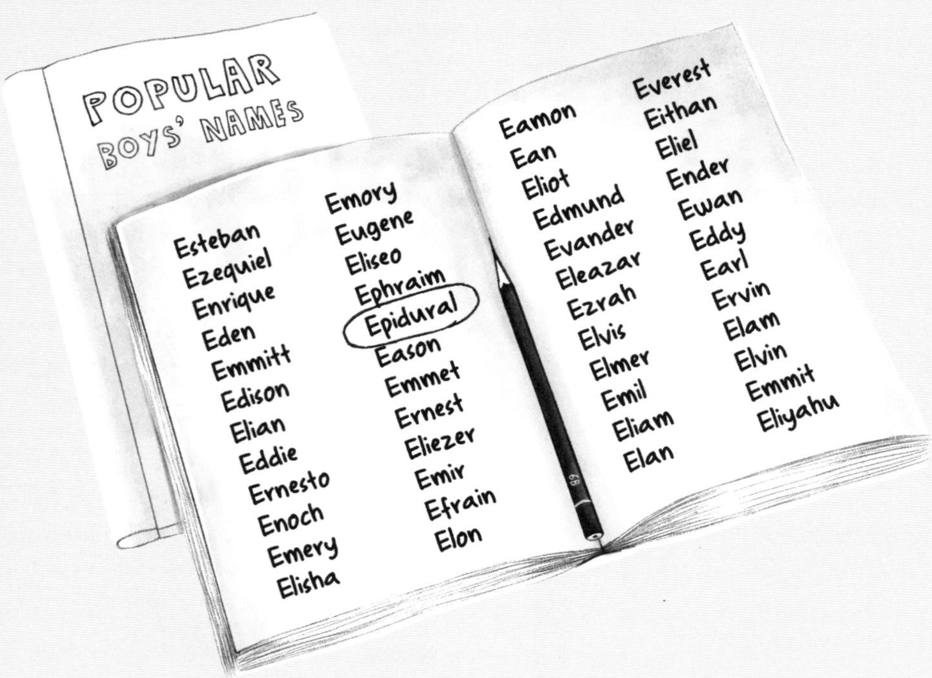
POPULAR
BOYS' NAMES
Esteban
Ezequiel
Enrique
Eden
Emmitt
Edison
Elian
Eddie
Ernesto
Enoch
Emery
Elisha
Emory
Eugene
Eliseo
Ephraim
Epidural
Eason
Emmet
Ernest
Eliezer
Emir
Efrain
Elon
Eamon
Ean
Eliot
Edmund
Evander
Eleazar
Ezrah
Elvis
Elmer
Emil
Eliam
Elan
Everest
Eithan
Eliel
Ender
Ewan
Eddy
Earl
Ervin
Elam
Elvin
Emmit
Eliyahu

N is a nurse who lives in Canada and has two kids. When I asked her for an interview, she said, 'I'm not sure I'm the best candidate for your book because I hated my pregnancies.' I said I wanted to hear all about it.

At some point in the conversation, she says, 'Gosh, I don't remember half of what I hated, but I know I hated it.'

It is her postpartum experience with her first baby that I'm going to focus on though. 'I had a rough time, I think I just went crazy,' she says. 'My milk didn't come in, I couldn't get H [her baby] to latch, her mouth was so small.' Her baby lost half her birth weight in the first few weeks and N was determined to breastfeed because it was such a big deal in nursing school. 'I was crying every single day. H hated my boobs and it made me feel bad.' Her mother didn't help when she said things like, 'It's easy, they all go to the breast!' And she recalls the tension and distrust she felt with her in-laws when they wanted to 'do it their way'.

She shares one example with her mother-in-law. 'I had finished dinner at their place and went to try and give H some breast milk, but my mum-in-law stuffed her dinner in so she could take H and feed her from the bottle, and I said, "No, I need her to get used to my breast!" She kept insisting. It really became an uncomfortable pulling match.'

Looking back at her postpartum experience, she says, 'I wish I didn't fixate on the need to breastfeed. It took away a lot of joy. Since a lot of people are not physically able to breastfeed and science today has developed formula which has the same ingredients as breast milk, except for the antibodies, we really don't need this propaganda that "breast is best".' She did, however, breastfeed her second daughter. She said it was easier the second time around. 'When it is your first, you have nothing to compare it to. Plus, Baby No. 2 had a bigger mouth!'

When I ask how she thinks things could change for first-time mothers, she says, 'We should stop lying to each other and acknowledge that it's really hard.' She also speaks about the stigma around mental health. When she was struggling with breastfeeding, her community nurse had referred her to a psychiatrist and she just refused to go because, 'You know, it felt like you're not coping well with motherhood.' She felt judged and took it as a wake-up call to 'snap out of it'. Only with the passage of time did she recognize that her mental health and well-being was affecting the whole family. She finds reasons why that happens so much. 'It's not like in the old days when women were at home. Today, we are expected to have a career, but we are also expected to keep the household together. That hasn't changed. Women are still the worriers and if there isn't a person to do that worrying, the world would fall apart, wouldn't it?' she asks.

I don't have an answer for her then, but she texts me an hour later, saying, 'Mamahood is so hard... I feel it's harder for us who haven't really been parented by our own parents... I say, as adults we have turned out okay!'

I think, like the rest of us, N is finding her own answers to the questions she is asking the world.

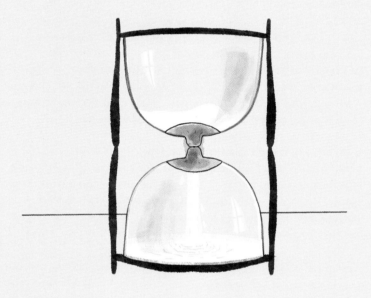

S works in theatre, and lives in Mumbai. Soon after she had her first baby, her partner got busy with work and was often out of town. 'I was alone with this baby quite a lot,' she says. She had no help so she would strap her son in the baby seat and go. She breastfed him at meetings. She breastfed him in the car. Despite comments like, 'Do you really need to do that here?', she breastfed him wherever and whenever she needed to. She ran her workshops and just looked for a lady working as a cleaner in the school and asked her to look after her baby. 'I would literally hand him over to whoever would take him,' she laughs. She continues to explain how support came from all kinds of places she didn't expect, while she could hardly rely on her own family for the same.

She opens up about how her mother is bipolar. When S was young and going to school, her mother would often not get up in the mornings to see her off to school. 'She loved us but she didn't like doing things for us,' she says, 'and I don't want to pass that on.' She is fighting hard to be present and involved in parenting her kids but also keeping her career going. 'Now that I've chosen this road, I ask myself how I will manage everything! It's an ongoing battle.'

She says that after six years of raising two children, she is 'only now clawing back at my career'. Like so many of us in India, she's been told she's lucky to have a partner who participates in parenting, and yet, she mentions how he never thought about whether to travel out of town when he thought about work, and during the Covid lockdown, she did thirty weeks of home-schooling, when he did none. 'You tell yourself that everybody goes through it but that doesn't actually make you feel better. It's my daily struggle to get over that resentment, to find joy.' We speak about the inherent misogyny that is still prevalent in Indian society. She shares a disturbing story; her grandfather while on his deathbed, told her father that he wanted to hand over his property to his second son because he had two boys, rather than to her father, who's children who were girls. We ask ourselves how this generation is supposed to remove the weight of such baggage, and she says that we need to open up about abuse, about our struggles, and only then will our children 'feel like they can say anything to anyone and be truthful'.

As her struggle continues with what she calls 'good days' and 'bad days', she is clear about one thing: 'I have a girl and a boy and I want to raise them both as feminists.'

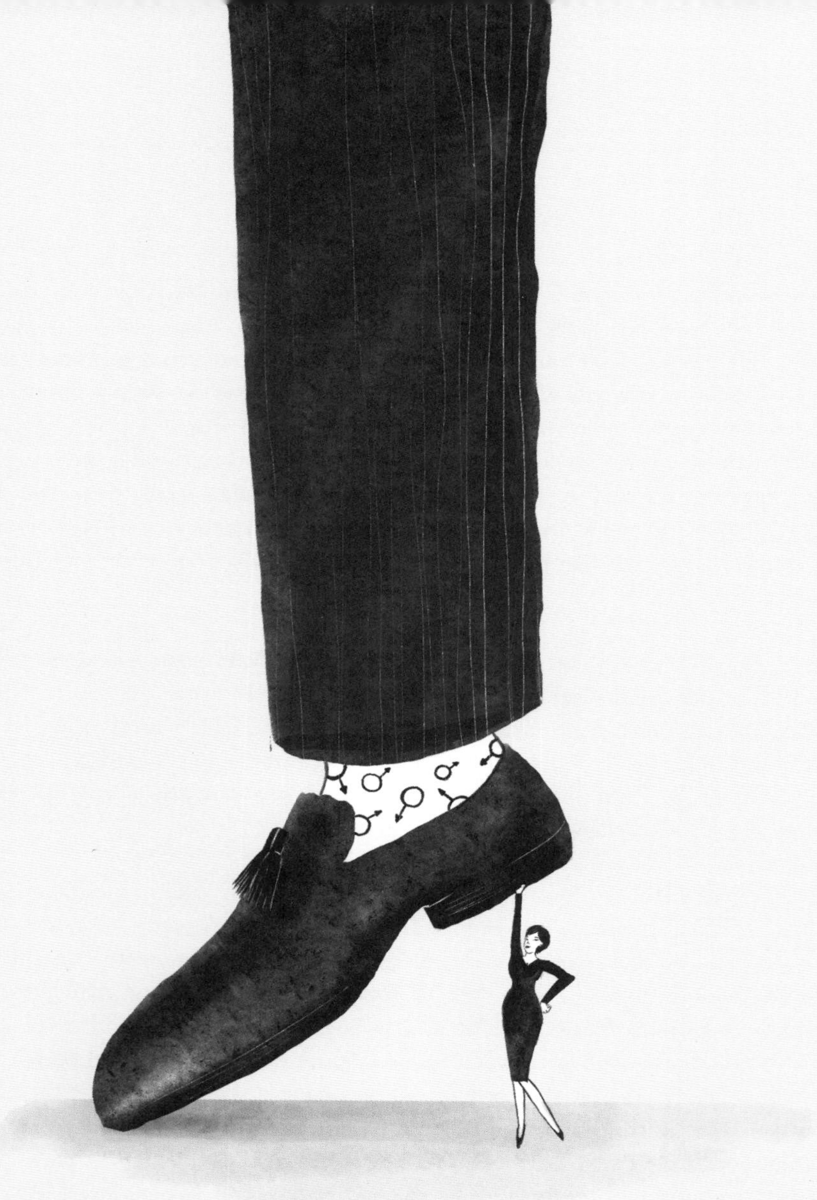

A Moment of Bliss

Bliss, like most gifts,
Comes in packages bright and unexpected.
As on a road through the desert
Where, between indistinctive dunes and endless drear
Between dry heat and dizzying sun
You chance upon a flaming, silent flower
That bears fruit among the thorns
And cacti of your delicate journey
But the sun does not wait
It's midday and there's not a spot of shade
Or a moment to waste
So you carry on
Leaving the flower in your encased mind
To drain away colour like a phantom.

Bliss, like a bout of mist
Can only be captured with distance.
And since you can't get a grip on the real thing
You make do with documentations,
So that when memory, in faithful alliance with longing,
Knocks at your heart,
You're ready.
You tear impatiently through boxes colourfully wrapped
Through scraps of old notes
And photographs of faded laughs
Only to put them aside
In alphabetical order, in neat piles
And curse yourself for rarely looking happiness in the
eyes
Or being ready enough for life.

Bliss is a scent or a kiss
Lodged between your throat and your lips
A lifelong trigger that is pulled
Each time you smell that scent
Or kiss that kiss again.
Like a sunrise, fluid and improvised
That, despite its daily occurrence,
Takes you by surprise every once in a while
So is bliss a warm glow of gold and a reminder
For noticing things that consistently go unrecognized.
And in this way,
You keep going every day
Even when you have no hold on the things you love
Because a moment of bliss, strangely, is enough

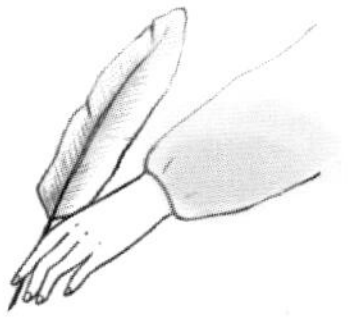

ACKNOWLEDGEMENTS

Writing this book gave me direction at a time when everything in the world came to a stop. I couldn't have done it without the practical help, mental strength and consistent love of my partner, Guy Hershberg. During the first lockdown in Mumbai, our cook, Sangeeta Kisane, agreed to work for us full-time for a few months, helping with housework and our newborn, and staying away from her own teenage daughter for half a year. Her support and love also helped me find time and energy to write. Throughout the creative process, I gained valuable insight and encouragement from my editor Manasi Subramaniam and I appreciate the meticulous and careful detailing of my copy editor Aparna Kumar and the technical expertise of Akangksha Sarmah that brought the work to completion. This book would not have been possible without my friend and illustrator, Valeriya Polyanychko, lending me her brilliance and sensitivity every step of the way. Sappho, my daughter was, of course, a giant source of inspiration throughout. And finally, to the mothers I spoke to, read from, followed on social media, cried and laughed with or simply sat next to while our children played together, thank you for the conversations.

BIBLIOGRAPHY

Chapter 2

Forbes.com, 'The surprising reason we lack so much knowledge about women's health', 24 August 2018.

'The gender health gap: Why women's bodies shouldn't be a medical mystery', www.globalcitizen.org, 6 October 2020.

Chapter 4

Aswathi Pacha, 'India might soon have the most caesarean births', the *Hindu*, 6 April 2019.

Kiran Kumbhar, 'Shunned for years, can trained midwives fix India's maternity mess?', 2 March 2016.

Quartz India, qz.com

Newbeginningz.in

ncbi.nlm.nih.gov

Chapter 5

Brilliantbeginnings, Surrogacy in Canada.

Marguerite Ward, '10 countries that show just how behind the US is in paid parental leave for new mothers and fathers', 6 May 2020.

'Feminism has failed women', the *New York Times*.

Chapter 6

'How long does postpartum depression last?', Medical News Today.

Chapter 7

'This isn't supposed to happen', Medical News Today.

Chapter 9

unicef.org

Jessica Grose, 'Fighting constantly after baby? Read this', the *New York Times*, 15 April 2020.

Daniela Ginta, 'What are the symptoms of low estrogen in women and how are they treated?', Healthline, 17 June 2021.

Martha F. Goetsch, 'Postpartum dyspareunia. An unexplored problem', researchgate.net, December 1999.

OTHER INFLUENCES

John Medina, *Brain Rules for Baby: How to Raise a Smart and Happy Child from Zero to Five*, Pear Press, February 2008.

Brett Finlay, Marie-Claire Arrieta, *Let Them Eat Dirt: Saving Your Child from an Oversanitized World*, Windmill Books, 12 October 2016.

Heng Ou, *The First Forty Days: The Essential Art of nourishing the New Mother*, Stewart, Tabori & Chang, 26 April 2016.

Dr Mahesh Balsekar and Malvika Choudhary, *0 to 2 Baby and You*, Vakils, Feffer & Simons Pvt. Ltd., 1 January 2015.

Katie Kirby, *Hurrah for Gin: A Book for Perfectly Imperfect Parents*, Coronet, 6 October 2016.

Emma, *The Mental Load: A Feminist Comic*, Seven Stories Press, 23 October 2018.

ONLINE SOLACE

The Birth Hour, thebirthhour.com.

Jon Fitzgerald, *The Milky Way*, Amazon Prime.

Babies, Netflix.

Jason Reitman, *Juno*, 4 December 2007.

James Cameron, *Aliens*, 11 July 1987.

@common_wild, Paul Kuka's official Instagram account.

Our quirky, cheeky and wonderful dog Kiara passed away on Friday, 2 April 2021, just as I was finishing the draft of this book. I thought of dedicating this book to her, but I think she would prefer a book on salami. Or just the salami. We miss her and draw her again and again, to remember her.